SUCCESSFUL

MANAGER'S

HANDBOOK

SUCCESSFUL
MANAGER'S
HANDBOOK

Edited by

Brian L. Davis, Ph.D.
Lowell W. Hellervik, Ph.D.
James L. Sheard, Ph.D.

With assistance from

Val J. Arnold, Ph.D.
Karen M. Grabow
Keith M. Halperin, Ph.D.
Lila A. Lewey
Molly Mulligan
Linda N. Schnappauf
Gwen W. Stucker

PERSONNEL DECISIONS, INC.
Building Successful Organizations

2000 PLAZA VII TOWER • 45 SOUTH SEVENTH STREET • MINNEAPOLIS, MN 55402-1608 • 612/339-0927

Third Edition, Fifth Printing
©1984, 1986, 1989 by
Personnel Decisions, Inc.

Printed in the United States of America.

ISBN 0-938529-00-5

CONTENTS

PREFACE

In 1984, Personnel Decisions, Inc. (PDI) published **Improving Managerial Effectiveness**—which was widely received by successful managers who wanted to be even better managers. That award-winning first volume led to a second edition entitled **Successful Manager's Handbook,** containing expansion of development suggestions and an update on readings and seminars. Like the first publication, this edition of the Handbook was a sellout in two printings. Certainly part of its extensive reception was due to its integration with PDI's **Management Skills Profile (MSP),** a development tool that provides managers feedback on their management skills from the perspectives of superiors, peers, and subordinates.

Now, in this 1989 Edition, we present updated suggestions for seminars and readings. These suggestions are representative of the available seminars, courses, articles, and books, and are by no means all inclusive.

PDI's Wheel of Managerial Success serves as the basic model for this Handbook and the MSP. You'll find the Wheel to be a particularly useful tool in management development—one that promotes an understanding of the success and improvement of managers.

Great organizations do not just happen—they are comprised of many individually successful managers who do the right things at the right time in the right circumstances. We're convinced that good managers can become better managers by the right kind of development—development which includes the proper use of experiences, relationships, education, and training. Those four avenues for development can be deployed to build on strengths and overcome limitations.

Over the past twenty-one years, Personnel Decisions, Inc. has developed revealing insights, especially in the areas of management assessment, growth, and development. Our orientation is an outgrowth of our backgrounds as organizational psychologists, innovators in the area of assessment and development, and practical, business-directed professionals.

Providing assistance in the preparation of development plans for managers is another area of expertise at PDI. This Handbook represents a compilation of the ideas and insights we've collected through our work. You can create your own development plans as well as guide others toward attainable development by using the principles and ideas presented in this Handbook.

We believe you will find these ideas to be immediately useful and a source of reference for the future. We encourage your feedback and ideas for use in compiling later volumes.

Lowell W. Hellervik, Ph.D.
President, Personnel Decisions, Inc.

SUCCESSFUL MANAGER'S HANDBOOK

Development Suggestions for Today's Manager

INTRODUCTION

The successful manager never stops growing and learning. He or she becomes successful through ability, motivation, and preparation for the challenges managers have to face. Since those challenges constantly change, the manager must continually develop to successfully handle those changing situations and to prepare for a new opportunity or advancement. Furthermore, managers have the responsibility for encouraging the growth of those they influence and manage. Ultimately, their own success is dependent on the growth and success of those they manage.

Even the most successful managers will have times when they face one or more of these situations.

- As you sit down to prepare a performance appraisal, you realize that you have no good suggestions for what the subordinate can do to develop his or her skills.
- You can't come up with any suggestions for a subordinate who needs to overcome a performance problem.
- You feel inadequate when you try to help someone grow in your organization.
- You're not sure how to help yourself grow as a manager.
- You realize that your supervisor wants input on your own development plan, but you can't think of anything more imaginative than listing courses out of the company's training catalog.

Obstacles to Management Development

A person's efforts to perform effectively as an individual and with others are rewarded in a number of ways. They can provide a sense of satisfaction in the current job, create opportunities for increased responsibilities, and provide chances for advancement. As a result, almost all managers and organizations acknowledge the need for management development.

However, far too few managers actually engage in development activities geared toward themselves or their subordinates. Although some of America's businesses and corporations rely on centralized human resource functions that provide training and development courses and outside programs, the majority provide too little development—on or off the job. Even organizations with outstanding development resources and programs often employ managers who don't use these resources effectively and do little to work with subordinates on the job. What are the reasons for this?

There are many obstacles to improving managerial performance through development, including the following.
- Those needing development don't recognize their needs.
- Many people think that all development activities involve missing work to attend some sort of training program.
- Most managers feel that they don't have enough time for development activities.
- Growth and development require planning and hard work.
- Development involves changing, and change can be difficult.
- Many people feel vulnerable in developmental settings.
- Many of us think of development as working on weaknesses that we don't want to expose to others.
- Many managers fail to develop specific action plans by which to manage their development.
- Many managers fail to set specific and measurable developmental objectives for themselves.
- Individual development is something that is easy to put off and always takes a "back burner" to other day-to-day priorities—thus, we procrastinate.

Perhaps the overriding reason that so little management development occurs is that individuals and their supervisors are unaware of individuals' development needs. Also, those who recognize development needs typically lack information or knowledge about the activities that could help individuals build on their strengths or overcome their limitations.

As a result, many people continue to perform at less than their potential. Their performance limitations, if not addressed, can cause these individuals to miss key promotions, be underutilized, and in some cases, be terminated. These limitations can signal the individuals' lack of preparation for future opportunities and growth in the organization. Organizations must realize the importance of viewing people as valuable, untapped resources who need the opportunity to develop their skills in meaningful ways.

Keys to Managerial Growth and Development

A sense of personal responsibility on the part of those involved in the development process is the primary key to successful growth and development. Each individual must take responsibility for planning and managing his or her own development progress. The person desiring to improve is in the best position to look after his or her own interests and to ensure that both the need to overcome limitations and the need to enhance strengths are addressed.

Managers and supervisors should take responsibility for encouraging, supporting, and guiding the development efforts of each subordinate. Although individuals can grow on their own, their efforts can be significantly enhanced with the help of managers and supervisors who provide direction and accountability.

Additional keys to success in improving managerial performance through development activities include:
- Exhibiting a willingness to take risks and try new things
- Focusing on the behaviors requiring change
- Remembering that growth includes both building on strengths and overcoming limitations
- Seeking and responding to feedback that will help shape behavior in the desired direction
- Taking a holistic approach to development so that all areas (health, stress, knowledge, attitudes, skills, etc.) are open for inspection and attention

The Development Process

Following is an effective process for approaching development. The five steps can be taken by individuals and their supervisors or, if necessary, by the individual alone.

1. Identify the individual's strengths, limitations, and specific performance problems using one or more of the assessment methods presented later in this introduction.
2. Read the related sections of this Handbook to identify potential development activities.
3. Determine and, if more than one person is involved, agree on development activities and a timetable for each activity.
4. Begin to implement these activities.
5. Periodically review and modify the development plan, and reassess the individual's strengths and limitations to check developmental progress and reestablish developmental objectives.

The following pages explain the assessment and development planning processes in more detail.

Assessment: Identifying Strengths and Limitations

Identifying areas of strength and limitation is an important step in the process of improving managerial performance. Most of us find this difficult to do on our own; we don't have a clear understanding of the areas in which we excel or those in which we need improvement. Furthermore, most supervisors find it difficult to clearly evaluate the strengths and limitations of those who report to them. The pages that follow describe a tool called the Wheel of Managerial Success and explain how this Wheel can be used in the assessment process.

The Wheel of Managerial Success

The Wheel of Managerial Success, developed by Personnel Decisions, Inc., is a tool that facilitates the assessment process. It outlines the eight major factors of performance/behavior that are important for success in nearly all managerial positions (supervisory, middle management, and executive). Certain factors are more critical in some positions than in others; overall, however, all eight factors are essential for success.

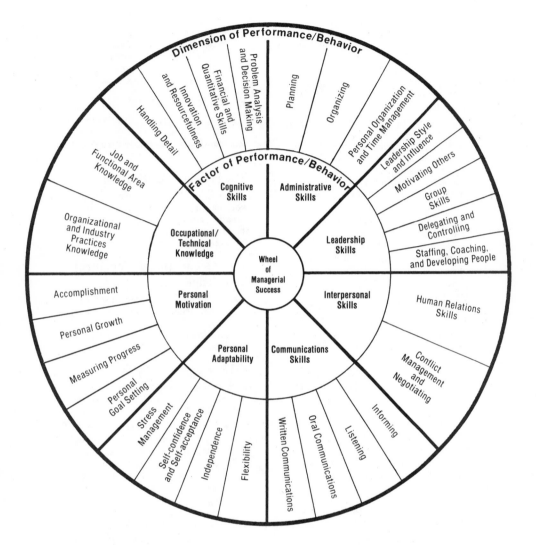

I. Administrative Skills

Structuring one's own activities and the activities of others; coordinating the use of resources in a way that maximizes productivity and efficiency.

- **Planning:** Setting goals, developing strategies and schedules for meeting those goals, and anticipating obstacles and alternative strategies.

- **Organizing:** Assigning responsibilities, allocating resources, and coordinating the activities of others to meet objectives efficiently and effectively.

- **Personal Organization and Time Management:** Allocating one's own time efficiently, arranging information systematically, and processing paperwork effectively.

II. Leadership Skills

Taking charge and making things happen through the effective action of others.

- **Leadership Style and Influence:** Taking charge and initiating actions, directing the activities of individuals and groups toward the accomplishment of meaningful goals, and adapting leadership strategy to different situations.

- **Motivating Others:** Creating an environment in which subordinates are rewarded for accomplishment of group and individual goals.
- **Group Skills:** Planning, conducting, and participating in meetings in which the collective resources of the group members are used efficiently.
- **Delegating and Controlling:** Clearly assigning responsibilities and tasks to others and establishing effective controls, ensuring that employees have the necessary resources and authority, and monitoring progress and exercising control.
- **Staffing, Coaching, and Developing People:** Hiring and evaluating employees, providing performance feedback, and facilitating professional growth.

III. Interpersonal Skills

Interacting with others in ways that enhance understanding and respect, perceiving the needs of others, developing smooth working relationships, and dealing effectively with conflict.

- **Human Relations Skills:** Showing an awareness of, and consideration for, the opinions and feelings of others; and developing and maintaining smooth, cooperative working relationships with peers, subordinates, and superiors.
- **Conflict Management and Negotiating:** Bringing conflict or dissent into the open and using it productively to enhance the quality of decisions; arriving at constructive solutions while maintaining positive working relationships.

IV. Communications Skills

Sending and receiving information clearly, accurately, thoroughly, and effectively.

- **Informing:** In a timely fashion, letting people know of decisions, changes, and other relevant information.
- **Oral Communications:** Speaking effectively one-to-one and in groups, and making effective presentations.
- **Listening:** Demonstrating attention to, and conveying understanding of, the comments or questions of others.

- **Written Communications:** Writing clearly and effectively; using appropriate style, format, grammar, and tone, in informal and formal business communications.

V. Personal Adaptability

Responding appropriately and confidently to the demands of work challenges when confronted with changes, ambiguity, adversity, or other pressures.

VI. Personal Motivation

Establishing high performance standards, working hard to attain those standards, taking initiative, and demonstrating commitment to the organization and to professional management.

VII. Occupational/Technical Knowledge

Applying the knowledge and skills needed to do the job, including technical competence in one's own field and familiarity with policies and practices of the broader function, the organization, and the industry.

VIII. Cognitive Skills

Processing information effectively to learn new material, to identify and define problems, and to make decisions.

- **Problem Analysis and Decision Making:** Identifying problems and recognizing symptoms, causes, and alternative solutions; making timely, sound decisions even under conditions of risk and uncertainty.
- **Financial and Quantitative Skills:** Drawing accurate conclusions from financial and numerical material, and applying financial principles and numerical techniques to management problems.
- **Innovation and Resourcefulness:** Developing original, unusual, successful approaches; encouraging the creativity of subordinates; and readily drawing on a large pool of diverse sources of information.
- **Handling Detail:** Processing or generating information without either overlooking important items or getting enmeshed in technicalities.

In addition, each factor is subdivided into dimensions that define that factor more specifically. The performance/behavior for these dimensions can serve as a guide for individuals and supervisors who are identifying areas of strength and limitation.

The Wheel of Managerial Success is the result of many years of PDI experience in developing assessment centers, performance appraisal systems, managerial selection and development programs, and integrated human resource systems. It also incorporates the findings of other organizational psychologists whose experience and research have helped to identify the most critical dimensions of managerial effectiveness. The Wheel has proven to be a particularly useful way of categorizing managerial behavior.

Using the Wheel in the Assessment Process

The factors and dimensions of performance/behavior shown on the Wheel can be used to guide the assessment process in a variety of ways. Following are three that Personnel Decisions, Inc., has found effective.

1. Individuals' effectiveness can be rated on each dimension using the five-point rating scale shown on page 10. Supervisors, peers, others who know the individuals and their work performance, and the individuals themselves can provide ratings.

    In addition, the individual and his or her manager may want to prioritize the relative importance of factors and/or dimensions for present and future positions. This can be done by rating each dimension and factor on a five-point scale:

    5: Extremely important
    4: Quite important
    3: Moderately important
    2: Slightly important
    1: Not important

    Similarly, the dimensions can be rated on this scale to indicate relative importance in the present or future position. This type of rating process is simply used to identify some priority of importance for that particular dimension and factor.

2. Any or all of the people mentioned previously can be asked to provide **behavioral observations** for each of the dimensions. (Behavioral observations are examples of the individual's behavior that help to explain a rating.) Emphasis should be placed on dimensions in which the individual was rated as high or low.

Management Skills Assessment

		Not effective		Moderately effective		Extremely effective		Not important		Moderately important		Extremely important
I. Adminstrative Skills	Overall Rating	1 2 3 4 5						1 2 3 4 5				
Planning		1 2 3 4 5						1 2 3 4 5				
Organizing		1 2 3 4 5						1 2 3 4 5				
Personal Organization and Time Management		1 2 3 4 5						1 2 3 4 5				
II. Leadership Skills	Overall Rating	1 2 3 4 5						1 2 3 4 5				
Leadership Style and Influence		1 2 3 4 5						1 2 3 4 5				
Motivating Others		1 2 3 4 5						1 2 3 4 5				
Group Skills		1 2 3 4 5						1 2 3 4 5				
Delegating and Controlling		1 2 3 4 5						1 2 3 4 5				
Staffing, Coaching, and Developing People		1 2 3 4 5						1 2 3 4 5				
III. Interpersonal Skills	Overall Rating	1 2 3 4 5						1 2 3 4 5				
Human Relations Skills		1 2 3 4 5						1 2 3 4 5				
Conflict Management and Negotiating		1 2 3 4 5						1 2 3 4 5				
IV. Communications Skills	Overall Rating	1 2 3 4 5						1 2 3 4 5				
Informing		1 2 3 4 5						1 2 3 4 5				
Listening		1 2 3 4 5						1 2 3 4 5				
Oral Communications		1 2 3 4 5						1 2 3 4 5				
Written Communications		1 2 3 4 5						1 2 3 4 5				
V. Personal Adaptability	Overall Rating	1 2 3 4 5						1 2 3 4 5				
(Stress management, self-confidence and self-acceptance, independence, flexibility)												
VI. Personal Motivation	Overall Rating	1 2 3 4 5						1 2 3 4 5				
(Accomplishment, personal growth, measuring progress, goal setting)												
VII. Occupational/Technical Knowledge	Overall Rating	1 2 3 4 5						1 2 3 4 5				
(Job and functional area knowledge, organizational and industry practices knowledge)												
VIII. Cognitive Skills	Overall Rating	1 2 3 4 5						1 2 3 4 5				
Problem Analysis and Decision Making		1 2 3 4 5						1 2 3 4 5				
Financial and Quantitative Skills		1 2 3 4 5						1 2 3 4 5				
Innovation and Resourcefulness		1 2 3 4 5						1 2 3 4 5				
Handling Detail		1 2 3 4 5						1 2 3 4 5				

3. Personnel Decisions, Inc., has developed a comprehensive instrument called the Management Skills Profile (MSP) to provide developmental feedback on the dimensions. This feedback is especially valuable, because it is:

- **Comprehensive,** in that it can come from superiors, peers, and subordinates
- **Anonymous** and therefore more likely to be candid and honest than face-to-face feedback
- **Specific and completely job related,** thereby providing a clear understanding of strength areas and development needs

This instrument is an excellent tool to use when a more comprehensive and objective approach is desired. For additional information, send in the enclosed information request card found at the end of this book or contact the Products Administrator, Personnel Decisions, Inc., 2000 Plaza VII Tower, 45 South Seventh Street, Minneapolis, MN 55402, (612) 339-0927.

This Handbook is designed to accompany the Management Skills Profile (MSP). At the back of the book, you will find an index referencing special development suggestions for each item contained in the MSP.

The assessment of an individual's skills and performance across the dimensions should not be a one-time event. Rather, it should be an ongoing process in which the individual continually assesses his or her performance and seeks feedback on it.

When assessing skills, recognize that the management factors and dimensions may be defined and used differently at different levels in the organization. For example, the nature of planning is likely to be different at the executive, management, and supervisory levels of an organization. These differences need to be considered and are particularly important for performance appraisal, assessment of potential, and evaluation of candidates for key positions in organizations. It may be important to consider these differences as one embarks on creating a development plan for him- or herself or someone else.

You should also recognize that there may be differences across organizations in terms of the relative importance of these dimensions/factors and differences in how the definitions may be refined for internal use. Typically, however, these types of tailoring are minor.

Creating a Development Plan

When the assessment step is complete, a plan should be developed to identify activities that will help the individual build on the strengths and overcome the limitations identified during the assessment. The following pages describe how to use this Handbook to identify development activities, how to create your own development suggestions, and how to format the final development plan.

Using This Handbook to Identify Development Activities

This Handbook is like having a management development consultant at your disposal to provide advice on development activities specifically suited to you or one of your subordinates. It represents a compendium of the best development ideas divided into carefully selected categories of importance to nearly all levels and types of managers. Activities can be selected by individuals alone or with the support and help of others. The Handbook offers a wide breadth and variety of suggestions in a format that is easy to understand and use.

The Wheel of Managerial Success forms the basis of this Handbook's organization, enabling you to easily locate suggestions in the various target areas. The suggestions have been categorized into the eight major performance factors and the dimensions within each of those factors. For example, you could get help with a problem concerning interpersonal skills by turning to the section dealing with that factor. There you would find descriptions of the two dimensions within the interpersonal skills factor— **Human Relations Skills** and **Conflict Management and Negotiating.** You could then examine the outline of development suggestions in either of these two dimensions. Following the outline in each dimension is a series of tips for improving performance in that particular dimension. Finally, you would find more comprehensive and specific on-the-job development suggestions, recommended readings, and seminars for that dimension.

In preparing a development plan for yourself or your subordinates, it is important to recognize that individuals have different learning styles. Some learn best through active experimentation and should use primarily on-the-job activities for their development. Others learn most easily through abstract conceptualization, and should rely more heavily on readings. Still others learn through reflective observation and can be trained most efficiently through seminars. Be sure to consider these differences in learning style when selecting development suggestions for yourself or others.

You'll probably find that some of the suggestions within a dimension don't apply to your needs or situation. You should search through the range of levels and types of activities within the dimension to find those that are most appropriate. The recommended approach is to skim all of the suggestions, then study in more depth those that are most relevant to your needs. Finally, tailor these suggestions to better fit your own situation and establish specific milestones, including a date by which each of your development goals will be accomplished.

Creating Your Own Development Suggestions

The suggestions in this manual won't cover every situation. Development needs and circumstances are diverse and variable, so you may need to come up with additional or modified ideas to help an individual grow and develop. In these cases, this Handbook can stimulate thinking about the kinds of activities that can help an individual grow in a particular area.

It's important that you recognize the breadth of the development activities included in this manual and the range of activities that can be applied to any given situation. Too often, we think of development as instructing someone to take a program or course. While this approach may be appropriate in some situations, other opportunities for development—both on and off the job—should be considered in most cases.

In creating your own suggestions to meet a particular need, choose from the following range of development activities. (Examples of all types of activities are included in this Handbook.)

Reading books, articles, and manuals

Observing other professionals and groups of professionals

Modeling, which involves:
- Observing individuals who possess the desired skills
- Discussing the observations noted
- Using the observations as models for behavior

Researching, which involves:
- Searching for information and materials in a certain area
- Asking questions and seeking information from other people

Practicing, which involves:
- Identifying the skill or behavior needing improvement
- Practicing that behavior in the actual work situation or away from work

Consulting with friends, bosses, associates, spouse, or others who can give advice in the area of concern

Coursework and study, including participation in:
- Company training programs
- Outside seminars
- Adult education classes
- Extension courses

On-the-job opportunities, including:
- Trying new projects
- Replacing employees who are on vacation
- Transferring to a different position
- Giving presentations
- Accepting special assignments
- Attending after-work practice sessions
- Assuming "lead person" responsibilities
- Joining or chairing task forces
- Representing the supervisor at meetings
- Switching jobs for a short period

Off-the-job applications, including:
- Joining and/or leading community groups
- Trying a new skill in a volunteer organization
- Giving presentations to civic organizations

Considerations for choosing the appropriate type of developmental activity include:
- Availability of the opportunity
- Level of comfort with the type of activity
- Type of behavior to be developed (knowledge, attitude, or skills)
- Time frame available for making the change
- Resources available

Format for Development Planning

The format shown on pages 16-18 can be used to structure development planning. The steps in structuring the plan are as follows:

Step 1.   Identify no more than three strengths and three development needs. Be careful not to try to change too much too fast. Development plans should not hurt the individual's performance in other areas or negatively impact the productivity of the department or organization. Thus, it is important to focus efforts on priority areas or changes that would be most beneficial to both the individual and the organization.

Step 2.   Specify a performance objective for each strength or development need. These objectives will help you determine whether the goals of the plan have been met. For example, in the listening area, an appropriate objective might be, "To better utilize my ability to listen well to others in group situations."

Step 3.   Identify action plans consisting of specific development activities to help attain the performance objective. This Handbook makes this part of the plan easy to complete, because, in many cases, you can simply list the page number and paragraphs that describe the development activity. Often, tailoring a suggestion can help you apply it to your own situation.

Step 4.   If appropriate, identify others who will be involved in the development process and specify their responsibilities. Changing job responsibilities can be difficult, so it's important to have support from others.

Step 5.   Specify the timetable for attaining each objective. Target completion dates will help encourage steady progress toward objectives.

Building on Strengths

In the spaces provided below, please record the strengths you have targeted for greater utilization, your specific objectives and action plans, the involvement of others you will require, and your target date for completion.

Step 1: STRENGTHS TARGETED FOR GREATER UTILIZATION	Step 3: ACTION PLANS	Step 4: INVOLVEMENT WITH OTHERS	Step 5: TARGET DATE
STRENGTH: PERSONAL MOTIVATION **Step 2: OBJECTIVES** • To better utilize strength in persisting at a task despite unexpected difficulties.	1. Assume project management responsibility for putting the 7X-25 model into production. (Currently six months behind schedule and 15% over budget.)	Meet with my manager to volunteer services and gain his support.	3/15
STRENGTH: OCCUPATIONAL/ TECHNICAL KNOWLEDGE **Step 2: OBJECTIVES** • To better utilize strong expertise in resolving technical problems and questions.	1. Serve as subject matter expert in the development of a 2-hr. training module on how to diagnose and correct operating problems on NEX-X-11 production equipment. 2. Compile notebook documenting most frequently occurring problems in the old X-7 equipment, most probable causes, and solutions.	Approval from manager and several meetings with technical trainers.	1/15 2/31
STRENGTH: CONFLICT MANAGEMENT **Step 2: OBJECTIVES** • To better utilize strength in addressing conflicts and discussing the reasons underlying them.	1. Resolve conflict between Development and Engineering on product introduction of 7X-25 Model.	Establish task force consisting of members from both groups to jointly work out production problems.	4/1

Addressing Development Needs

In the spaces provided below, please record the development needs you have targeted for improvement, your specific objectives and action plans, the involvement of others you will require, and your target date for completion.

Step 1: DEVELOPMENT NEEDS TARGETED FOR IMPROVEMENT	Step 3: ACTION PLANS	Step 4: INVOLVEMENT WITH OTHERS	Step 5: TARGET DATE
DEVELOPMENT NEED: COACHING & DEVELOPING Step 2: OBJECTIVES • Let subordinates know when they are doing well.	1. Read **The One Minute Manager** by Blanchard & Johnson. 2. Outline three ways to use principles in above book on a day-to-day basis with my subordinates. 3. Begin using above principles in dealing with subordinates at least three times a week.	None Discuss and brainstorm ideas with supervisor. Periodic (biweekly) feedback from subordinates on use of these principles.	3/15 3/22 4/1 6/31
• Give stretching and challenging assignments to subordinates.	Begin "grooming" Lee Smith as my replacement. 1. Meet with Lee to discuss her career goals and my desire to have her become my assistant. 2. Meet with Lee to provide overview of my responsiblities. 3. Bring Lee with me to all task force meetings, discussing our objectives for each meeting. 4. Have Lee represent department at all task force meetings and provide me with weekly progress reports. 5. Leave Lee in charge of department in my absence and discuss situations encountered upon my return.	Approval by supervisor.	4/1 4/15 4/22 5/1 6/31 7/1 9/31

Step 1: DEVELOPMENT NEEDS TARGETED FOR IMPROVEMENT	Step 3: ACTION PLANS	Step 4: INVOLVEMENT WITH OTHERS	Step 5: TIMETABLE
DEVELOPMENT NEED: ORGANIZING **Step 2: OBJECTIVES** • To coordinate work with other departments.	1. Establish Pat Layton as liaison between my department and manufacturing.	Clear with my manager and communicate to manufacturing.	3/15
DEVELOPMENT NEED: MOTIVATING OTHERS **Step 2: OBJECTIVES** • To recognize that different employees are motivated by different things.	1. Attend "Managing for Motivation" offered through Xerox Learning Systems. 2. Hold individual interviews with each subordinate to see what I can do differently to help them be more effective. Find out what turns them on about their jobs and where they want to go with their careers. 3. Identify what I've done or can do to provide rewards in the areas of achievement, recognition, work itself, responsibility, advancement, and growth. 4. Provide at least two "rewards" per week for effective performance to subordinates in the categories identified by them as being important. 5. Meet again with each subordinate for feedback over last three months and suggestions for additional improvements.	Approval by my manager and enrollment through personnel. Meetings with subordinate.	7/31 8/28 9/15 10/1 12/1 12/15

FACTOR 1

Administrative Skills

When Ed Jones took over a new division, his staff was impressed by his leadership abilities. Ed quickly and accurately assessed problems and made sound problem-solving decisions.

As the months went by, however, Ed's staff became less enthusiastic. Because Ed lacked the necessary administrative skills, his decisions were not effectively implemented. His inability to structure his own time made it difficult for his staff members to structure theirs; as a result, everyone's productivity suffered.

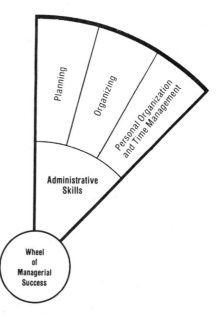

As this case illustrates, an effective manager possesses a balance of cognitive and administrative skills— cognitive skills to identify ways to **get** things moving, and administrative skills to **keep** them moving.

This section stresses the administrative aspect of management. It presents development activities in the following three areas to help you structure your efforts and those of others to attain maximum productivity.

Planning: setting goals, developing strategies and schedules for meeting these goals, and anticipating obstacles to goal attainment

Administrative Skills

Organizing: addressing changing department demands and employees' skills by improving organizational structure in numerous areas

Personal Organization and Time Management: allocating your own time, and efficiently and effectively arranging and processing paperwork

Planning

"Plans are nothing; planning is everything."
—Dwight D. Eisenhower

Many managers give lip-service to the importance of planning, then, when time is short, abandon it in favor of getting started on the "real" work.

Unfortunately, this is a shortsighted approach. Work performed without adequate planning often falls short of the desired goals or misses them entirely. And, in the long run, the required rework at the end of the project takes much more time than that required for adequate planning—living proof of the variation on Murphy's Law that states, "There's never time to do it right but always time to do it over."

The term "planning" applies to a broad range of skills. This section divides those skills into three parts.·

Part I, General Planning, contains suggestions that apply to planning in all situations.
- Establishing Goals and Objectives (p. 25)
- Establishing Schedules by Working Back for a Target Date (p. 25)
- Using Plans to Manage (p. 26)
- Consulting With Skilled Planners (p. 26)
- Involving Others in the Planning Process (p. 27)

Part II, Long-range Planning, applies to strategic planning situations—those that require a broad organizational perspective or deal with long-term issues.
- Developing Leadership Vision (p. 27)
- Developing a Greater Long-range Perspective (p. 28)
- Maintaining a Balance Between Overall "Big Picture" and Day-to-day Needs and Activities (p. 28)
- Preparing a Plan (p. 29)
- Anticipating Problems and Developing Contingency Plans (p. 29)
- Preventive Planning (p. 30)
- Identifying Projects (p. 30)

Part III, Project Planning, provides suggestions for managing specific projects.
- Preparing for an Absence (p. 31)
- Diagnosing Your Skills (p. 32)
- Making Plans That Are Realistic (p. 32)
- Assessing Project Needs (p. 33)

Tips

- Set aside one hour per day of "quiet time" for planning activities.

- Study the long-range plan for your company or division and consider its implications for your department.

- Read *Megatrends* by Richard Naisbitt.

- Attend a seminar on management by objectives.

- Read G.S. Odiorne's book, *Executive Skills.*

- Have subordinates submit an annual work plan for your review. Ask them to include specific objectives, priorities, and timetables. Use these ideas to construct an operational plan for your department.

- Read publications such as *Business Week, Fortune,* and *Wall Street Journal* to keep abreast of business developments. Determine any implications these developments might have for you or your company.

- To better balance attention to detail with broader planning, ask your supervisor to give you feedback when you are uneven in stressing one or the other.

- Seek opportunities for assignments requiring formal planning and organizing.

- Take care to use your calendar consistently to schedule all foreseeable events.

- Get your supervisor's help in budgeting your time.

- Add more details to your plans.

- Review with your manager your present methods of organizing and planning your work.

- Ask your manager for assignments that require careful planning and attention to detail.

- Set definite deadlines with your manager when taking on tasks.

- Seek your manager's feedback on your understanding of job priorities.

- Ask your manager to let you know of instances when your planning could be more effective.

- Write a three- to five-year plan for your department including strengths, weaknesses, human resource requirements, equipment, budget, etc.

- Attend one of the seminars on long-range strategic planning listed at the end of this section.

- Take on special assignments involving long-range planning for company operations. Devote one day a week to these broad assignments.

- Take on long-range projects; ask your manager to closely monitor your planning.

- Join a company task force dealing with a problem relevant to the company's future. Ask your manager for periodic reports on your performance.

- To improve broad planning skills, sacrifice minor details in favor of broad objectives.

- Attend a course on project planning.

- Break large projects into several smaller steps, with deadlines for each step. Ask your manager for feedback regarding the adequacy of your project plan.

- When managing several projects draw timelines on a big piece of paper for each one to help distribute the workload over time.

Part I: General Planning

Establishing Goals and Objectives

Setting goals and objectives is a task that is familiar to most business people, and most would agree that the identification of goals and objectives is important both personally, to establish a direction for their work, and organizationally, to help ensure the success of the company.

Time pressures, however, often cause the setting of goals and objectives to be pushed aside. If this is true in your case, the first step to take in improving your general planning is to set aside time for establishing your goals and objectives. The following guidelines can help you.

- Generate a list of the major goals and objectives you want to accomplish in a year's time.
- Identify the intermediate objectives you will have to meet to attain the major goals.
- Review your goals and objectives with your superior to ensure that your plans are on track and to determine the best way to go about accomplishing them.

Establishing Schedules by Working Back from a Target Date

When a project must be completed by a certain date, establishing schedules by working back from that date is the simplest way to ensure that the deadline will be met. This technique consists of the following five steps.

1. Create a list of ail tasks that must be accomplished during the course of the project. Arrange the tasks in chronological order.
2. Have a calendar, pencil, and paper handy. Look at the last task to be completed and determine how much time it will take. Then work back from this target date to set a start date for that task. Record this date on your schedule.
3. Work back from the start date of the last task to determine a start date for the second-to-the-last task.
4. Continue to work back in this manner until all tasks have been scheduled. If you find there is not enough time for all required tasks, extend the target date or reduce the time allotted for some or all of the tasks.
5. Review your schedule with your superior to determine whether your time estimates are realistic.

Using Plans to Manage

All too often, managers develop elaborate plans only to have them collect dust on a shelf or in a file drawer. For a plan to be an effective management tool, it must be continually monitored and updated. If you document performance against the plan (e.g., budgeted vs. actual labor, expenses, and schedule), others will take your plans seriously and you will be better able to develop realistic plans for future projects.

If your plan is well detailed and specific, it should be quite simple to manage through use of:
1. Target dates for various phases of the project
2. Intermittent reports from your subordinates on their progress toward goals
3. Monitoring and follow-up dates

By use of a tickler file or other valuable organizational tools, you can manage ongoing work and monitor subordinates' performance and progress toward goals against established objectives.

Consulting With Skilled Planners

Individuals in your organization who are known for their planning skills may be able to help you improve your skills. Here are three ways you can learn from these people.
- **Observe the planning process.** Ask your superior to help you become involved in various planning processes—personal planning activities, meetings, and so forth. Attend these activities and observe the techniques of the skilled planners. When deemed appropriate by your superior, contribute to the proceedings and ask your superior to provide feedback on your performance.
- **Review the written plans of skilled planners.** Notice what they included in their plans and how they organized them. Find out how the plans were developed and who was involved in their development. And finally, find out how the plans are used in the management process and whether they have proved effective.
- **Ask for advice on your plans.** Review your plans with someone who can offer constructive suggestions for improvement. Ask the person to comment on both the content and format of your plans.

Involving Others in the Planning Process

Why involve others in planning? Because when people participate in planning something, they also make a personal investment in reaching the goal. When you're making plans that affect subordinates, try the following process to involve others.

1. List all the individuals who will be affected by your plan. Review your list with a colleague to make sure you have included everyone.
2. Review your plan with each individual on the list, gathering information on how the plan might affect him or her.
3. Take time to explain to each person how her or his piece of the plan fits into the overall picture.
4. Ask each person for ideas on how to improve the plan, and incorporate them when possible.

By conveying mutual investment in the objective, you will be better able to get others to "buy into" your goal.

Part II: Long-range Planning

Developing Leadership Vision

Leadership vision involves developing a picture of where you see your company or department going. It is the cornerstone in setting objectives and goals for both yourself and your subordinates, and it is the driving force behind organizational growth and development.

- Use mental imagery to envision where you see your department or organization in five years.
    - What are your people doing?
    - What do your facilities look like?
    - What new directions do you see your department or organization taking?
- Record your thoughts and ideas on paper, and begin developing preliminary plans for meeting your objectives. The section in this chapter entitled **Long-range Planning** gives you some suggestions on how to create effective long-range plans.
- The final, but probably most important, step is to get buy-in to your vision from your team of subordinates. Refer to the section entitled **Motivating Others** for suggestions on how to do this most effectively.

Developing a Greater Long-range Perspective

Advancement to higher levels in the organization typically requires looking further into the future in various decision-making activities. Following are suggestions for developing this long-range perspective.

- Whenever you generate or analyze plans or major decisions, make a conscious effort to anticipate their long-range impact. In other words, develop the habit of long-range thinking.
- Periodically set aside time to anticipate potential problems or opportunities.
- Note trends and try to project them into the future based on available information and insight. Reading current publications in your field will help you become aware of these trends and their anticipated development.
- Solicit information from people inside and outside your organization regarding anticipated developments that may affect your industry, responsibilities, or career.
- Establish a network including customers, suppliers, regulatory agencies, and related industries from which you can obtain information prior to relevant occurrences rather than after the events have happened.
- Encourage subordinates to contribute and discuss ideas regarding anticipated developments or potential problem areas.

Maintaining a Balance Between Overall "Big Picture" and Day-to-day Needs and Activities

George L. Morrisey, a leading advocate of Managing by Objectives and Results (MOR), says that to maintain a big picture perspective, managers must:

1. Define roles and overall goal.
2. Determine key results areas.
3. Identify and specify indicators of effectiveness.
4. Select and set objectives.

By breaking the goal—or "mission," as Morrisey refers to it—into smaller, more manageable units, managers can evaluate daily activities against key objectives and, thus, maintain a big picture perspective.

Preparing a Plan

The best way to develop long-range planning skills is to actually create long-range plans. Following is a three-step process for identifying and generating these plans.

1. If you are not already doing so, identify a departmental objective that requires a long-range plan. Request that you be given responsibility for creating this plan. Also suggest a date by which you intend to complete the plan; this will help ensure that you complete your project in a timely way.
2. Create your plan. Following are topics or sections that are included in most long-range plans:
   - Goals
   - Objectives and subobjectives
   - Detailed schedule for accomplishment of objectives
   - Budget
   - Required resources
   - Constraints
   - Implementation process
3. Review your completed plan with your superior to assess its completeness and accuracy.

Anticipating Problems and Developing Contingency Plans

Identification of risk areas in the initial stages of work planning is one way you can anticipate and prepare for potential problems.

Each time you begin work on a project or long-term assignment over the next three months, initiate the following process:

1. Prepare a breakdown of all functional tasks.
2. Analyze each component to detect areas of risk. For example, information required for effective work planning might be unavailable, or a technical procedure new to employees might be required. Perhaps a service group which you utilize is undergoing staffing problems. Be a negative thinker for this moment; try to think of *everything* that could go wrong.
3. Categorize potential problems into high and low risk areas.
4. Prepare several possible approaches to such problems in the event that they occur.

5. Introduce safety factors into your planning for high risk areas. Consider allocating more time and/or funds to these phases. Also introduce tough control methods in the high risk areas; ensure that you are kept fully informed of all developments, either through actual observation or written reports.

Preventive Planning

Although there will always be many unforeseeable circumstances which remain out of your hands, preventive remedies can be successfully initiated in many instances.

1. Over the next month, keep a list of the problems you face on the job, recording cause, action, and final outcome.
2. At the end of this period:
   - Examine this list. Use the available hindsight to critically examine the extent to which these problems could have been prevented.
   - Try to classify the causes of the prevalent problems into broad categories for developmental purposes. For example, lists of similar problems might suggest a common cause such as a lack of planning, a failure to attend to detail, poor communications, etc.
   - Begin a program of development in the identified weak areas within the next two or three weeks.
3. After a three-month period, repeat the above process; you should find a decrease in the frequency of problems.

Identifying Projects

Some management positions require less long-range planning than others. Even if your current responsibilities do not include planning, you should work on attaining long-range planning skills. Although you may not need these skills at the moment, they will most likely be required for managerial advancement.

If you are unable to start any long-range planning projects in your current position, discuss with your superior the possibility of assuming responsibility for the planning of projects that are outside your immediate job area.

Part III: Project Planning

Preparing for an Absence

The absence of key people can cause bottlenecks in the work flow of an organization. Thus, it is important that you plan your absences and encourage your subordinates to do the same to prevent such delays. Following are suggestions for preparing for absences.

- Communicate your scheduled absences to all concerned individuals via memos, unit bulletin board, staff meetings, or other appropriate means. Encourage people who often need your help to plan their work and request whatever assistance they need before you leave.

- Delegate tasks as necessary to ensure that the work flow continues without interruption or delay while you are gone.
- Inform concerned persons of sources of assistance available during your absence. For example, your secretary may be able to locate copies of reports for those who need them.

If you return from an absence to find that work has been delayed or stopped, examine your planning process to determine what additional or different planning steps you should take prior to future absences.

Diagnosing Your Skills

Project planning is a skill that improves with experience; each plan you create and execute can yield valuable lessons for subsequent planning efforts. Following are suggestions for diagnosing your skills based on completed plans.

- Review the plans you have created in terms of the project-planning techniques listed in the preceding subsection. Did you use any of the techniques? Did they improve your plans? Were there other techniques you could have used to make your plans more effective?
- Ask others involved in your projects to help you assess your plans. What successes can be attributed to the strengths of your plans? What problems could have been avoided through improvements in the plans? A good way to ensure that project reviews occur is to incorporate them into the project plans (for example, make a review the final step of each project plan).

Making Plans That Are Realistic

Unrealistic plans can sometimes create more problems than they solve. For example, an impossible schedule set by one department may eventually affect the schedules of many other departments, causing inefficient use of resources, late introduction to the marketplace of an advertised product, and a general sense that things are out of control.

As a result, it's essential that managers include techniques for evaluating project plans as a part of the planning process. Following are suggested "reality checks" you can perform to help ensure your project plans are realistic.

- PERT charting and Gantt charting are techniques that can be used in all fields. Sources of information about these techniques include books, seminars, and individuals who have used them. Make a point of learning about and using the techniques that are appropriate for your projects.
- After composing a plan, have a trusted peer play the devil's advocate by confronting you with all possible things that could go wrong. Make changes to address problems you may have overlooked.

- In addition to evaluating individual plans, it's important to evaluate how one plan affects all of the others. Get in the habit of keeping a calendar large enough to chart all your projects simultaneously. Keeping track of the overall picture is the best way to avoid overcommitting yourself and gives you a quick reference when monitoring the availability of resources and time.
- Various groups of people affected by a plan should have contributed to it throughout its construction. When the plan is complete, ask each person to review the final plan one last time with the issue of realism as the focus of the review.

Assessing Project Needs

A major step in assuring the success of a project is planning the resources required for completion of the project. Without timely access to resources of all types, delays will occur. To ensure that you have adequately assessed your project needs, follow these steps:

1. Make a list of all required resources in each of the following areas:
   - Personnel needed to accomplish the task
   - Equipment needed and when
   - Other supplies
   - Information needed to make an informed decision
   - Time frames appropriate for the task
   - Preparations for anticipated problems

   To make sure your list is complete, ask your superior and those involved in the project to review it and suggest additions.
2. For each item on the list, determine:
   - When it will be needed
   - How much advance notice will be required to obtain it
   - The process to be followed in obtaining it
3. Make sure that all persons responsible for obtaining resources are informed, preferably in writing, of what is expected of them. Follow up as necessary.

Recommended Readings

Abell, Derek F. *Defining the Business: The Starting Point of Strategic Planning.* Englewood Cliffs, NJ: Prentice-Hall, 1980.

The author discusses the need to make basic decisions about a company's activity and the competitive arenas in which strategy will be implemented before any strategic planning is undertaken.

Allen, L. *Making Managerial Planning More Effective.* New York, NY: McGraw-Hill, 1982.

This book stresses planning as the most effective management tool. It explains what the problems in planning are, why it is an essential part of general management, how to build in accountability, and how to coordinate the various areas concerned with a plan. It also focuses on choosing products/customers, setting standards and performance measures, budgeting, and long-range strategies.

Argenti, J. *Practical Corporate Planning.* Winchester, MA: Allen & Unwin, 1980.

The author, an international corporate consultant, believes in simplification of the corporate planning structure. He begins by destroying some basic myths about corporate planning, stating succinctly what it is and is not. Additional chapters outline strategies for defining objectives, forecasting, appraising the company, and developing alternative strategies, action plans, and budgets. The book is directed at executives of small- and medium-sized companies.

Fink, Steven. *Crisis Management: Planning for the Inevitable.* New York, NY: AMACOM, 1986.

The author uses actual crises drawn from his own extensive hands-on management experience to vividly demonstrate how to identify, isolate, and manage a crisis; how managers can forecast their next crises and develop critical contingency plans; and how any individual at any rung of the management ladder can strive to create achievement out of adversity. The book gives four examples of actual mega-crises and the unfolding of each crisis.

Lorange, P. *Corporate Planning: An Executive Viewpoint.* Englewood Cliffs, NJ: Prentice-Hall, 1980.

Written by an authority on corporate planning systems, this book discusses how to determine planning needs and implement planning systems. Lorange covers pitfalls and problems, tailoring to a particular situation, modification, evolution, and the executive's role.

Makridakis, S., and Wheelwright, S.C., eds. *Forecasting.* Amsterdam and New York, N.Y.: North-Holland Publishing Co., 1979.

This book consists of a selection of essays by authorities covering recent concepts and knowledge about forecasting. The book concludes with a review of recent forecasting publications.

Naisbitt, John. *Megatrends: Ten Directions Transforming Our Lives.* New York, NY: Warner Books, Inc., 1982.

John Naisbitt, adviser to many of America's leading corporations, details America's shift from industrial production to providing services and information. From this book, the reader can project both business and career moves based on analysis of the trends and future of America's social structures.

Naylor, Thomas H. *Corporate Planning Models.* Reading, MA: Addison-Wesley, 1979.

The author outlines a systematic approach to design, development, and implementation of corporate planning models. He defines pragmatic steps required to achieve acceptance of computer-based planning models by top management. The book also describes typical political conflicts surrounding corporate planning models and includes five corporate modeling case studies.

Odiorne, G.; Weihrich, H.; and Mendleson, J. *Executive Skills.* Dubuque, IA: William C. Brown Publishers, 1980.

The authors have written this book to define and clarify the purpose of MBO. The book can supplement any general management textbook to help participants in executive development programs, or executives and managers who would like to know more about MBO.

Suggested Seminars

The seminars listed here were selected for their appeal to a managerial audience and have received good to excellent ratings from managers attending them.

Because of the dynamic nature of the seminar marketplace, some seminars may have been added, upgraded, or replaced, and others may no longer be offered. Additional information about these seminars may be obtained by calling the vendor directly, or through Seminar Clearinghouse International, a subscriber organization located in St. Paul, Minnesota. Call 612/293-1004 for information.

AMERICAN MANAGEMENT ASSOCIATIONS, P.O. Box 319, Saranac Lake, NY 12983, 518/891-0065.

Planning Techniques for Effective Management. This program includes: planning concepts; the planning process; corporate culture; problem analysis; Pareto analysis; setting your direction using objectives; and putting it all together: flow-charting and Pert techniques.
Length: 3 days
Cost: $795
Locations: Washington, DC; Chicago, IL; New York, NY.

Strategic Planning. The program covers key steps and end results, establishing a "climate" for planning, defining the corporate mission, key result areas that drive the business; how to conduct a situational analysis—internal and external factors; formulating assumptions about your business in the plan period; opportunities and threats in the key result areas; and implementation of the strategic plan.
Length: 3 days
Cost: $995
Locations: San Francisco, CA; Atlanta, GA; Chicago, IL; Bolton Landing, NY; New York, NY; Hilton Head Island, SC; Dallas, TX; Williamsburg, VA.

COLUMBIA UNIVERSITY, Executive Programs, 807 Uris Hall, New York, NY 10027, 212/280-3395, ext. 007.

Business Strategy. This program addresses itself to the development of such skills as strategic planning and implementation at the business-unit level, and a systematic approach to planning through continuous evaluation of competitors, customers, external environment, and internal resources.

Length: 2 weeks
Cost: $6000
Location: New York, NY.

MICHIGAN STATE UNIVERSITY, 7 Olds Hall, East Lansing, MI 48824, 517/353-8711, 800/428-4284 (in Mich.).

How to Prepare and Use a Business Plan. Three-day program which includes the following: developing a business plan; market forecasts and new business ventures; the Drucker Analysis for assessing markets; the situation analysis; the sales forecast; the planning gap; and innovative imitation.
Length: 3 days
Cost: $995
Location: Grand Rapids, MI.

Simplified Strategic Planning for Small to Mid-sized Companies. Overview of program topics being included in this seminar: the strategic planning process; external situation analysis; capabilities assessment; strategic analysis and decisions; goals and objectives; budgets; and schedules and agendas.
Length: 2 days
Cost: $795
Locations: Mackinac Island, MI; Traverse City, MI; Troy, MI.

PERSONNEL DECISIONS, INC., 2000 Plaza VII Tower, 45 South Seventh Street, Minneapolis, MN 55402, 612/339-0927, 800/633-4410, ext. 875 (outside Minn.).

The Emerging Manager: Skills & Strategies For Success. The Emerging Manager is a week-long (40-hour) program presenting a full range of management and leadership skills for first level managers at an early stage in their careers. Participants not only gain knowledge but also build skills and self-awareness in the following areas: interpersonal skills, adaptability skills, cognitive (thinking) skills, communication skills, personal motivation skills, administrative skills, and leadership skills.
Length: 5 days
Cost: $1750
Location: Minneapolis, MN.

SOUTHERN METHODIST UNIVERSITY, Edwin L. Cox School of Business, Management Center, Dallas, TX 75275, 214/692-3255.

Strategic Planning for Small and Mid-sized Companies. The objective of the program is to enable participants to create a vision of what your

company should be, define purpose and business mission, and learn how to face up to reality.
Length: 3 days
Cost: $995
Location: Dallas, TX.

STRATEGIC MANAGEMENT GROUP, INC., 3624 Market Street, Philadelphia, PA 19104, 215/387-4000.
Strategic Management Game. The Strategic Management Game, corporate training edition, is a powerful computer-based business simulation which reveals insights into many functional aspects of business management. Participants take control of a multi-million dollar company faced with several problems including: declining profitability, inefficient operations, and reduced liquidity.
Length: 5 days
Cost: Call vendor
Location: Hilton Head, SC.

TECHNOLOGY FUTURES INC., 411 West 13th Street, Suite 801, Austin, TX 78701, 800/832-3887.
Planning for the Technical Professional. Participants in this program will learn more effective use of people, funds, information, and time; basic planning principles in practical situations; integrating design, development, manufacturing, marketing, and service functions; integrating technical projects with other organizational activities; and using alternate scenarios in organizational planning.
Length: 3 days
Cost: $995
Location: Austin, TX.

UNIVERSITY OF MICHIGAN, School of Business Administration, Executive Education Center, Ann Arbor, MI 48109, 313/763-1000.
Strategy: Formulation and Implementation. The program provides a working knowledge of the following topics: basics of strategy; structural evolution of industries; competitor analysis as a basis for strategy formulation; global competitive challenges; diversification; strategy and technology; comprehensive model of strategy implementation; the role of structure in strategy implementation; and strategy and the management process.
Length: 6 days
Cost: $2850
Location: Ann Arbor, MI.

Organizing

As a manager or aspiring manager, you must be aware of the dynamic structure of your organization. Departmental demands and employee skills are constantly changing, and it's important that you be responsive to these changes. Monitoring them involves performing activities ranging from diagnosing structural problems by surveying employees to improving work flow by changing the office layout.

Personnel Decisions, Inc. offers a number of services to help you more effectively design your organizational structure. For more information, call or write to Personnel Decisions, Inc., 2000 Plaza VII Tower, 45 South Seventh Street, Minneapolis, MN 55402, (612) 339-0927.

In this section are other suggestions for staying on top of structural changes within your organization and department, including:
- Improving the Structure of Your Organization (p. 43)
- Improving the Span of Control in Your Organizational Structure (p. 46)
- Improving Coordination (p. 47)
- Organizing and Scheduling the Work of Subordinates (p. 48)
- Organizing an Effective Filing System (p. 49)
- Improving Documentation (p. 49)
- Improving Work Flow by Changing Office Layout (p. 50)
- Improving Efficiency Through the Use of Machines (p. 50)

Tips

- Draw your organization chart according to two or three different approaches and evaluate which would work best.

- Analyze how your organizational structure will need to be different one, two, and five years from now.

- Keep abreast of changes in other parts of the organization which may impact the way your organization should be structured.

- Determine if subordinates see their responsibilities and priorities in the same way you do.

- Make certain everyone working for you has an updated position description.

- Be alert to new technology which can increase your department's efficiency.

- Ask yourself who or what could be eliminated without any loss of production or goal achievement.

- Ask people in other departments for input about how your department could be better structured to improve cooperation.

- Talk to people in similar departments to see how they are organized.

- Look for ways to shift routine tasks from your higher paid people to your lower paid people.

- Read a book on process flow analysis and apply the principles to your department.

- If your work is highly dependent on expensive equipment, explore adding additional shifts to better utilize it.

- Delegate decisions to the lowest level possible.

- Clarify the steps and procedures to be used in accomplishing key tasks in your department.

- Have someone trace the flow of paperwork to assure efficiency and avoid duplication.

- Ask subordinates to identify tasks or procedures that should be eliminated or duplicated.

- Look for ways to reduce the duplication of effort in your department.

- Detail each step that must occur from the time work enters your department until it leaves your department. Try to eliminate unnecessary steps.

- Look at the physical layout of your department to see how it might be changed to improve communications or enhance efficiency.

Improving the Structure of Your Organization

The structure of an organization is dynamic. This means that a structure that worked well at one point in time may no longer be efficient or effective. As the demands of your department and the skills of your subordinates change, attention to the structural design of your department can help you identify potential problem areas. The following are four ways to examine the organizational structure of your work unit.

- Start by listing your work unit's goals. Then analyze the operations performed in your department. One way to perform this analysis is to draw a flow chart of the tasks that must be accomplished and indicate the flow of information necessary to meet these goals.
- Next, study your work unit's organization—who reports to whom and their responsibilities. Compare the current structure to your analysis of the work flow by asking yourself the following questions.
  - Does the chart reveal duplication of effort on any of the operational steps?
  - Are any employees performing functions not directly related to the accomplishment of departmental goals?
  - Does the work unit lack technical expertise that would help it attain its goals?
  - Does the department possess technical expertise it no longer needs?
  - Do individuals in the work unit have ready access to the information, expertise, or other resources needed to perform their functions?
  - Are too many or too few individuals available to accomplish the work load for any step of the process?
- Analyze the evolution of your organizational structure. How did it come to be structured the way it is today? Do elements of the structure no longer serve a purpose? For example, was the structure built around the capabilities of managers or employees who are no longer with the organization?
- Research the structure of other work units in your organization, or other organizations within your company, such as sister divisions or departments in other plants. Find out how they are set up and examine the ways in which they are satisfied or dissatisfied with their organizational structure.

Diagnosing Structural Problems by Surveying Employees

If your organization is experiencing serious problems and you are unsure of the causes of these problems, consider conducting a survey of the key members of your staff to determine if structural problems exist. Following are important questions, listed by subject area, to include in your survey.

Clarity of Responsibilities

- What is the main purpose of your job?
- Do you feel that your function is unclear to some people or work groups? If so, who are they and why do you think the confusion exists?
- Do overlapping responsibilities exist between any part of your operation and any other part(s) of the division/department? If so, identify the areas that overlap and the possible reasons for the overlap.
- Do employees under or around you ever express confusion about who is responsible for certain tasks or functions? If so, list areas of confusion.

Decision Making

What kinds of decisions:
- Get stalled and why?
- Do you think you should be making?
- Should your boss be making?
- Should your subordinates be making?

Organizational Structure

- Are you satisfied with the organizational structure beneath you? If not, what would you like to change?
- If you could make changes in the structure of any part of your organization, what would they be?
- To whom do you directly report? Do you report to anyone else in any capacity? If so, explain the situation and your opinion of its effectiveness.
- Does anyone who reports directly to you report to anyone else in any capacity? If so, explain the situation and your opinion of its effectiveness.

Span of Control

- Do you feel that you supervise too many or too few people to be efficient and effective? If so, what could be done to remedy the situation?
- To what extent do you feel that your boss supervises too many or too few people to be efficient and effective? How could the situation be improved?

Authority

- To what extent do you have sufficient authority to carry out your responsibilities?

General

- Describe any ways (other than those already listed) in which the present organizational structure makes it difficult for you to do your job.

Improving the Span of Control in Your Organizational Structure

If managers or supervisors are responsible for too many people, management time may be used inefficiently. Higher level tasks may be neglected because the managers must spend too much time dealing with subordinates' problems, and subordinates' time may be wasted because of inadequate control, poor guidance, and slow decision making.

If managers are responsible for too few people, they may supervise too closely, which can also result in inefficiency on the part of both managers and subordinates. In addition, managers may become insecure; if they don't have enough work to do, they may worry about the stability of their positions.

Researchers have found that no standard rules exist for choosing an appropriate span of control; different spans are appropriate for different situations. To analyze your situation, consider the following factors.

- **Manager's level in the organization.** Higher levels often spend more time on special projects that are unrelated to subordinates, thus leaving less time for supervision. Also, they typically have fewer direct reports.
- **Manager's experience level.** Experienced managers often accomplish tasks faster than inexperienced managers do and therefore can handle more direct reports.
- **Similarity of the functions the manager supervises.** If the functions being supervised are similar, less knowledge is required on the part of the manager. Also, more subordinates will be doing the same types of work and, therefore, will be available to assist each other, enabling the manager to handle more direct reports.
- **Geographic proximity of the functions supervised.** When functions are geographically separated, more time is spent traveling, mailing documents, making phone connections, and so forth, thus reducing the number of direct reports that can be effectively managed.
- **Complexity of the functions supervised.** Complex functions often require more supervision, especially if subordinates are inexperienced, which serves to lower the number of direct reports.
- **Direction and control needed by subordinates.** Employees with low levels of competence or experience require more supervision than do those with higher levels.

- **Degree to which functions or tasks must be coordinated.** Functions that require a great deal of coordination require more managerial time, again reducing the number of direct reports.
- **Extent to which the manager/supervisor must plan and review subordinates' activities.** If employees are at low levels of competence or experience, or if the tasks are extremely important, more managerial time must be spent on planning and review. This also reduces the number of direct reports.
- **Amount of available organizational assistance and support.** If the organization provides assistance in areas such as training and guidance, the manager can spend less time on these functions, which increases the number of direct reports that can be effectively managed.
- **Amount of supervision required for vendors and other people who do not formally report to the manager.** If the manager must supervise a number of vendors, distributors, franchises, etc., less time will be available for working with direct reports, which, of course, reduces the number of direct reports.

You may also wish to ask the other managers in your organization to evaluate their own situations using these factors. Then compare your assessment with theirs and work together to arrive at an appropriate span of control.

Improving Coordination

In some cases, confusion in an organization may be due to a lack of coordination rather than flaws in the organizational structure. Following are mechanisms you should examine if coordination becomes a problem.

- **Chain of command.** Managers and supervisors at every level should clearly understand their responsibilities and have the authority and procedures to carry them out. Formal policies should be developed for issues that arise consistently.
- **Horizontal communications.** Individuals on the same level, especially managers of different departments, must communicate effectively and efficiently if an organization is to run smoothly. Consider the current state of horizontal communication in your department. Is communication blocked or hampered in any way? What could be done to improve it?
- **Liaisons.** Persons acting as liaisons can help managers coordinate the activities of their organizations. Product managers, customer

representatives, and project managers are examples of individuals responsible for communicating with the various people and coordinating the various functions for particular products, clients, or projects.

- **Formal committees.** Several kinds of committees can be used to improve coordination. Descriptions of three of them follow.
    - **General management committees** make joint decisions across departments, setting policies for and overseeing the operations of the company as a whole. Members are senior managers.
    - **Special area committees** consist of managers with special areas of interest, such as salary determination, capital expenditures, research and development, and planning.
    - **Multiple-level management committees** facilitate vertical communication and coordination. Typically, top managers hold regular meetings with their immediate subordinates. Each of these subordinate managers then meets with employees on the next level down.

        Take care to ensure that committees are not overused and that all active committees continue to serve useful purposes.

Organizing and Scheduling the Work of Subordinates

Do you sometimes observe some of your subordinates working feverishly to juggle many tasks while others are sitting around with nothing to do? You can greatly improve work flow and efficiency in your department by carefully scheduling the work of your subordinates. To do so, follow these guidelines:

1. When setting project objectives, examine the process from inception to the final output.
    - Determine the steps necessary.
    - Chart out these steps, looking for possible bottlenecks in the process.
    - If bottlenecks occur, attempt to circumvent these by shortening or breaking down the various steps to distribute the work more evenly.
    - If efficiency is slowed due to confused accountability, streamline the process where possible so authority for various stages of the project changes hands minimally.
2. Combine your final process plan with a running time log for each individual involved to see where time is actually being spent.

3. Based on your analysis, determine whether or not your department needs reorganization in terms of subordinates' responsibilities, accountabilities, and so forth.

Organizing an Effective Filing System

Poor filing systems waste time and can even stop the flow of work if they inhibit people from finding the needed documents. Often, secretaries are the most competent people for setting up effective filing systems. They have been trained in this area and are experienced in identifying the most commonly referenced subject areas. Thus, you might want to team up with your secretary or set up a committee of secretaries to streamline your office files.

Following are guidelines that such a committee should consider in creating its system design.

- The system should be understandable to those who do not use it on a daily basis. This ensures that information can be retrieved even when the person in charge of the files is on vacation or leaves the organization.
- The most used folders should be readily accessible.
- The filing cabinets should be placed near those who use them most often.
- Guidelines should be established regarding the length of time different types of files should be retained. Experts suggest that current operations files should include no more than one year's correspondence. However, your organization should determine its own policies based on the use and importance of its filed materials.

Improving Documentation

Information and decisions which are trusted to memory may easily be forgotten or unavailable for use when they are needed. To ensure the documentation and accessibility of information, consider the following suggestions.

1. Document decisions made at meetings by asking someone to take notes of the proceedings.
2. Organize the notes or minutes of the meeting in useable form for future reference, and file them so that they can be readily located when needed.

3. Document decisions reached by phone or in one-to-one meetings in the same way, and make certain they are filed for future reference.
4. If appropriate, carbon copy the documentation to others involved with, or affected by, the decision so that everyone has a chance to react and make corrections if necessary.

Improving Work Flow by Changing the Office Layout

Professional office designers study offices to determine the most effective layout of furniture and equipment. You can apply their techniques on a less sophisticated level to eliminate inefficiencies in your work area.

Draw a diagram of your current office layout, then trace work flow and travel patterns on this diagram by determining who walks where to get what or to talk to whom. You might want to trace the flow of a particular job, such as the flow of a product through a plant. After you have determined the current flow, ask yourself the following questions to determine if the current work flow and placement of work stations, files, desks, and so forth are as efficient as possible.

- Are equipment and supplies located near those who need them most often?
- Are the work stations of people who must communicate frequently placed close together to facilitate communication?
- Are high-traffic or noisy areas located too close to areas in which people require relative quiet in order to concentrate?
- Should the office be rearranged to minimize tiring work conditions, such as poor ventilation, fumes, dust, or poor lighting?

Improving Efficiency Through the Use of Machines

In many cases, the productivity increases realized through the use of machines quickly make up for the cost of the machines. To determine whether your department has enough machines, ask yourself the following questions.

- Are tasks that could be partially or totally performed by a machine performed by hand?
- Is anyone using obsolete or poorly functioning equipment that causes downtime or slowdowns in the work flow?

- Would the productivity gained by investing in updated models of equipment offset the cost of the new equipment?
- Is there enough equipment so that employees don't waste time waiting in line to perform their tasks?

Recommended Readings

Bain, D. *The Productivity Prescription: The Manager's Guide to Improving Productivity and Profits.* New York, NY: McGraw-Hill, 1982.

This practical guide for managers at all levels provides a set of guidelines, techniques, and procedures that can be used to measure productivity, analyze productivity problems, and devise solutions that can be implemented at minimal cost. Numerous examples and illustrations plus four extended case studies serve to dramatize how these techniques and procedures can be successfully applied in diverse business situations.

Fitzsimmons, James A., and Sullivan, Robert S. *Service Operations Management.* New York, NY: McGraw-Hill, 1982.

This book discusses how to design and manage service operations. Decision models are discussed and applied to such topics as service facility location, work design, utilization of service capacity, service vehicle scheduling and rating, and measuring and controlling service quality.

Januz, Lauren R., and Jones, Susan K. *Time Management for Executives.* New York, NY: Charles Scribner's Sons, 1981.

In the chapter on filing, the authors discuss six ways to organize a personal filing system and explain how to use each type of system. Practical suggestions on filing, cross-referencing, and purging are provided.

Neuschel, R. *Management Systems for Profit and Growth (2nd ed.).* New York, NY: McGraw-Hill, 1976.

In this book systems and procedures are treated not as mere paperwork and clerical detail, but as one of the basic administrative techniques through which the complex business organization acts and by which it controls and coordinates its actions.

Salvendy, G. *Handbook of Industrial Engineers.* New York, NY: John Wiley & Sons, 1982.

Chapter 2 of this book is written by Louis E. Davis and deals with organization and job design, as well as process flow analysis.

Suggested Seminars

The seminars listed here were selected for their appeal to a managerial audience and have received good to excellent ratings from managers attending them.

Because of the dynamic nature of the seminar marketplace, some seminars may have been added, upgraded, or replaced, and others may no longer be offered. Additional information about these seminars may be obtained by calling the vendor directly, or through Seminar Clearinghouse International, a subscriber organization located in St. Paul, Minnesota. Call 612/293-1004 for information.

ARTHUR ANDERSEN & CO., Center for Professional Education, 1405 North Fifth Avenue, St. Charles, IL 60174, 312/507-7460.

Planning and Managing Your Time. Some of the key topics included in this one-day seminar are: developing an action plan, proper planning, establishing achievable goals, setting priorities, avoiding wasted time, handling interruptions, what makes a good meeting, delegating tasks, and procrastination.
Length: 1 day
Cost: $250
Location: Chicago, IL.

ASSOCIATED MANAGEMENT INSTITUTE, 3820 Industrial Way, P.O. Box 2001, Benicia, CA 94510, 800/556-5522.

Fundamentals of Management & Supervision. One-day program which covers: nature of management and supervision; the planning process; establishing clear objectives; communicating the objectives; management control means self-control; creating organizational support through motivation; and building the team.
Length: 1 day
Cost: $195
Locations: Anaheim, CA; San Jose, CA; Chicago, IL; Dedham, MA.

BRYANT COLLEGE, The Center for Management Development, 450 Douglas Pike, Smithfield, RI 02917, 401/232-6200.

Time Management Seminar. A one-day program which focuses on effectiveness vs. efficiency; self-diagnostic exercises; the planning component; managing your day; and organizing your office.
Length: 1 day
Cost: $295
Location: Lexington, MA.

INSTITUTE FOR APPLIED LEARNING, P.O. Box 3543, Boulder, CO 80307, 303/494-3871.

Managing Multiple Demands. A program with topics in the following areas: what you can do when; being in control of the many demands made on you; reading, prioritizing; doing your own demand and priority analysis; negotiating your demands mix; different reactions to different demands; when you should say "no" or maybe even "yes"; taking command; and evaluating your payoffs and priorities.
Length: 1 day
Cost: $149.00
Locations: Fresno, CA; San Francisco, CA; San Jose, CA; Indianapolis, IN; Minneapolis, MN; Buffalo, NY; Rochester, NY; Cincinnatti, OH; Columbus, OH; Pittsburgh, PA; Milwaukee, WI.

LEARNING INTERNATIONAL, 200 First Stamford Place, P.O. Box 10211, Stamford, CT 06904, 203/965-8400.

Planning and Directing Performance. This program covers: how to evaluate risks and decide who should do the job; how to carefully think through an assignment; how to anticipate problems before turning over a project to someone else; motivating others; how to communicate the whats, hows, and whens of the assignment as the manager; planning; organizing; motivating; and directing.
Length: 2 days
Cost: Call vendor
Locations: Atlanta, GA; Schaumburg, IL; Bellevue, WA.

PADGETT THOMPSON, Padgett Thompson Building, P.O. Box 8297, Overland Park, KS 66208, 800/255-4141.

Time Management. The topics in this program include recognizing and overcoming time wasters, basic strategies for improvement, managing yourself, meetings—how to make every minute count, and avoiding supervising by crisis.
Length: 1 day
Cost: $99
Locations: Chicago, IL; Indianapolis, IN; Wichita, KS; Minneapolis, MN; Kansas City, MO; St. Louis, MO; Cleveland, OH; Columbus, OH; Madison, WI; Milwaukee, WI.

UNIVERSITY OF WISCONSIN, Business Outreach, Schneider 113A, Eau Claire, WI 54701, 715/836-5637.

Managing Your Workday. A one-day program focusing on: overcoming disorganization, designing work flow systems, planning, and delegation.

Length: 1 day
Cost: Call vendor
Location: Eau Claire, WI.

UNIVERSITY OF WISCONSIN, Management Institute, 432 North Lake Street, Madison, WI 53706, 800/362-3020 (in Wisc.), 800/262-6243.
  Developing Management Skills. Workshop provides a solid foundation in the management skills needed to perform effectively. Content includes communicating to get results, motivating for improved performance, delegating and time management, and how you manage time.
  Length: 3 days
  Cost: $495
  Location: Madison, WI.

WATERLOO MANAGEMENT EDUCATION CENTRE, Suite 619, Waterloo Square, Waterloo, Ontario, Canada N2J 1P2, 519/886-4740.
  Management 2. This seminar provides experienced managers with a complete, systematic approach to management with topics that include strategic planning, objective setting, management control, organization design, and leadership.
  Length: 4 days
  Cost: $595
  Location: Waterloo, ON.

WEBER ASSOCIATES, INC., 849 Chestnut Lake Drive N.E., Marietta, GA 30067, 404/971-3362.
  Leadership Development Workshop Unit III. This 4-day program has topics which include: how to plan effectively; organizing for results; managerial delegation; conference leadership skills; group communication skills and techniques; presentations and image projection; and tapping organizational and personal creativity.
  Length: 4 days
  Cost: $595
  Location: Marietta, GA.

Personal Organization and Time Management

The ability to manage time effectively affects every other aspect of a manager's work. No matter how competent a person is in a skill area, that competence can't be exercised if: 1) there is no time to perform the job, or 2) the time allotted is insufficient for the production of a quality product or the development of quality service procedures.

References devoted exclusively to the subject of time management can provide dozens of tips. For the purposes of this reference, however, PDI has chosen to address the time management problems that: 1) are most common among managers, and 2) have the most impact on overall managerial performance. The guidelines offered here include:

- Reducing Job Overload (p. 59)
- Reducing Outside Commitments (p. 59)
- Reducing Excessive Interruptions (p. 60)
- Overcoming Procrastination (p. 61)
- Determining Priorities (p. 62)
- Dealing With Higher Priority Items and Tasks First (p. 62)
- Promptly Returning Phone Calls and Responding to Written Requests (p. 63)
- Assessing Your Daily Accomplishments (p. 63)
- Handling Paperwork by Organizing Your Desktop (p. 64)
- Creating a More Efficient Office Space (p. 65)
- Eliminating Unnecessary Memos (p. 66)
- Capturing Inspirations Without Disrupting Work-in-progress (p. 66)

Tips

- Have your secretary organize your files so that he or she can easily locate items when you are out of the office.

- Record due dates for assignments on your calendar.

- Maintain a "tickler" file for items needing periodic follow-up.

- Use three-part "speed memos" when delegating assignments requiring follow-up.

- Use "hanging folders" for files requiring fast and easy access.

- Clear your office of infrequently used files.

- Archive or throw away files not accessed in the last one or two years.

- Have your secretary maintain a day file for all of your written correspondence.

- Sort your in-basket according to priority and work on high priority items first. Skim or throw away low priority items.

- Have your subordinates represent you at meetings when appropriate.

- Schedule your personal time more carefully, being sure to include time for administrative "nitty gritties."

- Keep a daily memory jogger.

- Set aside time in your weekly calendar for follow-up procedures in your work.

- Keep a generalized list of things that need to be done further in the future.

- Before leaving work each evening, list the things that need to be done the next day.

- Develop your "priority-setting skills" by periodically writing down those tasks that are pending and those your manager considers to be most critically important. Ask your manager for feedback about your priorities.

- In order to facilitate the planning and organizing of your work week, limit it to 40 hours.

- Set your own deadlines for tasks and don't reinforce yourself until you've met them.

- Take the time to just sit still and plan, organize, and attend to detail.

- Monitor how you spend your time for a week. Alter your schedule so it is in line with your job priorities.

- Delegate all filing tasks to your secretary.

- Take a course in time management.

- Schedule "quiet time" every day for work requiring uninterrupted thinking or planning.

- Return phone calls early in the day or near the end of the day to increase your chances of getting through.

- Have your secretary screen your calls and handle those not requiring your attention.

- Use a Day-Timer.

- Be more careful in scheduling foreseeable events in your weekly calendar.

- Delegate routine assignments to subordinates and spend more of your time planning.

Reducing Job Overload

Job overload usually means poor performance in the short term and exhaustion and burnout in the long term. When people are overloaded with work, both the people and the organization suffer.

To determine if you are overloaded, analyze your job performance the way your would analyze one of your employee's performance. Do you meet deadlines? Do you accomplish what you say you will accomplish? If your analysis shows that you are trying to do too much, the suggestions that follow can help you reduce your workload.

- Concentrate on your most important objectives. Delegate the less important tasks to others or let them go undone.
- Do more jobs alone. Because working in groups or committees is time-consuming, try to eliminate some committee work. Other committee work can be accomplished quickly outside of a committee, then taken to the committee for review and approval.
- Delegate routine tasks.
- Look ahead and divide your work load into time stages to make it more manageable. Determine what should be done tomorrow, next week, next month, and next year, and plan accordingly.
- Schedule time for essential work. If appointments tend to fill your calendar, leaving no time for important tasks, block out time on your calendar for these tasks.
- Look at your job in new ways to determine if it can be simplified. Select a task, break it down into details, question each detail, determine better ways to handle the details, then apply the improvements.

Reducing Outside Commitments

Commitments to outside activities can multiply over the years to a point where you have no time of your own. Committees, volunteer activities, and organized recreational activities can end up taking much more time than you had anticipated. If your commitments leave you with no time to yourself, analyze each activity and ask yourself the following questions.

- **Does this activity help me continue to grow in some way?** You may find that activities that were challenging initially have become routine and unfulfilling. You may want to turn these activities over to someone who is more enthusiastic about them.
- **Is this activity worthwhile?** Some commitments are not pleasant but need to be done. If you feel a sense of obligation and no one else can

handle the job, you might decide to stay involved. However, if you view the situation realistically, you may find that your talents are no longer required and that the activity is no longer worthwhile to you. In this case, you can drop the commitment.

- **Do I enjoy this activity?** Sheer enjoyment is a good reason to participate in an activity. Some activities, however, should provide enjoyment but do not. For example, perhaps your recreational softball league has become too competitive.

Reducing Excessive Interruptions

Excessive interruptions might be a major source of that "where has the day gone?" feeling at the end of the day. To help minimize interruptions, follow this procedure:

1. For one week, keep a log of interruptions and the reason for each interruption.
2. Using your analysis of your log and a chart with two columns labeled "Reasons for Interruptions" and "Possible Solutions," implement a plan that will help you handle each of those situations in the future.

Reasons for Interruptions	Possible Solutions
People stop by to socialize; they interrupt you because of your accessibility.	Decrease your accessibility. Close your office door when you do not want to be interrupted. Establish set times when you are available for impromptu talks.
Individuals are insecure about making decisions on their own because of lack of experience or confidence, so they come to you more often than is necessary.	Establish programs to help these individuals develop their skills and increase their confidence.

(Chart continued on next page.)

Reasons for Interruptions	Possible Solutions
People who could make decisions on their own are coming to you for approval.	Consider delegating more authority. Analyze the topics discussed during the interruptions to determine which areas should be delegated.
People have questions about coordination of staff members' duties.	Consider scheduling more staff meetings.
People lack information.	Consider establishing a better means of disseminating information—better project plans, more informational memos, more discussion at staff meetings.

3. After you have implemented your plan, keep another log of your interruptions for a week to determine if they have decreased.

Overcoming Procrastination

People procrastinate in different ways, to different degrees, and for different reasons. But most people habitually put off things they know they should be doing. The following tips are designed to help you get a start on overcoming procrastination.

- Make firm deadline commitments with your superior, subordinates, and customers, and note them on your calendar to force yourself to start the projects.
- If you procrastinate on follow-up tasks, block out time on your weekly schedule and dedicate it to follow-up.
- If you put off projects that seem too difficult or overwhelming, make a list of the small, easy tasks involved in the project and do these tasks first. Their momentum may carry over into the more difficult tasks.
- If you find a particular project unpleasant, consider delegating it, or do the most interesting tasks involved in the project first and let the momentum of these tasks carry over into the less interesting tasks.

- Tell yourself you'll work on a project for a half-hour to see how it goes (you know that you can handle it for a short period of time). By the end of the half-hour, you may have found that the task isn't so difficult or distasteful after all.
- Establish ways to reward yourself along the way—for example, a coffee break after writing the introduction to a report or a day off after completing a major project.

Determining Priorities

Do you sometimes feel immersed in unimportant details at the expense of high-priority tasks? To determine whether you are using your time wisely, complete the following exercise.

1. For the next few weeks, keep a record of how you spend your time. Write down the tasks you perform and how much time you spend on them. At the end of this period, list the types of tasks you performed, starting with those on which you spent the most time.
2. On a separate sheet, list your primary job responsibilities according to importance and the amount of time they should receive.
3. Compare your lists to determine whether you are devoting the bulk of your time to high-priority tasks.

Dealing With Higher Priority Items and Tasks First

Do you often reach the end of the day feeling as if you have done a lot but accomplished very little? Charles Hobbs, a noted expert on time management, suggests that many managers tend to confuse urgent matters with truly vital ones, resulting in the accomplishment of urgent trivialities rather than high payoff tasks.

Hobbs suggests creating a prioritized to-do list by grouping daily tasks into three categories:
- Vital (high payoff) tasks
- Important (yet less vital) tasks
- Tasks with limited payoff

For each of these three lists, prioritize the items by asking yourself the following questions:
1. Which of these tasks will be of most benefit to the organization?
2. Which tasks do organizational or departmental policies and priorities suggest are most important?

3. Which of these tasks does my boss consider most important?
4. What are the consequences of not completing these tasks today?
5. If I have time to complete only three or four of these tasks today, which should I plan to do?
6. Which task completion would make me feel best?

When you've prioritized all three lists, create a to-do list, focusing on the most vital tasks first. When an urgent matter arises, determine how it fits into your daily plan (is it urgent **and** vital or simply urgent?) and act accordingly.

Promptly Returning Phone Calls and Responding to Notes and Written Requests

Returning phone calls and responding to written correspondence are important, yet often cumbersome responsibilities for most managers. To become more efficient, follow these guidelines taken from Charles Hobbs' "Insights on Time Management" series:

1. Work with your secretary to ensure that he or she takes clear, complete, and accurate phone messasges. Your secretary can then determine if he or she can be of help and, if not, will have a message clear enough that you can respond to the caller appropriately.
2. Develop a system whereby your secretary inserts all phone messages into your calendar for your reference.
3. Schedule time on your calendar each day during which you return phone calls. Between 8:00-8:30 in the morning and 4:30-5:00 at night are often good times to catch people in their offices.
4. If you return a phone call and the person is out or unavailable, schedule a telephone appointment with him or her and record this appointment on your calendar.
5. Respond to notes and memos by hand writing your response directly on the correspondence. Make a copy for your files if necessary.
6. With your secretary, develop a system for establishing priorities on written notes by having him or her screen your in-basket for urgent messages and order the remaining correspondence appropriately.

Assessing Your Daily Accomplishments

This exercise will help you more accurately predict the time required for various short-term tasks and show you which tasks are taking the majority of your time.

1. At the beginning of each day, plan—in detail—the work you expect to complete that day. List the tasks according to priority and determine the amount of time you expect to spend on each.
2. At the end of the day, review your list to determine how much of the work you accomplished and how long it took to accomplish it.

If your analysis reveals a considerable discrepancy between what you plan to accomplish and what you actually accomplished, try to determine the reason for the discrepancy (too many interruptions?, procrastination?).

Handling Paperwork by Organizing Your Desk

If your desk is covered with stacks of paper, you probably waste quite a bit of time sorting through the stacks as you look for documents you need to complete your work. To eliminate this problem, consider establishing a filing system for organizing your paperwork.

Develop a categorization system that fits your needs. The following series of files comprises a sample system that one manager found effective.

- A "review" file—for paperwork generated by others that had to be reviewed in a timely way in order for work to progress. (This manager chose to attend to this file in the early morning and late afternoon, when interruptions were minimal and interaction with others was not required to keep projects moving.)
- A "reading" file—for papers that did not require a response or carry associated deadlines. (This file was attended to in the manager's spare time.)
- A "file" folder—for papers that had been processed and should be retained. (This folder was given to the manager's secretary periodically for filing.)
- An "action item" file—for lists of tasks to be performed and work-in-progress.
- A "delegate" file—for papers concerning activities that could be performed by others.

Creating a More Efficient Office Space

Charles Hobbs, in his "Insights on Time Management" series, recommends a "fingertip management" system for organizing your desktop, based on the frequency with which you use items in your office. His suggestions include:

1. Dividing your desk into three parts.
   - A-items such as your calendar, that you need right at hand
   - B-items such as your phone, that are not immediate needs but that must be within reach
   - C-items such as books, that are used infrequently

   Hobbs suggests keeping in front of you only what you are working on immediately (A-items) and removing all else (B- and C-items). He suggests keeping those items categorized as B-items within reach and locating the remaining C-items where you must get up from your desk to reach them.
2. Putting your in-basket in your credenza drawer. Put "in" items in the front of the drawer and "out" items in the back.
3. Working with your secretary to have him or her prioritize your in-basket. Use your calendar to keep control of urgent in-basket items.

Eliminating Unnecessary Memos

Although some memos are necessary, informal surveys reveal that employees in most organizations spend far more time writing and reading memos than is advisable—and at great cost to the organizations. To determine whether the memos you and your subordinates write promote efficiency, periodically ask yourself the following questions.

- Are the messages of the memos short and to the point? If not, take steps to make memos more concise.
- Would a phone call or brief personal visit be a more effective method of communication? Memos involve one-way communication; phone calls and discussions allow people to read each other's reactions, ask questions, and clear up misunderstandings immediately.
- Does the memo describe a task that could be done in less time than it takes to write the memo?
- Are formal, typed memos sent when handwritten, short-form memos or notes would suffice?
- Finally, time management specialist R. Alec Mackenzie recommends that you take an occasional inventory to assess the efficiency of your department's memo writing practices. Examine the memos written and received in a one-month period. How many could have been shorter? How many were unnecessary?

Capturing Inspirations Without Disrupting Work-in-progress

"Idea people" are sometimes inefficient because they are frequently distracted by "inspirations." If you find yourself frequently distracted by a good idea or the thought of another task you should be doing, try the following suggestions:

- Keep a pad of paper readily available for jotting down a word or phrase to help you remember your thought later. Then put the thought out of your mind and give your full attention to your initial task. The best places to record your ideas are in a daily diary or a special notebook that you can keep with you. This ensures quick access to paper and quick retrieval of your information.
- Some managers keep "idea files" on their desks as catch-alls for concepts not yet sufficiently developed to be categorized and placed in a subject file.

Recommended Readings

Douglass, Merrill E., and Douglass, Donna N. *Manage Your Time, Manage Your Work, Manage Yourself.* New York, NY: AMA, 1978.

The authors discuss how to get rid of the time wasters in your business day and get more done faster and easier. The book discusses many aspects of time management and includes dozens of charts and forms for evaluating and reorganizing your work and time habits.

Januz, Lauren R., and Jones, Susan K. *Time Management for Executives.* New York, NY: Charles Scribner's Sons, 1981.

The authors present easy, step-by-step instructions to help you use your time more effectively. Topics covered include eliminating unnecessary paperwork, delegating more responsibility to subordinates, using otherwise wasted travel or waiting time, avoiding unnecessary tasks, and performing unpleasant jobs quickly and systematically. They also discuss how to plan for and attain definite goals, deal with people (including bosses) who take up your time needlessly, run productive meetings, extend concentration, and handle interruptions.

Love, Sydney F. *Mastery and Management of Time.* Englewood Cliffs, NJ: Prentice-Hall, 1978.

The author offers practical tips on how to reduce your work load; budget, prioritize, and control your time; and get more done in less time. Also discussed are time-saving techniques for storing and retrieving information and for managing new projects.

Mackenzie, Alec. *The Time Trap.* New York, NY: McGraw-Hill, 1972.

This book offers advice on the executive management of time. Suggestions are well thought out and explained in sufficient detail. The appendix contains a useful reference chart of time wasters, their probable causes, and how to handle them. In this book, Mackenzie demonstrates how time management affects the most important activities in a manager's fulfillment of his or her responsibilities. The book complements the usual time-management suggestions (such as those for dealing with interruptions) with especially helpful discussions in areas not often addressed, such as getting more from meetings, combatting reverse delegation, and recognizing and managing the time-use pattern that corresponds to your management style.

Mackenzie, Alec, and Waldo, Kay C. *About Time!: A Woman's Guide to Time Management*. New York, NY: McGraw-Hill, 1981.

This book on time management is tailored to the needs of today's businesswoman. Techniques for work and home reveal how to: discover the top ten time wasters, defeat the paperwork monster, say no, get rid of the superwoman syndrome, increase decisiveness, enlist a househusband, tame the telephone, delegate, and set attainable performance goals.

Oncken, W., Jr. *Managing Management Time: Who's Got the Monkey?* Englewood Cliffs, NJ: Prentice-Hall, 1984.

Based on Oncken's highly successful "Managing Management Time" seminars, this book outlines, in step-by-step detail, powerful time management strategies that can help managers at all levels achieve more visible, far-reaching results through others, both inside and outside one's own organization.

Suggested Seminars

The seminars listed here were selected for their appeal to a managerial audience and have received good to excellent ratings from managers attending them.

Because of the dynamic nature of the seminar marketplace, some seminars may have been added, upgraded, or replaced, and others may no longer be offered. Additional information about these seminars may be obtained by calling the vendor directly, or through Seminar Clearinghouse International, a subscriber organization located in St. Paul, Minnesota. Call 612/293-1004 for information.

AMERICAN MANAGEMENT ASSOCIATIONS, P.O. Box 319, Saranac Lake, NY 12983, 518/891-0065.

Time Management. A practical course designed to help individuals at all levels make the best possible use of time. Topics included are: take charge of your time clock; Pareto's principle; priority systems; real vs. stated objectives; managing vs. doing; clarifying objectives; tracking time use patterns; matching activities to objectives; wiping out timewasters; and turn your team on to time management.
Length: 2 days
Cost: $795
Locations: Irvine, CA; San Francisco, CA; Washington, DC; Atlanta, GA; Chicago, IL; New York, NY.

BRYANT COLLEGE, The Center for Management Development, 450 Douglas Pike, Smithfield, RI 02917, 401/232-6200.

Time Management Seminar. The key topics for this one-day seminar include: effectiveness vs. efficiency; self-diagnostic exercises; the planning component; managing your day; and organizing your office.
Length: 1 day
Cost: $295
Location: Lexington, MA.

CAREERTRACK INC., 1800 38th Street, Boulder, CO 80301, 303/447-2300, 800/334-6780 (outside Colo.).

Getting Things Done. This program enables participants to learn how to say no when you mean no (and not feel bad about it); how to overcome changing priorities, the start-stop syndrome, and incomplete work assignments; human "downtime" and how to make it productive; "team time"—why it's essential; and the delegator's checklist.

Length: 1 day
Cost: $49
Locations: Burlingame, CA; Corte Madera, CA; Milpitas, CA; Atlanta, GA; Duluth, MN; Asheville, NC; Atlantic City, NY; Cherry Hill, NJ; Binghamton, NY; Buffalo, NY; Chattanooga, TN; Johnson City, TN. For additional locations, contact the vendor.

CHARLES R. HOBBS CORPORATION, 2290 East 4500 South, Suite 220, Salt Lake City, UT 84117, 801/278-5381, 800/332-9929.

Insight on Time Power. This high-intensity seminar covers such topics as: coping with impossible demands; handling priorities; retrieving important data; retaining every worthwhile idea; remembering every meeting; reducing crisis management; doing more in less time; delegating more effectively; dealing with interruptions; handling lengthy phone calls; and avoiding proscrastination.
Length: 2 days
Cost: $395
Locations: Irvine, CA; Los Angeles, CA; Okland, CA; Atlanta, GA; Boston, MA; Baltimore, MD; Rochester, NY; White Plains, NY; Philadelphia, PA; Pittsburg, PA; Dallas, TX, Houston, TX. For additional locations, contact the vendor.

DUN & BRADSTREET BUSINESS EDUCATION SERVICES, P.O. Box 803, Church Street Station, New York, NY 10008, 212/312-6909.

Managing Multiple Priorities. Program designed to help participants increase their skills in juggling tasks, maintaining quality, handling more than one person's priorities, discovering your pressure points, and remaining calm under deadlines.
Length: 1 day
Cost: $160
Locations: Danbury, CT; Chicago, IL; Itasca, IL; Midland, MI; Albany, NY; Buffalo, NY; New York, NY; Akron, OH; Cincinnatti, OH; Corpus Christi, TX; Everett, WA; Kelso, WA. For additional locations, contact the vendor.

PADGETT THOMPSON, Padgett Thompson Building, P.O. Box 8297, Overland Park, KS 66208, 800/255-4141.

Time Management. Program participants will learn concepts of recognizing and overcoming time wasters; basic strategies for improvement; managing yourself; meetings—how to make every minute count; and avoiding supervising by crisis.

Length: 1 day
Cost: $99
Locations: Chicago, IL; Indianapolis, IN; Wichita, KS; Minneapolis, MN; Kansas City, MO; St. Louis, MO; Cleveland, OH; Columbus, OH; Madison, WI; Milwaukee, WI.

STEFFEN, STEFFEN & ASSOCIATES, 652 Glenbrook Road, Stamford, CT 06906, 203/359-4100.
   Public Time Mastery Seminars. This seminar explains the ten tools that participants need to maximize productivity and increase effectiveness. Practical steps are provided for integrating these skills into daily life.
   Length: 2 days
   Cost: Call vendor
   Locations: New York, NY; Dallas, TX.

UNIVERSITY OF PENNSYLVANIA, The Wharton School, 200 Vance Hall, Philadelphia, PA 19104, 215/898-1776.
   Executive Self Management. This practical two-day seminar is designed to help participants in understanding time, energy and effectiveness, managing time, understanding behavior and managing others, and understanding and managing self.
   Length: 2 days
   Cost: $1195
   Location: Philadelphia, PA.

WILLIAM ONCKEN CORPORATION, 8344 East R.L. Thornton Freeway, Suite 408, Dallas, TX 75228, 214/328-1867: Dallas, 612/473-2404: Minneapolis.
   Managing Management Time. Also known as "Get Them Monkeys Off Your Back," this program goes beyond the "daily diary" approach—it examines the causes and effects of time management problems; and deals with the realities of getting performance through other people.
   Length: 2 days
   Cost: $450
   Locations: Washington, DC; Chicago, IL; New Orleans, LA; Minneapolis, MN; Dallas, TX; Houston, TX; Seattle, WA.

FACTOR 2

Leadership Skills

Leadership: the ability to "take charge"—to make things happen by encouraging and channeling the contributions of others.

In the past, leadership was simpler. Yesterday's managers could **demand** performance. Today's managers, faced with a more educated and democratically oriented work force, must consider employee concerns as well as corporate goals and objectives.

In addition, while yesterday's managers relied primarily on their own resourcefulness and creativity, today's managers must encourage and apply the contributions of all of the company's human resources, both individually and in groups.

This section contains developmental activities in five major areas of leadership skills that PDI has identified as essential to managerial success.

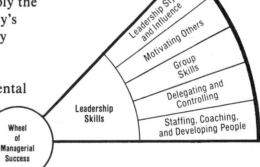

Leadership Style and Influence:
taking charge and initiating action, directing the activities of individuals and groups toward the accomplishment of meaningful goals, and adapting leadership strategy to different situations

Motivating Others: creating an environment in which subordinates are rewarded for accomplishment of group and individual goals

Leadership Skills

Group Skills: maximizing personal effectiveness in group situations; planning, conducting and participating in meetings; and improving group processes to maximize the effectiveness of group members

Delegating and Controlling: assigning responsibilities and tasks to others, ensuring that employees have the necessary resources and authority, and monitoring progress

Staffing, Coaching, and Developing People: hiring and evaluating employees, providing performance feedback, and facilitating professional growth

Leadership Style and Influence

It's possible to develop a working knowledge of effective leadership skills by reading articles in business magazines and books on the subject. As with the development of any skill, however, it's the hands-on experience that counts. Individuals hoping to increase their competence as leaders must have the opportunity to participate in situations that will provide experience in the use of leadership skills. Tasks that require these skills include managing meetings, motivating others, building and directing project teams, and training new employees.

This section provides the following suggestions for:

- Gaining Leadership Experience (p. 80)
- Gaining Experience Outside Your Organization (p. 80)
- Improving Your Leadership Skills by Incorporating Techniques Used by Others (p. 81)
- Increasing Your Leadership Impact (p. 82)
- Finding Time to Meet With Subordinates (p. 82)
- Improving Leadership Through Feedback (p. 83)

Tips

- Meet with subordinates to show them how their contributions support the goals of the organization.

- Encourage subordinates to set ambitious goals. Reward performance, whether or not they achieved their goals.

- Clearly communicate departmental objectives and solicit input from each subordinate on what they can do to help achieve them.

- Be willing to take the ideas of your people to the next higher level and support them enthusiastically. Give credit where credit is due.

- Communicate the achievements of your unit and people to higher level management in a visible and positive way, showing pride in, and support for, your subordinates.

- Schedule an annual retreat for your group to build esprit de corps and commitment to goals.

- Give positive reinforcement to your people immediately through oral or written comments.

- Take the time to get to know your people's personal side; inquire about their spouse, kids, etc. Show genuine interest.

- Identify the persons in your organization whose leadership you most admire. Determine specifically what they do that helps them be effective and try some of those behaviors with your subordinates.

- Attend the Leadership Development Program offered through PDI and apply the principles with your own subordinates.

- Assess your decision-making style, soliciting subordinates' ideas. Look for opportunities to be more participative.

- Ask peers how your leadership style is perceived and solicit suggestions for improvement.

Leadership Skills

- Use a feedback instrument such as the Management Skills Profile (MSP) offered through PDI to get feedback on your leadership skills from your superiors, peers, and subordinates.

- Discuss with your manager the impact of your leadership style and some possibilities for new approaches.

- Seek opportunities for assignments to projects which would place a premium on your being forceful and persuasive.

- Become more dominant in meetings, if necessary, to assure that others understand your point of view.

- Adopt a "can-do" attitude and approach challenges from a problem-solving perspective. Look for alternative solutions rather than why things can't be done.

- Read Hershey and Blanchard's book on Situational Leadership. Identify the maturity level of each subordinate for various tasks and define the appropriate leadership style.

- Identify the behaviors you feel are critical to success in your organization and then lead by example.

- Read *In Search of Excellence* with subordinates and evaluate your organization on each of the eight factors, identifying areas you can improve.

- Work to balance your "task" and "people" orientation as described in *The Managerial Grid* by Blake and Mouton.

- Become quicker to offer your ideas in a group setting, especially as a subordinate, rather than sitting back and waiting for others.

- Attend a Management Development Center offered by Personnel Decisions, Inc. to receive feedback and acquire new skills in managing your subordinates.

- Volunteer for a leadership role in your community, church, service organization, etc. that will help you develop your leadership skills.

- Show your enthusiasm for the organization and your superior's role in the organization through your comments and actions.

- Serve as an example to others by performing tasks at a high level of excellence.

- Initiate new ideas, objectives, and projects with your superior and with your subordinates.

- Take on extra work to help the organization meet its objectives.

Gaining Leadership Experience

Although you can learn the theories of leadership behavior through a reading program, you must also gain actual experience to develop your skills. If you are not currently in a leadership position, ask your supervisor to assist you in developing leadership skills by arranging for short-term leadership roles, such as chairing a task force or leading a group discussion.

When your assignment is complete, ask your supervisor or trusted group members to critique your performance as a leader.

After you have performed as a leader in numerous situations, you will gain an understanding of your leadership strengths and weaknesses.

Gaining Experience Outside Your Organization

Volunteer leadership positions in organizations such as churches, nonprofit organizations, social service agencies, professional organizations, and youth organizations provide opportunities to develop and improve leadership skills and, at the same time, to make valuable contributions to your community.

Depending on your development needs, look for opportunities to practice your skills in areas such as:
- Managing meetings
- Motivating others
- Speaking before groups
- Delegating
- Identifying and developing the skills of others
- Giving feedback
- Team building

Also look for opportunities for growth in such facets of organizational management as finance, public relations, and marketing.

The opportunities provided by these organizations will allow you to practice your skills in relatively nonthreatening settings. You will be exposed to a variety of situations and individuals under circumstances in which the impact of your actions on your career is not nearly as great as it would be in the work environment. And when the time comes, you are much more likely to be successful in a leadership role in your work place.

Improving Your Leadership Skills by Incorporating Techniques Used by Others

You can learn a great deal about effective leadership by observing those with experience in leadership situations. To benefit from their experience, periodically implement the following guidelines.

1. Identify an effective leader within your organization and arrange to observe that person's behavior in settings such as staff meetings, training sessions, and problem-solving sessions. Take notes on behaviors that make this person a successful leader.
2. Try out some of these behaviors in your own group situations. Keep in mind that new behaviors often seem awkward at first.
3. After several weeks of practicing your new behaviors, ask for feedback from others on the success of your leadership efforts.
4. As you gain leadership experience, you will probably discover that no one individual in your organization possesses all of the characteristics of a successful leader. At this point, you may want to redefine and narrow your definition of the term "effective leader." For example, one leader may be skilled in delegating, whereas another is especially successful in coaching and developing subordinates. At this point, select individuals and situations according to the areas in which you want to develop specialized leadership skills.

Increasing Your Leadership Impact

The ability to command the attention of others is necessary for effective leadership. If you suspect that your impact is low, there are several things you can do.

- When meeting with individuals and groups, stand up quickly and introduce yourself, if necessary.
- With subordinates, be firm and direct when stating expectations or confronting poor performance. Don't dilute your comments with phrases such as "...don't you think?", "It seems to me," "Maybe I'm wrong but," etc.
- If you are uncomfortable stating your point of view directly, consider enrolling in an assertiveness training course to build your skills and develop your confidence in presenting your opinions in a more forceful manner.
- Pay attention to your vocal qualities when giving direction or feedback to others. If you tend to be soft-spoken, work on delivering your message in a more forceful and confident tone.
- Join Toastmasters or other organizations which offer opportunities to assert yourself in group situations. Often it is just getting used to the feeling of being the "lead" with others that makes the difference.

Finding Time to Meet With Subordinates

One of your primary management responsibilities is to make yourself available to subordinates to answer their questions and address their concerns. If you find that the press of daily activities tends to make you unavailable to your subordinates, try these approaches.

- If you are out of the office much of the day, examine your schedule and set up times with your secretary during which you will check in at the office by phone or in person. Let your subordinates know that your secretary will have this information.
- Make it a point to schedule all your appointments through your secretary. In this way, if a subordinate needs to see you for any reason, he or she can easily contact your secretary to set up an appointment.
- Initiate contact with subordinates, particularly those with whom you have little contact. While these do not have to be formal meetings, taking time to talk with your subordinates will keep you abreast of the day-to-day happenings in your department.
- Set up regular meetings (e.g., weekly, monthly, quarterly) to answer questions and keep abreast of what your subordinates are working on.

Improving Leadership Through Feedback

Most managers do not have clear perceptions of their leadership styles and impact on others. Some feedback is gained through observing others' reactions and through the feedback others provide in formal and informal settings. In-depth feedback is often helpful, yet others may be hesitant to provide it unless you actively solicit it. Ways to obtain this feedback are outlined in the following guidelines.

1. Ask several individuals whom you trust and respect to give you feedback by answering specific questions, such as:
   - How would you describe my leadership style?
   - What do you feel I do particularly well as a leader? In what areas do I need work?
   - To what extent do I tend to be oriented more toward the work tasks or the people doing the work? Do I need to change my emphasis in any way?
   - Have you observed specific situations in which I could have performed better in areas such as motivating others, managing meetings or groups, coaching subordinates, delegating, handling crises, and so forth?

   You may also wish to ask the same people to provide you with feedback in the future as you take steps to improve your leadership skills.

2. Use a formal instrument (questionnaire or rating scale) to obtain ratings of your performance in a number of areas. Some instruments ask for the input of the concerned individual only; others solicit feedback from subordinates, peers, and/or superiors. When completed, these instruments summarize the ratings and provide you with feedback and, occasionally, suggestions for improvement.

   Professionally designed instruments of this type are available from Personnel Decisions, Inc., 2000 Plaza VII Tower, 45 South Seventh Street, Minneapolis, MN 55402. The Management Skills Profile (MSP) is designed to provide feedback from subordinates, peers, and/or superiors, based on the factors of the PDI Wheel of Managerial Success.

3. Attend a seminar or assessment center designed to provide personal feedback on leadership behavior.

   The **Leadership Development Program** is a six-day program offered by Personnel Decisions, Inc. to help managers learn the skills and strategies of leadership. The Program blends assessment exercises and feedback with training experiences to help managers be more productive and successful.

   The **Management Development Center** is an intensive three-day program offered by PDI. It is built around a realistic simulation of the manager's job and provides immediate feedback and individualized coaching on a full range of managerial and leadership skills. PDI also offers a comparable four-day program for executive level managers called the **Executive Development Center.**

   For information on these programs, write to Personnel Decisions, Inc., 2000 Plaza VII Tower, 45 South Seventh Street, Minneapolis, MN 55402, or call 612/339-0927.

Recommended Readings

Albrecht, Karl, and Zemke, Ron. *Service America! Doing Business in the New Economy.* Homewood, IL: Dow Jones-Irwin, 1985.

Service America! shows how service management can turn a company in any kind of service field into a customer driven and service-oriented business. Based on the idea of managing the critical incidents in which customers come into contact with the organization, this book presents a workable approach for instilling service excellence into every niche of an organization.

Argyris, C. *Increasing Leadership Effectiveness.* New York, NY: John Wiley & Sons, 1976.

This book describes a technique designed to develop leaders who know how to anticipate problems, create viable problem-solving networks, and generate and channel human energy and commitment to implement solutions.

Baird, Bruce F. *The Technical Manager: How to Manage People and Make Decisions.* Belmont, CA: Wadsworth, Inc., 1983.

This book is for engineers, scientists, and computer professionals who have been trained in solving physical and technical problems, but have been promoted to managers. The aim of *The Technical Manager* is to develop in the reader an understanding of the attitudes, perceptions, and techniques required to be a successful manager.

Bittel, Lester R. *Essentials of Supervisory Management.* New York, NY: McGraw-Hill, 1981.

An abridged edition of Bittel's *What Every Supervisor Should Know,* this book is designed for self-study or reference. It covers the two primary responsibilities: administration of the management process within a department, and management and motivation of the employee work group. Key concepts summarize the basic tools of each chapter. The Question and Answer format, Review Questions, Real-life Cases in Point, Action Summary Checklists, and Self-checks facilitate on-the-job application and learning. Major topics include: planning, organizing, and controlling work; managing people; handling sensitive problems; and improving employee performance.

Blake, R., and Mouton, J. *Managerial Grid III (3rd ed.).* Houston, TX: Gulf Publishing Company, 1984.

This is a reexamination of *The Managerial Grid*, which was first published in

1964. Major changes include further identification, clarification, and comparison of the motivational dimensions of each grid style of leadership.

Block, Peter. *The Empowered Manager: Positive Political Skills at Work.* San Francisco, CA: Jossey-Bass, 1987.

In this book, Block shows managers how to break out of the bureaucratic mode of thinking and take more responsibility for the workings of their unit. He explains how managers can become empowered to make positive changes in their organizations and develop an entrepreneurial spirit in themselves and in members of their unit.

Burby, R.J. *Managing with People.* Reading, MA: Addison-Wesley, 1976.

This is a self-instruction, programmed text designed for first-line supervisors. Its primary objective is to examine in some depth the area of worker motivation and its relation to job productivity.

Burley-Allen, Madelyn. *Managing Assertively: How to Improve Your People Skills.* New York, NY: John Wiley & Sons, 1983.

An assertiveness training manual directed specifically to first-line supervisors, it gives the reader step-by-step guidance on responding confidently and effectively to the "people problems" faced on the job. Examples, self-assessment exercises, and questionnaires are included to help the reader increase supervisory skills, self-awareness, and assertiveness. The author uses a building blocks approach to help the reader analyze his/her own management style and identify obstacles to managing assertively.

Burns, J.M. *Leadership.* New York, NY: Harper & Row, 1978.

Burns attempts to make a definitive analysis of the nature of leadership. While he mainly discusses political leadership, corporate executives can draw inferences that apply to their own organizational situations.

Cannie, Joan Koob. *The Woman's Guide to Management Success: How to Win Power in the Real Organizational World.* Englewood Cliffs, NJ: Prentice-Hall, 1979.

Showing how you can gain managerial power and status and use it to be successful in your management career, this guide offers scores of practical strategies for: dealing with criticism without getting defensive or frazzled; initiating and maximizing employee satisfaction and morale; enriching communications by breaking down barriers; handling men who flatter, flirt with, or bully you; overcoming the fear of making decisions, and more.

Cuming, Pamela. *The Power Handbook: A Strategic Guide to Organizational and Personal Effectiveness.* New York, NY: Van Nostrand Reinhold, 1981.

This book contains numerous planning guides and self-scoring questionnaires designed to help the reader build a plan of action which responds to his/her unique problems and opportunities. *The Power Handbook* is designed to give the reader more precise goal definition, a better understanding of personal strengths and weaknesses, and an overall attitude of "can do" confidence.

Davis, George, and Watson, Glegg. *Black Life in Corporate America: Swimming in the Mainstream.* New York, NY: Van Nostrand Reinhold, 1979.

This book, which deals with the human issues that concern all managers, black or white, male or female, and what these managers have experienced and revealed, has profound implications for the future of American motivation, productivity, and bottom-line profitability. It is the first in-depth look at men and women trying to "make it" in a world created by and for white males.

Ellis, A. *Executive Leadership: A Rational Approach.* New York, NY: Institute for Rational Living, Inc., 1978.

Ellis has developed a system to help executives cope with the inanities and insanities of the organizational world so that they can organize both their business days and their personal lives with minimum stress and maximum satisfaction.

Fordyce, Jack K., and Weil, R. *Managing with People: A Manager's Handbook of Organization Development Methods (2nd ed.).* Reading, MA: Addison-Wesley, 1979.

This book explains organization development and serves as a handbook with methods and examples. Included are five case studies and a bibliography of other sources.

George, Claude S. *Supervision in Action (4th ed.)* Englewood Cliffs, NJ: Prentice-Hall, 1985.

This work provides a clear and practical approach to understanding and dealing with the problems faced by first-line supervisors. It assumes no prior training, understanding, or knowledge of supervision.

Gordon, Thomas. *Leader Effectiveness Training.* New York, NY: Bantam Books, 1980.

This is an excellent introduction to the interpersonal coaching and leadership aspects of management. It includes practical problem-solving techniques and communication skills necessary to: get people to work with you, not just for you; resolve conflicts between individuals; develop a work team that gets results; evaluate others without damaging their self-esteem; and make meetings more productive and enjoyable.

Hersey, P., and Blanchard, K.H. *Management of Organizational Behavior: Utilizing Human Resources (4th ed.).* Englewood Cliffs, NJ: Prentice-Hall, 1977.

This book examines the behavioral approach to management, develops an outline of change theory, and presents various strategies for planning and implementing change. Among the topics discussed are motivation and behavior, the motivating environment, leader behavior, determination of effectiveness, ways to diagnose the environment, and management for organizational effectiveness and planning.

Hersey, Paul. *The Situational Leader: The Other 59 Minutes...* New York, NY: Warner Books, Inc., 1985.

Based on the Situational Leadership model, this book provides a brief and succinct guide on how to develop people and effectively utilize human resources. Hersey outlines a practical model to help managers meet the ongoing challenges faced by individuals in leadership situations.

Jackson, J.H., and Keaveny, T.J. *Successful Supervision.* Englewood Cliffs, NJ: Prentice-Hall, 1980.

This book is for practicing supervisors and those about to assume a supervisory role. It presents case examples based on real-life supervisory problems, plus sections on supervisory "tools" and "how-to-do-it" hints. Also included is an important section on the supervisor and the law: equal employment opportunity, occupational safety and health, and labor-management legislation.

Kanter, Rosabeth Moss. *The Change Masters: Innovation for Productivity in the American Corporation.* New York, NY: Simon and Schuster, 1983.

The Change Masters vividly demonstrates that when environments and structures are hospitable to innovation, people's natural inventiveness and power skills can make almost anything happen. Dr. Kanter's book is an indispensable guide for individuals who seek to realize their entrepreneurial potential, for corporate leaders who want to see their companies grow, and for all those concerned with the economic future of the nation. Included are some searches for innovation by companies such as Hewlett-Packard, General Electric, Polaroid, General Motors, Wang Laboratories, and Honeywell.

Kotter, John P. *Power in Management: How to Understand, Acquire, and Use It.* New York, NY: AMACOM, 1979.

The author's purpose of this book is to help managers and students of management gain a basic understanding of the acquisition and use of power in managerial jobs.

Morrisey, George L. *Management by Objectives and Results for Business and Industry (2nd ed.).* Reading, MA: Addison-Wesley, 1983.

This book is designed as a guide for managers at all levels of the organization who are dedicated to setting clear objectives and attaining results. The author has taken a "how to" approach to MBO, providing a large number of "real world" illustrations drawn from a wide variety of business, industrial, commercial, and service organizations.

Morrison, Ann M.; White, Randall P.; Van Velsor, Ellen, and The Center for Creative Leadership. *Breaking the Glass Ceiling: Can Women Reach the Top of America's Largest Corporations?* Reading, MA: Addison-Wesley, 1987.

Based on a three-year study, this book examines the factors that determine success or derailment in the corporate environment, shows how women can break the glass ceiling (a transparent barrier at the highest level of management that only a handful have been able to break), and looks at the new obstacles on the road to the top. Invaluable advice is also provided from the women executives themselves on learning the ropes in a company, getting the right kind of support, and integrating work and life.

Natemeyer, W.E., ed. *Classics of Organizational Behavior.* Durham, NC: Moore Publishing Company, Inc., 1978.

The topics of this book include: "Management and the Behavioral Sciences," "Individual Behavior and Motivation," "Interpersonal and Group Behavior," "Leadership and Power," "Behavioral Dimensions of Organizations," and "Organizational Change and Development."

Peters, Tom. *Thriving on Chaos: A Handbook for a Management Revolution.* New York, NY: Alfred A. Knopf, 1987.

Peters maintains that organizations merely aspiring to be excellent will prove disastrous; the only winning companies will be constantly adapting ones. Developing such flexibility will require a revolution in both management theory and day-to-day management practice. *Thriving on Chaos* is the essential guide to this revolution. Forty-five prescriptions specify what managers at every level must do if the organizations are to survive and flourish in today's and tomorrow's environment.

Peters, Tom, and Austin, Nancy. *A Passion for Excellence.* New York, NY: Random House, 1985.

To succeed at a high level of excellence requires great commitment on the part of managers and supervisors at all levels of the organization. This book seeks to show how managers at every level, in all kinds of organizations, can participate in maintaining and enhancing the long-term excellence of their department and organization. The authors offer examples and suggestions for practical actions that can be taken immediately.

Reber, Ralph W. *Behavioral Insights for Supervision.* Englewood Cliffs, NJ: Prentice-Hall, 1975.

This book presents a practical approach to understanding the behavior of people at work plus exercises to promote application of behavioral concepts to real situations. It covers supervisory style, motivation, and influence of job design on employee performance.

Shafritz, J.M., and Whitbeck, P., ed. *Classics of Organization Theory.* Durham, NC: Dorsey, 1987.

Topics covered in this book include: classical organization theory, neoclassical organization theory, the systems perspective, organizational structure, patterns of organizational adaptation, and contemporary organizational analyses.

Stewart, Nathaniel. *The Effective Woman Manager.* New York, NY: John Wiley & Sons, 1978.

In this book, the author, a nationally recognized authority in the field of management development, offers the upwardly mobile manager a practical, realistic guide to the skills that can "make or break" a career. It describes how to develop the seven vital managerial skills—planning, coordinating, delegating, evaluating, problem solving and decision making, time allocating, and training and guiding—to create the all-important aura of competence needed on the job. Self-tests, questionnaires, and checklists are provided at the end of each chapter for self-evaluative purposes.

Tichy, Noel M., and Devanna, Mary Anne. *The Transformational Leader.* New York, NY: John Wiley & Sons, 1986.

This book is about leadership, corporate America's scarcest natural resource. Transformational leadership is about change, innovation, and entrepreneurship. The authors use the concept of the three-act play to enable one to think about and take action on the transformational issues facing organizations. These are: recognizing the need for revitalization; creating a new vision; and instituting change. Throughout the book are integrated true, inside stories of transformation taking place at many companies.

Wilcock, Keith D. *The Corporate Tribe.* Excelsior, MN: Wyer-Pearce Press, 1984.

This book helps managers clarify their career goals and understand some fundamental anthropological principles of modern corporations. It shows how all corporate functions have evolved from earlier tribal roles. Those who understand the implications of this newly discovered concept become more firmly committed to their companies. The knowledge enhances their power and effectiveness as leaders.

Suggested Seminars

The seminars listed here were selected for their appeal to a managerial audience and have received good to excellent ratings from managers attending them.

Because of the dynamic nature of the seminar marketplace, some seminars may have been added, upgraded, or replaced, and others may no longer be offered. Additional information about these seminars may be obtained by calling the vendor directly, or through Seminar Clearinghouse International, a subscriber organization located in St. Paul, Minnesota. Call 612/293-1004 for information.

AMERICAN MANAGEMENT ASSOCIATIONS, P.O. Box 319, Saranac Lake, NY 12983, 518/891-0065.

Developing Executive Leadership. A program specifically designed for experienced managers wanting to equip themselves with the latest techniques. Included in the course outline are the following topics: leadership in today's business environment; analyzing your leadership capabilities; adapting your leadership techniques to fit specific situations; communication techniques to help you put your messages across clearly; adapting your leadership abilities to shifting needs; conflict resolution; developing effective group members; implementing change; and setting direction with leadership.

Length: 3 days
Cost: $850
Locations: Irvine, CA; San Francisco, CA; Washington, DC; Orlando, FL; Atlanta, GA; Chicago, IL; Boston, MA; New York, NY.

BATTELLE, 4000 N.E. 41st Street, P.O. Box C-5395, Seattle, WA 98105, 800/426-6762, 206/527-0542.

Manager As Leader. Participants enrolling in this program will have the opportunity to learn about the leader as change agent, developing the team, clarifying the values, creating the vision, positioning, communicating, empowering, coaching, and measuring.

Length: 3 days
Cost: $825
Locations: Phoenix, AZ; San Diego, CA; San Francisco, CA; Denver, CO; Washington, DC; Indianapolis, IN; Boston, MA: Detroit, MI; Cleveland, OH; Columbus, OH; Philadelphia, PA, Seattle, WA. For additional locations, contact the vendor.

CENTER FOR CREATIVE LEADERSHIP, 5000 Laurinda Drive, P.O. Box P-1, Greensboro, NC 27402, 919/288-7210.

Leadership At The Peak. This meeting of top executives is designed to discuss innovation; international management; power, personality, and politics; handling the media; feedback for development; self-evaluation and goal planning.
Length: 4 days
Cost: $4800
Location: Colorado Springs, CO.

Leadership Development Program. Participative in nature, this program offers participants learning opportunities in the areas of: assessment of one's abilities; creative leadership; decision making; situational leadership; utilizing group resources; innovative problem solving; peer and staff feedback; and setting and achieving goals. Extensive use is made of small groups, face-to-face sessions, videotaping, questionnaires, formal input, and discussion.
Length: 6 days
Cost: $3000
Locations: San Diego, CA; Colorado Springs, CO; Greensboro, NC; San Antonio, TX.

LEVINSON INSTITUTE, INC., 275 Concord Avenue, Belmont, MA 617/489-3040.

On Leadership. This course has three objectives: to teach executives the basic principles of human behavior; to give them practice in applying these principles to enhance their leadership roles and resolve organizational problems; and to provide them with a reliable basis for making their own critical evaluations of various psychological techniques in management.
Length: 6 days
Cost: $2800
Location: Andover, MA.

LMA INC., 365 Melendy Road, P.O. Box 140, Milford, NH 03055, 603/672-0355.

Positive Power and Influence. Before this five-day course begins, attendees collect information about current styles of influence. Participants explore alternative methods of influence based on learning objectives, select program activities to develop and refine skills, and select and practice new strategies in real life influence situations.

Length: 5 days
Cost: $950
Locations: Manchester, NH; Merrimack, NH; Nashua, NH.

PERSONNEL DECISIONS, INC., 2000 Plaza VII Tower, 45 South Seventh Street, Minneapolis, MN 55402, 612/339-0927, 800/633-4410, ext. 875 (outside Minn.).

Leadership Development Program (LDP). The Leadership Development Program helps leaders be more productive and successful, and helps them promote the productivity and success of others. The LDP has affected the lives and careers of executives, professionals, supervisors, military officers, civil servants, teachers, and many others in leadership positions—proving its value both to the people who attend and to their organizations. Through **assessment and constructive feedback,** participants become more aware of their abilities and shortcomings. Through **participative learning action planning** they set specific, attainable goals for continued development. Designed by the Center for Creative Leadership in 1973, the LDP is offered monthly in Minneapolis by Personnel Decisions, Inc.
Length: 6 days
Cost: $3000
Location: Minneapolis, MN.

The Emerging Manager: Skills & Strategies For Success. The Emerging Manager is a week-long (40-hour) program presenting a full range of management and leadership skills for first level managers at an early stage in their careers. Participants not only gain knowledge but also build skills and self-awareness in the following areas: interpersonal skills, adaptability skills, cognitive (thinking) skills, communication skills, personal motivation skills, administrative skills, and leadership skills.
Length: 5 days
Cost: $1750
Location: Minneapolis, MN.

The Executive Development Center. Offered two to three times a year, this four-day program is similar to the Management Development Center in features and benefits, but is designed to capture the complex skills and dynamic challenges of the general manager's role. For new and prospective executives, it provides a realistic preview of the demands, issues, and daily activities they will face. For experienced executives, it provides an opportunity to renew and refine their skills and personal operating style.

Length: 4 days
Cost: $5000
Location: Minneapolis, MN.

The Management Development Center. A three-day program, offered five to six times yearly, helps managers assess their strengths and development needs in a wide range of managerial and leadership skill areas. This intensive and stimulating program engages participants in a realistic simulation of the manager's job. It provides an opportunity to receive immediate feedback and individualized coaching from fellow managers and highly trained management consultants. A summary report outlining development suggestions and a follow-up development discussion are included.
Length: 3 days
Cost: $3100
Location: Minneapolis, MN.

SANTA CLARA UNIVERSITY, Executive Development Center, Santa Clara, CA 95053, 408/544-4521.

Leadership Challenge: Getting Extraordinary Things Done in Organizations. This workshop is designed for experienced managers and corporate executives with responsibilities for getting multifunctional groups to work together in profit centers, divisions, large projects, or headquarters operations. Participants will see dramatic videotapes and study cases of how leaders model their values in daily actions, present their unique vision and values for their team at work, and commit to taking specific actions that will turn dreams into realities.
Length: 4 days
Cost: $2195
Location: Watsonville, CA.

UNIVERSITY OF WISCONSIN, Management Institute, 432 North Lake Street, Madison, WI 53706, 800/262-6243 (outside Wisc.), 800/362-3020 (in Wisc.).

How to Influence Without Direct Authority. This program offers topics such as: developing special skills to influence others; building, using, and sustaining your influence; and generating creative ideas.
Length: 2 days
Cost: $450
Location: Madison, WI.

Motivating Others

Imagine that one of your most capable employees, Sarah, has reached a "productivity plateau." For the past month, she's seemed bored with her job and has done only what's needed to get by. Plus, she hasn't shown any interest in a promotional opportunity you discussed with her six months ago. You're not sure what the problem is, but it's obvious that Sarah's motivation level has dropped.

It's possible that Sarah isn't sure what is expected of her. (Have you set specific objectives for her, clearly defined her responsibilities, and expressed your expectations of her?) More likely, she hasn't received feedback on and reinforcement of her accomplishments. Other factors that might have contributed to her low motivation level include inadequate compensation, poor physical environment, no sense of achievement, mismatched responsibilities and abilities, and a lack of opportunity for advancement or personal growth (although you doubt that, because of the promotion you'd discussed with her).

This section provides guidelines for handling motivation-related issues like the one involving Sarah. It examines the importance of:

- Using Basic Principles of Motivation (p. 99)
- Learning Approaches to Motivating Others from Colleagues (p. 100)
- Individualizing Your Approach to Motivation (p. 100)
- Establishing High Standards of Performance for Subordinates (p. 102)
- Creating an Environment Where Subordinates Work Their Hardest (p. 103)
- Conveying the Attitude That Everyone's Work Is Important (p. 104)
- Conveying Enthusiasm About Meeting Department Objectives and Deadlines (p. 105)
- Enriching Jobs to Increase Motivation (p. 105)
- Giving Good Reasons When Asking Subordinates to Change (p. 106)

Tips

- Have lunch with individuals to inquire about how their jobs are going. Look for opportunities to compliment effective performance sincerely.

- Recognize that people are both **similar** and **different** in what turns them on. List the three strongest and three weakest motivators for each of your subordinates and specify what resources you have available to provide the necessary motivation.

- When you assign a task, follow up on resource allocations. If you find you are unable to provide the support on which you agreed, discuss alternatives.

- Establish a "group identity" and work at building pride in group membership—"esprit de corps."

- Consider individuals' motivational needs in the context of fairness for the whole group and determine outside opportunities for satisfying these needs.

- Recognize that some people may be happier outside your organization and encouraging their departure might be best for all concerned.

- Take time to listen to the joys and concerns of your subordinates on a one-to-one basis.

- Find ways to build in feedback so that people know how they are doing on a periodic or constant basis.

- Read *The One Minute Manager* by Blanchard and Johnson and apply the principles where appropriate.

- "Go to bat" for one of your employees who has a good idea that has been rejected or overlooked.

- Be supportive of your subordinates' efforts to try new ideas, test new talents, or exercise authority.

- If a work environment issue keeps your employees from doing their best, work with them to overcome it.

- Recognize that, depending on their maturity, subordinates will require different leadership styles on different tasks.

- When trying to change the behavior of subordinates, specify both the current and the desired behavior and identify the positive and negative consequences for each.

- Make a table with the names of your subordinates in the left margin and two columns (positive and negative feedback). Record the number of times you give each person positive and negative feedback during each of the next ten weeks. Try to increase the frequency of positive feedback by 10 percent each week until, on the average, 80 percent of all the feedback you give is positive.

- Find ways to enrich the jobs of your subordinates with activities that are challenging and rewarding.

- Establish achievable goals with people.

- Readjust goals if they prove to be unattainable.

- Establish group goals for and with the full group.

- Readjust the group's goals if they later prove to be unattainable.

- Establish quantifiable annual objectives and, on a monthly basis, have subordinates chart their progress against these objectives.

Using Basic Principles of Motivation

The subject of motivation in the work environment is one on which volumes of information have been compiled, countless books have been written, theories proposed, and research studies conducted. Thus, the following summary of these principles is obviously abbreviated. These few key principles, however, can help guide managers who are learning to establish a motivational climate.

1. Employees are likely to perform more effectively when they know what is expected of them. This principle relates to ensuring that objectives are set for each employee, ensuring that employees know their responsibilities, and clarifying your expectations. Literature on management by objectives and performance standards provides information on this principle.

2. Employees are likely to perform more effectively when they receive feedback on and reinforcement of their performance. Literature on feedback and reinforcement provides information on this principle.

3. Managers can improve the motivational climate by removing barriers to employee motivation. Some conditions in the work environment have little direct impact on performance, yet their absence can be a source of distraction. Examples include appropriate salary compensation and some types of physical improvements. F. B. Herzberg is one of the better-known authors on this subject.

4. Additional factors that influence motivation include an employee's:
   - Sense of achievement
   - Match between responsibilities and abilities
   - Opportunities for advancement
   - Opportunities for personal growth

As a manager, you have a great influence on an employee's ability to attain these factors.

Many managers believe they have no impact on the motivation of others because motivation occurs within an individual or because they have no control over some of the factors that impact employee satisfaction, such as working conditions and benefits. However, as the preceding principles point out, managers play a major role in distributing many of the rewards employees seek and in eliminating many of the barriers to satisfaction that employees encounter.

See the readings at the end of this section and the section entitled **Leadership Style and Influence** for more sources of information on motivation.

Learning Approaches to Motivating Others from Colleagues

Colleagues who are recognized for their abilities in providing a motivational environment can be excellent sources of approaches. They can provide models upon which you can base your own behavior. To benefit from their experience, follow these guidelines.

1. Arrange to attend meetings led by these colleagues. Take note of the behaviors that are effective in bringing about the desired results. In addition, meet with these people outside the meetings to discuss approaches they have found effective.

2. Develop a plan to try out some of these people's approaches with your subordinates. For your first attempt, choose a relatively simple approach with which you are comfortable; this will improve your chances of success on your first try.

3. After implementing your plan, watch for improvement in your department's motivational climate. Seek feedback from others on the results of your innovations.

As you come closer to approximating the behavior of your role models, you should also come closer to attaining a motivational climate similar to those established by your models.

Individualizing Your Approach to Motivation

Individuals vary in how they value various rewards. The following guidelines will help you gear your motivational techniques to the employees in your work group.

1. As a starting point, write each subordinate's name on a separate sheet of paper. Use these sheets of paper as follows.
   - List the needs and corresponding rewards you believe to be most relevant to each subordinate, based on your current knowledge of that subordinate.
   - Initiate a discussion with each employee to learn, directly from the source, what that employee perceives his or her needs to be. Compare the lists supplied by the employees to the lists of your perceptions to determine your level of sensitivity to employee requirements.

- Observe employees over time and add to or alter your list of requirements. Examples of situations that indicate requirement changes include cases in which employees did not mention certain needs because they thought them inappropriate (for example, employees who consider it inappropriate to indicate that they require frequent recognition or salary increases) and those in which employees mention certain needs they do not have but believe you expect them to have (for example, employees who are not interested in advancement but who believe that they will be penalized for lack of ambition should this fact become known).
- In addition, observe employees to determine the optimum timing for rewards. For example, some employees may appreciate frequent encouragement and recognition throughout a project while others may prefer to receive these rewards upon project completion.
- Most important, develop and implement a list of ways in which you can provide the rewards that influence employees' individual motivation levels.

2. To further develop your skills:
   - Seek feedback on your motivational abilities from colleagues skilled in this area. If appropriate, arrange for coaching to improve your skills.
   - Observe skilled colleagues in action and incorporate their approaches into your own program. (See the subsection entitled "Learning Approaches to Motivating Others from Colleagues" for more information.)

As you make changes in the way you deal with employee motivation, watch for indications of improvement in the motivation level of your department.

Establishing High Standards of Performance for Subordinates

While most employees will generally fulfill their job responsibilities, it is the rare individual who will take the initiative to go above and beyond what is expected by management. It is up to you, then, to set standards of performance for your subordinates that test their skills and push them to reach their full potential. Here is a procedure for doing so:

1. The best and most convenient time to set performance expectations is during the employee's annual performance review. Prior to this, you should give careful consideration to each subordinate's skills, experience, special training, career goals, past performance, etc.
2. With basic job requirements as a base line, determine what will be required to achieve a satisfactory level of performance which meets the job requirements.
3. Then, with consideration of the factors listed in #1 above, determine what you feel would be appropriate "stretch objectives" for each individual, that is, standards of performance that exceed the job requirements, and are challenging, yet obtainable. (Obtainable is a key word here. It's important that you don't set your subordinates up for failure by setting standards they cannot possibly reach.)
4. The next step would be to discuss your expectations with your subordinate, giving careful consideration to his or her concerns, ideas, and any factors you may have overlooked when setting your standards. It's important that your subordinate feels he or she has input into performance expectations and that he or she "buys into" the appropriateness of the standards. If this does not occur, it is likely that your subordinate will not be highly motivated to meet objectives.

5. Once you and your subordinate have come to an agreement on expectations, document them and each take a copy for reference. Agree to meet periodically to see how his or her progress measures up to expectations. Revise the performance standards if the situation warrants, but remember to keep the goals challenging.

Creating an Environment Where Subordinates Work Their Hardest

One primary factor in productivity is the reinforcement employees receive for their behaviors. If employees receive consistently positive reinforcement for desirable behaviors, productivity levels will tend to be high; if, on the other hand, employees perceive that unproductive behaviors are rewarded or—even worse—that productive behaviors are punished, productivity will tend to be low.

If your subordinates are not meeting your expectations, one approach is to determine whether something in the work environment is reinforcing their behaviors inappropriately. The following process can help:

1. Examine your subordinates' motivational make-up.
   - What do they value (autonomy, recognition, challenging work assignments, etc.)?
   - How do they prefer to receive rewards for their work (consistently, intermittently, etc.)?
2. Determine the consequences of current behavior using the following Behavior/Consequences matrix.

		Consequences	
		+	**-**
Current Behavior	*Desirable*	A	B
	Undesirable	C	D

- In Box A: List the positive consequences the employee experiences as a result of engaging in desirable behaviors.
- In Box B: List the adverse consequences of engaging in desirable behaviors.

- In Box C: List the positive consequences of engaging in undesirable behaviors.
- In Box D: List the negative consequences of engaging in undesirable behaviors.

Be sure to consider these consequences from the employee's perspective, not your own. Consequences that you label adverse from your perspective are positive from the employee's point of view—or they wouldn't continue. For example, from your point of view, the consequence of an employee leaving early is that work is not completed on time; from the employee's point of view, the only consequence may be that he or she has more time for personal pursuits.

3. Identify the consequences that need to be changed to change the behavior. Do this by determining how to remove the positive consequences of undesirable behaviors and create positive consequences for desirable behaviors.
4. Discuss the desired goals with the employee, putting them in behavioral, observable terms.
5. Make the relationship between the behavior and its consequences very clear. For example, the consequence of meeting productivity goals may be receiving more challenging projects, if that is something that would motivate the individual.
6. Once the desired behavior is performed, reward it immediately. Positive consequences increase the probability that the behavior will occur again. Delaying reinforcement can be a form of negative consequences that reduces the chance of the behavior recurring.

Conveying the Attitude That Everyone's Work Is Important

While some individuals have more complex and involved responsibilities than others, it is important to convey the attitude that everyone's work is important. You may want to try these techniques:

- Meet with your subordinates individually and show them how their responsibilities fit into the running of the department and organization.
- Highlight the importance of what they are doing by showing them how dependent you and others are on their work.
- Frequently reinforce their effective performance, emphasizing how it impacts you and the rest of the organization.

- Be particularly careful to reinforce persons performing "low visibility" responsibilities with equal frequency as those whose work is in the "limelight." The research assistant who gathers the necessary data for the manager needs to share in recognition for a winning proposal that brings in an important piece of business.

Conveying Enthusiasm About Meeting Department Objectives and Deadlines

Managers may assume that their commitment to department objectives and deadlines will automatically be communicated to subordinates. To some extent, that's true. However, using the following techniques can help you make sure your subordinates recognize your commitment:

- When you assign new projects to subordinates, take the time to explain how the project fits in with overall department objectives. When employees understand how their work contributes to the whole, their commitment to it increases.
- Make it a point to regularly reinforce the importance of each individual's contributions and their value to overall department objectives.
- Remind your subordinates often that the success of the department is key to the success of the organization.
- Emphasize your own commitment to the department and organization and praise the commitment demonstrated by your staff.

When your commitment to department objectives and deadlines is obvious to your subordinates, their motivation and involvement in the overall success of the company will increase.

Enriching Jobs to Increase Motivation

Researchers have found that job enrichment—changing jobs to make them more satisfying—is a technique that can lead to higher quality work. Following is a list of ideas from which you can choose.

- Discuss how your employee's role supports your department or organization objectives, and how they in turn impact the company performance. Employees will be more involved when they see how their piece fits into the total picture.
- Add new tasks to the job to widen the variety of skills used in performing the job. This can increase motivation by reducing boredom.

- Loosen managerial controls to give subordinates increased responsibilities for managing their own work. (See the "Delegating" section for guidelines for determining the appropriate amount of control.)
- Increase the subordinate's visibility. For example, a subordinate who formerly prepared reports for your signature might now be allowed to submit reports under his or her own signature. (Of course, this individual would also be held accountable for those reports.)
- Increase the subordinate's authority and accountability. Give the subordinate full decision-making responsibility in areas for which approval was formerly required.
- Increase the meaningfulness of assigned tasks. A subordinate who previously completed only a portion of a task might be permitted to handle the entire task alone or with others to have the satisfaction of producing a total product. This concept was successfully applied in a Swedish automobile-manufacturing plant; workers were given responsibility for assembling an entire engine rather than simply tightening a single bolt.
- Increase the amount of feedback on performance. Feedback can be provided by you—the manager—or employees can provide their own feedback. For example, a machine repair person can keep a tally of the number of "call back" service calls received on the equipment serviced.
- Assign special projects periodically to provide challenges and visibility.

Giving Good Reasons When Asking Subordinates to Change

To remain competitive, organizations must constantly innovate with changes in technology and methodology. With these changes comes the need for change among the individuals performing functions within the organization. Often, however, change creates uncertainty and suspicion among subordinates, especially if they are not fully informed of the reason for change. Next time you find yourself in a position where you must explain reasons for changes to your subordinates, try these steps:

1. Call a meeting for all individuals affected by the changes. Emphasize that this will be a discussion of the proposed changes and for them to come prepared with questions.
2. After explaining the changes, open the meeting to questions and comments. Often more than one person has the same concern, and this will give each a chance to voice his or her opinion.

3. Pay particular attention to signs of animosity or resistance and address these immediately. By showing that you know and care how your subordinates feel, you can gain their cooperation more quickly.
4. Finally, emphasize to them that you will be available and willing to answer any questions they may have.

Recommended Readings

Albrecht, Karl. *Successful Management by Objectives: An Action Manual.* Englewood Cliffs, NJ: Prentice-Hall, 1978.

The author explains the philosophy and techniques of management by objectives. He discusses how to motivate and encourage employees by giving them reasons and rewards for a job well done and how to teach employees to set and reach meaningful goals.

Bradford, David L., and Cohen, Allan R. *Managing for Excellence: The Guide to Developing High Performance in Contemporary Organizations.* New York, NY: John Wiley & Sons, 1987.

This book is written for middle managers who must turn the grand designs of CEOs and presidents into personal commitment on the part of individuals in a department. It focuses on the manager as developer and discusses how to develop overreaching goals that tie employees' interests to the needs of the department, build shared-responsibility teams, and motivate employees to get even routine jobs done creatively and productively.

Donaldson, Les. *Behavioral Supervision: Practical Ways to Change Unsatisfactory Behavior and Increase Productivity.* Reading, MA: Addison-Wesley, 1980.

This book describes how superiors and managers on any level can deal with and correct subordinates' behavioral problems. It explains how techniques of behavioral change can be used to deal with uncooperative subordinates.

Dowling, W., and Sayles, L. *How Managers Motivate (2nd ed.).* New York, NY: McGraw-Hill, 1978.

Focusing on face-to-face supervision, this book emphasizes research based on direct observation of first-line managers on the "firing line" and helps provide readers with the material they need to cope with changing management requirements.

Gordon, Thomas. *Leader Effectiveness Training.* New York, NY: Bantam Books, 1980.

This is an excellent introduction to the interpersonal coaching and leadership aspects of management. It includes practical problem-solving techniques and communication skills necessary to: get people to work with you, not just for you; resolve conflicts between individuals; develop a work team that gets results; evaluate others without damaging their self-esteem; and make meetings more productive and enjoyable.

Harris, O.J., Jr. *Managing People at Work.* New York, NY: John Wiley & Sons, 1983.

Innovative, theoretical, and practical approaches to motivation and handling of interpersonal conflict are described.

Hersey, P., and Blanchard, K.H. *Management of Organizational Behavior: Utilizing Human Resources (4th ed.).* Englewood Cliffs, NJ: Prentice-Hall, 1982.

This book examines the behavioral approach to management, develops an outline of change theory, and presents various strategies for planning and implementing change. Among the topics discussed are motivation and behavior, the motivating environment, leader behavior, determination of effectiveness, ways to diagnose the environment, and management for organizational effectiveness and planning.

Kelley, Robert E. *The Gold-Collar Worker.* Reading, MA: Addison-Wesley, 1985.

Management consultant Robert Kelley maintains that a new breed of workers demanding a new kind of management has come into play. These he terms as the "gold-collar workers"—the brain power of American business. Intelligent, independent, and innovative, these employees are incredibly valuable. In this book, Kelley takes a close look at these new workers, examines their impact on corporations, and offers practical advice for the people who manage them.

McGinnis, Alan Loy. *Bringing Out the Best in People.* Minneapolis, MN: Augsburg Publishing House, 1985.

The author portrays fascinating case studies and anecdotes about Lee Iacocca, Sandra Day O'Connor, and many others, sharing their motivational secrets. He details 12 key principles and shows how these can be put to work in bringing out the best in people in your family or organization.

Rosenbaum, Bernard L. *How to Motivate Today's Workers: Motivational Models for Managers and Supervisors.* New York, NY: McGraw-Hill, 1981.

This book provides ideas for dealing with specific coaching and motivating problems. It is a set of active skill-building exercises and models that show how to build improved behavior models for poor, average, and dissatisfied performers. Included are keys to: dealing with disciplinary action, resistance to change, conflict between employees, absenteeism, and unrest.

Ullrich, Robert A. *Motivation Methods that Work.* Englewood Cliffs, NJ: Prentice-Hall, 1981.

The author uses a behavioral approach to improve productivity. He explains how to overcome major types of management problems and offers suggestions on how to get the most from employees. Included are techniques that help overcome alienation among workers, methods that turn self-interest into teamwork, strategies for helping committed employees become high achievers, and an explanation of how to identify the appropriate management technique for your situation.

Suggested Seminars

The seminars listed here were selected for their appeal to a managerial audience and have received good to excellent ratings from managers attending them.

Because of the dynamic nature of the seminar marketplace, some seminars may have been added, upgraded, or replaced, and others may no longer be offered. Additional information about these seminars may be obtained by calling the vendor directly, or through Seminar Clearinghouse International, a subscriber organization located in St. Paul, Minnesota. Call 612/293-1004 for information.

ARTHUR ANDERSEN & CO, Center for Professional Education, 1405 North Fifth Avenue, St. Charles, IL 60174, 312/507-7460.

Managerial Skills: Motivation and Leadership. Key topics included in this one-day seminar are the following: history of productivity research, how expectations affect productivity, how personal needs influence leadership behavior, and situational approach to leadership.
Length: 1 day
Cost:$ 250
Locations: Chicago, IL; New York, NY.

HILLSDALE COLLEGE, Dow Leadership Development Center, Hillsdale, MI 49242, 517/437-3311.

Motivating Individuals for Peak Performance. Understanding how leaders and subordinates see each other; developing coaching and training techniques; pinpointing problems and using counseling effectively; interpersonal communication skills; creating an effective motivational system; turning around negative attitudes; analyzing and rewarding individual performance are the major topics highlighted in this 5-day program.
Length: 5 days
Cost: $800
Location: Hillsdale, MI.

KEPNER TREGOE, Research Road, P.O. Box 704, Princeton, NJ 08542, 800/223-0482, 609/921-2806, 800/268-6685 (in Canada).

Managing the Performance System. Designed to help individuals deal interpersonally, this program identifies for participants ways to effectively troubleshoot performance problems, improve substandard performance, make adequate employee performance excellent, set standards for

optimum job performance, identify key human resource developing needs, and design an effective employee incentive system.
Length: 1 day
Cost: $295.00
Locations: Atlanta, GA; Chicago, IL.

IOWA STATE UNIVERSITY, 110 EES Building, Haber Road, Ames, IA 50011, 515/294-7612.
Leadership and Motivational Skills for Supervisors. Participants in this program will: learn how to deal with obstacles to employee performance; set goals; learn concepts of situational leadership, get feedback on leadership style; and get the job done.
Length: 2 days
Cost: $275
Location: Ames, IA.

MW CORPORATION, One Croton Point Avenue, Croton-On-Hudson, NY 10520, 914/271-5568, 914/271-6659.
Motivation Workshop. This workshop is designed to give participants an in-depth look at what motivates people, how to motivate people, and how motivation impacts on productivity. Content areas include customer service, managing the boss, performance appraisal, coaching, delegating, counseling, confronting, influencing, empowering.
Length: 3 days
Cost: $795
Locations: Danbury, CT; Atlanta, GA; Boston, MA; Baltimore, MD; Crotonville, NY; Tarrytown, NY.

NTL INSTITUTE, P.O. Box 9155, Rosslyn Station, Arlington, VA 22209, 703/527-1500.
Developing Your Staff: How to Improve Morale, Motivation, and Productivity. Participants attending this program will be involved in increasing your understanding of factors leading to high morale and achievement motivation; getting feedback on your own style, strengths, and limitations as a staff developer; developing skills in gathering and analyzing work-group data; giving feedback; developing skills in intervention to improve morale and productivity; and exploring the impact of power, access, and opportunity on work groups.
Length: 6 days
Cost: $795
Location: Bethel, ME.

PERFORMEX, The Ferry Building, #3045, San Francisco, CA 94111, 415/543-7733.

Personal Performance Program. This three-phase program allows participants to get feedback from bosses and subordinates on their strengths and weaknesses, learn best ways to manage self, receive coaching, and achieve improved performance. Within two weeks of completion of workshop, participants again meet with counselor to review workshop and follow up on the development planning.

Length: 3 days
Cost: $995
Location: San Francisco, CA.

PSYCHOLOGICAL ASSOCIATES, INC., 8201 Maryland Avenue, St. Louis, MO 63105, 314/862-9300

Dimensional Management Training I. This program focuses on people skills and provides a five-step system for working out problems with subordinates, as well as skills to help participants communicate, motivate, and manage behavioral barriers.

Length: 5 days
Cost: $595
Location: St. Louis, MO

RUMMLER-BRACHE GROUP, P.O. Box 4537, Warren, NJ 07060, 201/757-5700.

Performance Design Workshop. The purpose of this program is six-fold: developing a model of actual and ideal organization performance; identifying where the greatest opportunities to impact performance and obtain results reside; determining what is causing the gap between desired and actual performance at these pivotal points; specifying the changes required in the individual, the process, and the organization to achieve improved performance; implementing the changes to obtain the desired result; and evaluating the changes that occur to determine whether desired results have been achieved.

Length: 3 days
Cost: $745.00
Locations: Washington, DC; Chicago, IL; Summit, NJ.

WATERLOO MANAGEMENT EDUCATION CENTRE, Suite 619, Waterloo Square, Waterloo, Ontario, Canada N2J 1P2, 519/886-4740.

Motivation and Leadership. This five-day seminar covers such key topics as a practical look at Maslow; motivational power of past experience;

Leadership Skills

what makes people perform—a plan for action; leadership; generating
enthusiasm—the optimistic leader; leadership styles—management
approaches; team building; and group dynamics and team leadership.
Length: 5 days
Cost: $800
Location: Waterloo, ON.

Group Skills

In any position that involves management or supervisory duties, the ability to work effectively with groups of people is an important part of the job. The skills involved in accomplishing work with and through others become as important as individual technical skills.

This section has been divided into three parts.

Part I: Individual Skills
- Evaluating Your Impact on Groups (p. 118)
- Increasing Your Impact in Group Situations (p. 119)

Part II: Meeting Management Skills
- Setting Up Meeting Facilities (p. 120)
- Constructing Effective Agendas (p. 121)
- Organizing the Meeting (p. 122)
- Managing Meetings (p. 123)
- Evaluating the Effectiveness of Your Meetings (p. 123)

Part III: Improving Group Processes
- Acknowledging and Dealing With Informal Leaders (p. 125)
- Encouraging Group Interaction (p. 126)
- Improving Group Problem Solving (p. 127)
- Improving Group Decision Making (p. 128)
- Using the Nominal Group Technique to Improve Group Problem Solving (p. 130)
- Converting Decisions Into Group Action (p. 130)

Tips

- Find opportunities to lead groups where the risk of failure is low.

- Analyze ways in which you hold back members of your group. Work on eliminating those disruptive behaviors.

- Prepare for your next meeting by looking over the agenda and thinking about contributions you can make.

- Join a task force in your organization. Use it as an opportunity to practice styles of leading and contributing to a group effort.

- Seek the leadership responsibility for a task force in your community, church, school, etc. Use it to hone your group skills, as well as to contribute.

- Ask a subordinate to chair meetings in which you wish to actively participate.

- Prior to forming any group, ask yourself if the task or goal is best handled by a group; write a charter or purpose for each group you have established.

- Seek feedback from your boss on your meeting behavior. Probe for both strengths and weaknesses.

- Be sure to take your fair share of "air time" in meetings with your boss. Express your point of view but be sensitive to others' needs for air time.

- Use good "active listening" skills to summarize, acknowledge, and reinforce contributions of other group members.

- When speaking in group situations, talk longer and expand more fully on the concepts you are presenting.

- Practice being more forceful in situations like church meetings where the costs, risks, and implications are not great.

- In group decision-making situations, spend less time processing data, and make earlier entry into the group's decision-making process.

- Participate more in group decision-making situations and express yourself with more conviction.

- In groups, force yourself to say things even when you are uncertain about their impact.

- Make a conscious effort to be more consistently persuasive in meetings by standing behind your ideas.

- Concentrate on both task and maintenance functions in your next meeting.

- Allow yourself plenty of time to prepare for your meetings.

- Meet individually with group members to get their ideas on how the group meetings are going.

- Assign a "process observer" for the meeting to help keep the group functioning effectively.

- Publish the agenda for the meeting in advance and advise people of any required preparation.

- Use a flip chart at meetings to keep track of contributions of group members.

- Hold informal communications meetings periodically with your staff off site to avoid disruptions.

- At the end of each meeting, recap action items. Clarify person(s) responsible and completion dates.

- Assure that your meetings start and end on time. Do not wait for "latecomers."

- Try to keep your meetings no longer than one-and-one-half hours. Set up another meeting if more time is required.

- Under your manager's direction, take charge of conducting certain aspects of meetings, particularly where assignments have to be made.

- Make a list of the key strengths and limitations of each person in your group. Find ways to utilize the strengths.

- Use new techniques to help your group generate ideas—brainstorming, brainwriting, nominal group, etc.

- Find a way to involve the most quiet member of the group without embarrassing the individual.

- Use open-ended questions and reflective listening to draw out quieter members of the group.

- Train your staff in group process by listing the various elements of "task" and "maintenance" behavior, discussing their importance, and evaluating which person is best at each of these functions.

- Examine each group you have established for correct membership—consider expanding it or changing its composition from time to time.

- Make more input to group's focus on issues rather than individuals.

Part I: Individual Skills

Evaluating Your Impact on Groups

How effective are you in group situations? Do you contribute too much? Too little? Does the impact you have on a group depend on the circumstances? In developing a plan for improving your group skills, you should first sharpen your awareness of how you currently function. The following process and accompanying chart should help you develop this insight.

1. For the next several months, keep a record of your contributions in committees, meetings, or other group settings. Also keep track of ideas, plans, and solutions that you could have contributed but did not.

2. Determine your overall impact at each meeting. Did you contribute a great deal? Very little? Was the effect of your participation positive, negative, or neutral?

3. Evaluate the reasons for your performance in each meeting by checking the appropriate responses to the following questions.

   - If you contributed a great deal, what were the reasons?
     ____ Good preparation
     ____ Knowledge of the area
     ____ Interest in the topic
     ____ Felt at ease with other group members (other members expected and/or welcomed contributions, the opinions of other members warranted responses/rebuttals, other members were quiet, etc.)
     ____ Other (describe: _____)
   - If you did not contribute very much or very often, what were the reasons?
     ____ Lack of preparation
     ____ Lack of knowledge of the area
     ____ Lack of interest in the topic
     ____ Discomfort with other group members (shyness, intimidation due to their status levels, other members were too vocal, etc.)
     ____ You participated in situations in which you were the formal leader but held back in other situations
     ____ You contributed, but if your ideas were not accepted, you immediately let them drop
     ____ Other (describe: _____)

Settings	Contri-butions Made	Contri-butions With-held	Overall Level of Contri-butions (high, med., low)	Impact (+, -)	Reasons

At the end of several weeks, make an overall analysis of your skills to determine whether you would like to change your impact in group settings.

Another way to determine your impact is to ask a trusted coworker or superior to critique your performance in group settings. Ask the person to focus on the cases in which you present your point of view effectively and those in which you hold back or are not as effective in interjecting your opinions. Analyze the feedback you receive to determine if your behavior forms a pattern that you would like to change.

Increasing Your Impact in Group Situations

If you exhibit a low-key or withdrawn style of group participation, it may cause others to believe that you lack leadership potential. To become a well-rounded leader, consider increasing your impact in group situations. The following suggestions should help you develop a more assertive style.

- Make a conscious effort to increase the level of your contributions; in other words, make suggestions more often.
- Work at becoming more assertive in groups. In addition to speaking up more often, develop forcefulness in stating your opinions. Don't hesitate to voice your thoughts or to label them as your own. Take steps to ensure that other group members take your contributions seriously and consider them when making decisions.
- Because impact in group situations is increased by advance preparation, take time to study the meeting agenda beforehand. Having facts and figures before you may help you to be more forceful in stating your opinions.

- If you sometimes need more time to absorb information and solve problems, you may be able to increase your impact by anticipating the topics to be discussed and the decisions to be made; that way, you will not be forced to think on your feet. Again, studying the meeting agenda can help you prepare ahead of time.
- Examine the reasons you checked in the preceding subsection for not contributing in group situations. Then identify other elements that prevent you from asserting yourself and techniques for overcoming each element. For example, if you tend to make suggestions, then withdraw them if they are not immediately supported by other group members, you may decide to voice your suggestions at least twice before dropping them if you believe they are viable.

Practice one of these behaviors per week for a month, making sure you've tried each one several times before going on to the next one. Set definite goals for yourself, such as spending 15 minutes preparing for each meeting or speaking at least five times during each meeting. Monitor the impact you are having in the group as a result of these behaviors and keep applying those that have proved most helpful to you.

Part II: Meeting Management Skills

Setting Up Meeting Facilities

When the logistics of setting up meetings are attended to in advance, less time is wasted, and meeting initiators and leaders appear more competent. Important elements in setting up meetings include:

- **Meeting time.** Choose a time when all necessary facts and people are available. Also, select a time that will help ensure that the meeting ends at a logical time—just before lunch or quitting time, for example.
- **Location.** Select a location that is accessible to all who will attend.
- **Room size.** Select a room that is of the appropriate size for your group—neither so large that participants may sit far away from the action and each other nor so small that participants have insufficient room to write or sit comfortably.
- **Ventilation and temperature.** Ensure that the room is not too stuffy, drafty, hot, or cold.
- **Equipment.** Be sure that all necessary equipment is on hand and set up. Meeting time should not be wasted while someone looks for a flip chart or threads a film projector.

- **Furniture arrangement.** If you have the flexibility to do so, set up the room to maximize group attention and participation. If the group is small, use a semicircular seating arrangement that exactly accommodates the number of people involved. If you must use rows, use more short rows rather than a few long rows so people aren't too spread out and the speaker's eye-span will not have to be too wide.
- **Seating.** Encourage participants to sit close to the speakers and each other rather than spreading out across the room. This will promote equal participation.

You may wish to create a checklist of these points to use when setting up your meetings.

Constructing Effective Agendas

Agendas are instrumental in conducting efficient meetings. They allow group members to prepare for meetings and ensure that all necessary items are addressed. When preparing agendas, check to see that you have taken the following steps.

1. **State the purpose of the meeting at the top of the agenda.** This will help participants determine whether they should attend.
2. **State a definite start and stop time for the meeting.**
3. **Determine the type of action desired on each agenda item.** You are likely to have "information only," "discussion only," and "decisions required" items. Organize your agenda according to these item types and communicate them to group members. This will help members prepare for the meeting and determine the goal to be attained in addressing each item.
4. **Establish priorities.** Establish priorities for each agenda item so that group members focus on addressing the most important items.
5. **Determine the order of the agenda items.** Most experts recommend placing the most important topics toward the beginning of the agenda; that way, if time runs out, the lower priority items are left unaddressed. You may, however, wish to run through any informational items on your agenda at the beginning of the meeting to ensure that they are covered.
6. **Establish time limits on items.** Decide on an approximate amount of time to be spent on each agenda item. Enforce your time limits on "information only" and "discussion only" items. On "decision required" items, acknowledge when the time limit has been reached; then ask the group to decide whether and how to continue with these items.

Organizing the Meeting

Organizing the meeting in advance is just as important as arranging for the appropriate facility. Your attention to organizational considerations can greatly affect the efficiency of the meeting and the way in which others evaluate your meeting-management skills. Over the next several months, pay special attention to the following steps required for meeting organization.

1. **Prepare an agenda.** (See the suggestions in the preceding subsection.)
2. **Distribute the agenda well in advance of the meeting.** This enables participants to gather materials and prepare their arguments.
3. **Limit the number of participants.** Invite only those people who are needed for decision making or who require the information that will be presented. To encourage equal participation by all members, try to restrict the size of a problem-solving meeting to 10 or 12 participants.

Managing Meetings

Managing meetings effectively takes practice. Over the next several months, take steps to ensure that you have the opportunity to lead several meetings. Then, during the course of the meetings, refer to the following guidelines for practicing the principles of good meeting management. You may wish to take a copy of these guidelines with you to the meetings until you feel that they have become a natural part of your management style.

1. **Start the meeting on time.** When people expect meetings to start late, they arrive late. If, on the other hand, they must walk in after a meeting has started, they are likely to take steps to arrive at future meetings on time.
2. **Begin with a reminder of the time allotted** for the meeting and with an assurance that the meeting will end on time.
3. **Review the agenda and the amount of time to be allotted to each item.**
4. **Ensure that someone monitors the time and takes minutes.** Have the timekeeper inform you of the time remaining and whether the meeting is running behind schedule.
5. **Minimize digression** by politely curtailing any interjections that are unimportant or unrelated to the topic of discussion.
6. **End with a summary** of what has been accomplished and agreed upon. Restate any assignments and associated deadlines.
7. **Inform participants of future events;** announce any follow-up meetings and times for those meetings, or let people know how and when the times will be established.
8. **End the meeting on time.**
9. **Follow up** by distributing copies of meeting minutes and reminders about assignments and deadlines to all persons who attended.

Periodically evaluate your performance of each of these steps.

Evaluating the Effectiveness of Your Meetings

To further improve your meeting-management skills, you may wish to solicit feedback on the effectiveness of your meetings. One way of doing this is to periodically ask participants to complete the following evaluation form. Distribute copies of the form toward the end of the meeting, and use the feedback you receive to increase the effectiveness of your future meetings.

Leadership Skills

	Y/N	Comments
Setup Arrangements		
Were the date, time, and location appropriate?	Y/N	
Was the room the proper size?	Y/N	
Were the ventilation and temperature satisfactory?	Y/N	
Was the required equipment on hand and set up?	Y/N	
Was the furniture adequate?	Y/N	
Did the seating arrangements promote equal participation?	Y/N	
Meeting Management		
Were the appropriate people invited?	Y/N	
Was the size of the group appropriate?	Y/N	
Were the essential preparatory materials distributed?	Y/N	
Did the meeting start on time?	Y/N	
Was the purpose of the meeting clear?	Y/N	
Was the agenda distributed in advance?	Y/N	
Was the agenda appropriate (number of items, priority of items, etc.)?	Y/N	
Did the group follow the agenda?	Y/N	
Were assignments and deadlines established?	Y/N	
Did the environment promote participation?	Y/N	
Did the meeting end on time?	Y/N	

Part III: Improving Group Processes

Acknowledging and Dealing With Informal Leaders

Informal leaders exist in almost all groups. They are the people who are the "natural" influencers of others—those to whom others tend to turn for advice, opinions, and help in making decisions.

Before they can lead effectively, new leaders who come into a group often need to: 1) identify the informal leadership, and 2) be accepted by the informal leaders. Failure to do so may result in their reduced acceptance as leaders or, even worse, sabotage by the informal leaders and the group.

1. To identify informal leaders, watch for:
   - Who talks to whom
   - Who listens to whom
   - Who interrupts whom
   - The extent to which individuals' comments and suggestions are attended to
   - How the group arrives at decisions

   The informal leaders are those people who have the most influence in these matters.

2. Once you recognize the informal leaders, it is usually effective to **legitimize their power in some way or recognize their special status.** For example, unless the informal leaders are disrupting the group, you may wish to stand back a little and allow the group to continue to function in its normal way. You can also recognize the status of these leaders by holding a separate discussion in which the informal leaders fill you in on the goals of the group and how the group has operated in the past.

It is usually counterproductive to try to reduce the power of informal leaders in any overt manner. If you are competent in your new role, the group will soon recognize your competence and respond to your influence naturally.

Look for opportunities to practice your skills in identifying and dealing with informal leaders. In addition to evaluating situations in which you assume the role of the formal leader, analyze the dynamics of groups in which you are a participant or an observer. Practice spotting the informal leaders in those situations and determine how you would deal with them. Compare your analyses to the analyses and actions of the actual leaders.

Encouraging Group Interaction

Interaction in meetings typically takes one of three forms:
- The group is largely silent, with the leader doing most of the talking.
- Group members interact with the leader.
- Group members interact with each other.

The third form represents the most effective type of interaction. When group members interact, the resources of all members are used most fully, and problem solving is promoted. Following are ways to encourage group interaction.

- **When deciding where to sit, choose a place that deemphasizes your leadership role.** For example, instead of sitting at the head of the table, sit to the side.
- **Establish a norm of group interaction immediately upon formation of the group.** One way to accomplish this is to provide a minimum of information yourself and then immediately provide an occasion for each group member to talk. For example, you might ask group

members to introduce themselves and discuss their expertise relevant to the group task or to express their opinions on the group task.

- **Invite group members to respond to each other's comments.** For example, you might ask, "Is there anything anyone else would like to ask George about this position?"
- **Whenever possible, avoid interrupting members.** By interrupting, you redirect attention to yourself and your role as director of the discussion.
- **Use nonverbal behavior to direct group members' comments away from you and toward other group members.** For example, a group member responding to a comment made by another group member might look to you for your reaction rather than at the other group member. In this case, avoid reacting and look toward the group member who made the original comment.
- **Explicitly redirect comments that are inappropriately directed to you.** For example, you might say, "That sounds like a comment on George's position. What do you think, George?"
- **Ask group members to lead sessions or facilitate group discussion of particular points.** In other words, temporarily forfeit your leadership power to facilitate group interaction.

Improving Group Problem Solving

To develop skills that will enable you to improve the effectiveness of group problem solving, follow these suggestions when you lead problem-solving sessions over the next few months. Watch the groups you lead for signs of increased participation and the generation of more and better solution alternatives.

- As group leader, you should **facilitate rather than direct the group discussion.** The preceding subsection points out that group interaction allows the resources of all members to be used most fully and explains techniques for encouraging interaction.
- **Protect minority opinion.** The most obvious or popular suggestions are not always the best. To ensure that innovative suggestions are given full consideration, the facilitator must ensure that those who propose minority solutions are provided with an environment in which they feel comfortable voicing their ideas.
- Encourage sessions that are **problem-oriented rather than solution-oriented.** Too often, participants in problem-solving sessions jump immediately into the generation of solutions before the problem is fully defined; this practice encourages the adaptation of solutions that solve only part of the problem.

To ensure adequate emphasis on problem definition, institute a strict sequential structure (e.g., "We will spend 15 minutes on problem definition, then 20 minutes on the generation of solution alternatives").

- Use **brainstorming to generate alternate solutions.** When brainstorming, group members strive for quantity rather than quality, piggyback on the ideas of others, and avoid judgment of alternatives. This approach results in increased quality of the ultimate decisions and great creativity in problem solving. (The subsection entitled "Brainstorming" in the "Innovation" section of this Handbook explains the brainstorming process in greater detail.)
- Look for a second solution after a first solution is arrived at to encourage additional creative approaches.

Group members should be informed of the steps you will take to improve group problem solving and your reasons for taking these steps. For example, you might start the session by saying, "Today I'm going to help the discussion along but not participate in or direct it. I'll try to protect minority opinion so that the full range of alternatives will be presented and encourage group interaction to ensure that we all benefit from each individual's experience."

Improving Group Decision Making

When a group has problems making decisions, it is usually because its members are confused or in disagreement about one or more of the following:

- **What** decision they are trying to make
- **Who** should be involved in making the decision
- **How** individuals should be involved (as information sources, decision makers, etc.)
- **When** the decision must be made

You can increase the effectiveness of group decision making by asking the following series of questions at the start of each session.

1. **Do we all agree on the decision to be made?** This question should be asked after someone has stated an interpretation of the decision to be reached. Another question that can help clarify this point is, "What part of the problem-solving process are we in?" The five parts are:
   - Defining the problem
   - Generating alternatives
   - Selecting an alternative

- Implementing a plan
- Evaluating the plan

Each of these stages requires different kinds of decisions.

If anyone disagrees with or is confused about the decision to be made, the group must make sure that the goal of the session is clarified before proceeding.

2. **Who should be involved in this decision?** The answer to this general question depends on the answers to the following specific questions.
    - Who possesses the knowledge to ensure that the decision is logical and sound?
    - Who will be involved in the implementation of the decision? (It's important that those responsible for implementation be included if they are to fully accept the decision.)
    - Who must approve the decision? (Decisions are meaningless unless they are approved by the persons with the authority to do so. Approval may be easier to obtain if those in authority are invited to participate in the decision-making process.)

3. **How should each person be involved?** Not everyone involved in a decision-making session is a full-scale decision maker. Group members may be involved directly (actually make the decisions) or consulted (provide information or opinions).

    The people who are involved directly fall into one of three categories:
    - Those with "power veto" (they can veto any suggestion or decision)
    - Those with "technical veto" (they can veto only those ideas or decisions that are within their areas of expertise)
    - Those without veto power (they can contribute information, vote, or reach consensus, but do not have veto power)

    Before beginning the session, all group members should know the categories into which they fall.

4. **When will the decision be made?** Always set a time frame so people know when to expect a decision to be made. Give one person responsibility for managing the decision-making process. This person need not be the head decision maker but must be identified from the start as the individual who ensures that the decision is made by the agreed-upon time.

Using the Nominal Group Technique to Improve Group Problem Solving

The Nominal Group Technique is a specialized technique designed to improve group problem solving by combining the advantages of group and individual problem solving. Try this procedure the next few times you lead a group problem-solving session.

For each stage of group problem solving, proceed as follows:
1. Ask all members to write down as many ideas as they can think of in five minutes.
2. Solicit one idea from each member and list it on a blackboard or flip chart exactly as stated. No criticism of ideas is permitted at this stage.
3. Continue to solicit one idea at a time from members until all ideas have been recorded.
4. After all ideas have been listed, review each idea for clarification to ensure that all members understand all ideas.
5. Ask each member to identify the best two or three ideas, from his or her perspective. Tally the preferences and give priority to those ideas most frequently endorsed.

Converting Decisions Into Group Action

Most managers have, at some time in their careers, served on task forces or have been in groups which seem to continually "rehash" the same issues, meeting after meeting, with little or no action being taken to resolve them. When you are leading a group, you can bring meetings to a closure by:
1. Reviewing the decisions that were made in the meeting.
2. Identifying action steps required to implement those decisions or to prepare for the next meeting.
3. Assigning the responsibility, time tables, and deadlines for each action step.
4. Setting an agenda for the next meeting, if any.

Immediately following the meeting, write a one- to two-page summary of points 1 through 4 and distribute it to all group members. Begin the next meeting with a status review of the action items.

Recommended Readings

Carnes, William T. *Effective Meetings for Busy People: Let's Decide It and Go Home.* New York, NY: Institute Electrical, 1987.

Focusing on committees, boards, panels, working groups, and other "decision-makers," this book explains how to use the "goldfish bowl" process for deliberative conferences, i.e., those open meetings which must produce "decisions that stick." It pinpoints the reasons why too many deliberative meetings fail to meet the expectations of the participants and the leaders and discusses such issues as: when and when not to schedule a meeting, the various types of meetings, the pros and cons of parliamentary procedures, and effective conference speaking.

Doyle, Michael, and Strauss, David. *How to Make Meetings Work.* New York, NY: Berkley Publishing Group, 1986.

This book focuses on the interaction method, based on four well-defined roles (facilitator, recorder, chairperson, group member) which collectively form a self-correcting system of checks and balances and are equally responsible for a group's success. It teaches the reader how to be effective in each of these roles. Also covered: developing agendas, planning and organizing a meeting, different types of meetings, making a presentation, group problem solving, and "problem" people at meetings and what to do about them.

Mackenzie, R. Alec. *The Time Trap.* New York, NY: McGraw-Hill, 1975.

One section of this book covers the following topics: the why, who, when, and where of meetings; the high cost of meetings; discouraging time overruns; roles people play in meetings; starting meetings on time; getting and sticking to the point; time-limiting the meeting agenda; ending meetings on time; summarizing; and twenty-one rules for getting more from meetings.

Suggested Seminars

The seminars listed here were selected for their appeal to a managerial audience and have received good to excellent ratings from managers attending them.

Because of the dynamic nature of the seminar marketplace, some seminars may have been added, upgraded, or replaced, and others may no longer be offered. Additional information about these seminars may be obtained by calling the vendor directly, or through Seminar Clearinghouse International, a subscriber organization located in St. Paul, Minnesota. Call 612/293-1004 for information.

AVATAR INTERNATIONAL INC., 7101 Tree Mountain Parkway, Stone Mountain, GA 30083, 404/934-9799.

> **Basic Facilitator Workshop.** Participants in this program concentrate on the characteristics of effective facilitators, facilitator communication skills, consensus decision making, constructive management of conflict group dynamics, meeting management, building organizational support, and persuasion and presentation skills.
> *Length:* 3 days
> *Cost:* $675
> *Location: Los Angeles, CA.*

CENTER FOR CREATIVE LEADERSHIP, 5000 Laurinda Drive, P.O. Box P-1, Greensboro, NC 27402, 919/288-7210.

> **Targeted Innovation.** This workshop presents the tools of the trade for creative problem solving and focuses on the applied side of the creative process.
> *Length:* 6 days
> *Cost:* $1800
> *Locations:* San Diego, CA; Greensboro, NC.

COLLEGE OF ST. THOMAS, The Management Center, 2115 Summit Avenue, St. Paul, MN 55105, 612/647-5219.

> **Conducting Effective Meetings.** This program provides participants with methods for making meetings more productive and handling difficult situations. The content includes types of meetings and when to call them, dynamics of group interaction, and ways to keep on the subject and get full participation.
> *Length:* 4 hours
> *Cost:* $90
> *Location:* Minneapolis, MN.

CREATIVE EDUCATION FOUNDATION, 437 Franklin Street, Buffalo, NY 14202, 716/884-2774.

Creative Problem Solving Institute CPSI. This institute is designed for those who feel that they have little or no previous experience in the study of creative problem solving. Three major tracks are available: Business/Industry; Creative Learning; and Heterogeneous (for those seeking an expanding experience involving a variety of resources within the group).
Length: 5 days
Cost: Call vendor
Locations: San Diego, CA; Orlando, FL; Buffalo, NY.

INTERACTION ASSOCIATES INC., 185 Berry Street, China Basin Bldg., Suite 150, San Francisco, CA 94107, 415/777-0590.

Mastering Meetings for Results. Participants identify what does and does not work in conducting productive meetings, and learn techniques in setting up for success, following up effectively, and mastering meetings for results.
Length: 2 days
Cost: $500
Locations: San Francisco, CA; Washington, DC; Atlanta, GA; Boston, MA; Detroit, MI.

UNIVERSITY ASSOCIATES, 8517 Production Avenue, San Diego, CA 92121, 619/578-5900.

Group Facilitation. A five-day program designed to enable participants to enhance group facilitation skills and knowledge; increase knowledge of intervention theory; broaden repertoire of interventions; and increase awareness of your own intervention style.
Length: 5 days
Cost: $465
Location: Toronto, ON.

Understanding Group Dynamics. The topics of this week-long program include how to recognize the phases of group development, assess and diagnose group functions and dysfunctions, power and influence strategies, individual and group problem solving strategies, and how to set goals and make decisions in group settings.
Length: 5 days
Cost: $825
Locations: San Francisco, CA; Toronto, ON; Atlanta, GA; Chicago, IL.

WEINBERG AND WEINBERG, Rural Route Two, Lincoln, NE 68520, 402/781-2542.

Problem Solving Leadership Workshop. This program focuses on the process aspects of problem solving leadership. Its purpose is not merely to convey thoughts, but to change behavior.

Length: 6 days
Cost: $725
Locations: Jacksonville, FL; Lincoln, NE; Portland, OR.

Notes:

Delegating and Controlling

In some poorly managed companies, "delegation" refers to managers' random assignment of undesirable tasks to powerless subordinates. Handled correctly, however, delegation is something quite different. In addition to getting work accomplished through the efforts of others at a lower level, it can show employees that their managers have confidence in their abilities and are willing to let them try new tasks and receive recognition for accomplishing them. Delegation requires a careful evaluation of all activities performed within the work group as well as an analysis of the skills of all employees in the group. Based on that information, you can make a determination of which tasks would best be performed by which employees.

This section provides guidelines for using delegation effectively within your work group. Included are suggestions for:

- Increasing Your Willingness to Delegate (p. 140)
- Identifying Tasks to Be Delegated (p. 140)
- Assigning the Appropriate Degree of Authority to Subordinates (p. 141)
- Using Employee Strengths When Delegating (p. 142)
- Deciding When to Supervise and Coach Subordinates and When to Leave Them Alone (p. 143)
- Providing Adequate Instructions and Guidance When Delegating (p. 143)
- Delegating the Appropriate Amount of Work (p. 144)
- Monitoring Progress Toward Goals (p. 145)
- Avoiding Upward Delegation (p. 145)
- Developing Follow-up Systems (p. 147)

Tips

- Identify a task which you are unlikely to accomplish on your own and delegate a portion or all of it.

- Ask several people in positions similar to yours what sort of tasks they typically delegate.

- Delegate a challenging task to your secretary—it may involve monitoring, recording, writing, etc.

- Identify responsibilities you are personally handling that could be handled by each of your subordinates and delegate accordingly.

- Find ways to individualize delegation to meet the needs and abilities of each person.

- Use three-part "speedimemo" forms to delegate assignments and file your copy in your "tickler file" for follow-up.

- When delegating assignments orally, ask subordinates to summarize your request to ensure understanding.

- Evaluate the workload of each of your subordinates. If work does not seem to be evenly distributed, redistribute responsibilities.

- Seek feedback from your subordinates about whether you delegate too much detail instead of giving them enough latitude in their assignments.

- When delegating work to subordinates, work at providing more guidelines without controlling too closely.

- Create a tickler file and use it as a means of following up on delegated tasks.

- Use a weekly or monthly meeting (of one or several subordinates) as a means of keeping delegated projects on track.

- Use delegation as a way of helping a key subordinate learn a function important for his/her promotion.

- Set aside time each week to meet with subordinates and review delegated items.

- Set up a source of information which will allow you to monitor the progress and success of subordinates.

- Spend more time face-to-face with subordinates finding out how things are going.

- Ask your secretary to help you track delegated assignments.

- Review material in your tickler file and on your desk once per month with your boss, secretary, or with experienced and trusted subordinates. Analyze why you still have the material and whether that is appropriate.

- Establish a routine for yourself and your secretary to have all memos produced by you to include a target completion date or dates as well as automatic "tickling" for follow-up a few days before those dates.

- If dates are missed, be sure to schedule new dates with your people.

- Have your subordinates set their own deadline dates, but then hold them firmly to them—with "no excuses" except on rare occasions when clearly justified.

- Seek guidance from your manager in setting up control and follow-up procedures.

- Don't allow a subordinate to dump a delegated task back in your lap for you to resolve.

- Read *No-Nonsense Delegation* by McConkey and find five concepts to apply immediately.

- Ask subordinates for ideas on how to improve your style of delegating and controlling.

- If a delegated assignment is not up to your expectation, do not redo it yourself. Show your subordinate what needs to be changed and have him/her rework it.

- Don't worry about whether you know how to handle a problem when delegating. Ask your subordinate to "fix it"—that's his/her job.

- Do "Decision Charting" occasionally with your staff on a variety of decisions. For each decision, determine each person's role in the decision according to this code:

  R = Responsible for making the decision

  A/V = Approval/veto authority

  C = Must be consulted prior to decision

  I = Must be informed after the decision is made

Increasing Your Willingness to Delegate

It's not uncommon for managers to resist the delegation of tasks for which they once had responsibility.

To increase your willingness to delegate, first determine the reason for your resistance, then identify ways to overcome it. Following are common reasons for managers' reluctance to delegate.

- **Lack of confidence in subordinates' abilities.** If you lack confidence in your subordinates' abilities, begin your delegation assignments with relatively minor tasks, where subordinates' mistakes will have negligible impact. After employees have mastered these tasks, assign increasingly complex or important tasks.

- **Desire for perfection.** If you feel that you are the only person who can do certain tasks well enough, start by delegating tasks that do not require perfection. In addition, you can use control and coaching to help subordinates develop the ability to perform tasks to your satisfaction, thereby giving yourself more time for activities that require perfectionism.

- **Insufficient time to explain the task or train someone to do it.** This may be an acceptable reason for not delegating for short-term projects or projects that will be done only once. However, for time-consuming or repetitive tasks, spending time teaching employees tasks will save you time in the long run. Remind yourself of this fact whenever you are tempted to use insufficient time as an excuse for completing a delegatable task yourself.

- **Personal satisfaction and/or reward from task accomplishment.** If you enjoy a task or receive recognition from others when you perform it, you may tend to reserve it for yourself when you should be delegating it. In such a case, identify other, higher level tasks that give you as much satisfaction and recognition. You may find that expanding your accomplishments enables you to obtain even greater rewards.

Identifying Tasks to Be Delegated

In order for delegation to occur, a manager must take the time to identify and assign tasks that can be accomplished by others. To determine activities to be delegated, follow these guidelines.

1. Make a list of all activities for which you are currently responsible. Then classify each activity as a task that:

- You must retain and perform yourself
- Can be shared with subordinates
- Can be delegated to subordinates

The following chart will help you structure your analysis.

Task	Retain	Share	Delegate
1.			
2.			
3.			
4.			

2. Compare your current activity assignments to those reflected on your chart. Develop a plan for eliminating any discrepancies.

Assigning the Appropriate Degree of Authority to Subordinates

Assigning the appropriate degree of authority goes hand-in-hand with delegating. If subordinates don't feel they have the authority to proceed on their own, they must go to you for approval, which takes you away from tasks that require your attention.

To establish the degree of authority you wish to delegate, follow these guidelines.

1. On the following chart, build on the chart you just created in the preceding subsection. For each task you have decided to share or delegate, indicate the degree of authority you wish to grant by checking the appropriate column:
   - Proceed without approval
   - Proceed, but inform me of your actions
   - Obtain approval before proceeding

Your chart should now look something like this:

Task	Retain	Share	Dele-gate	Proceed w/o Approval	Proceed but Inform	Obtain Approval
1.						
2.						
3.						
4.						

2. Inform each employee of the degree of authority you wish him or her to assume for each task.
3. In the future, look for assignments for which you can grant complete authority; these will save you the most time in the long term. Also, conscientiously examine each assignment to determine if you are retaining authority unnecessarily.
4. Periodically hold discussions with individual subordinates to determine whether you have given them the appropriate level of authority. Try to determine whether you are assigning too much or too little authority. Take notes on employees' comments and consider their concerns when making future assignments.

Using Employee Strengths When Delegating

Assigning tasks to subordinates who possess the required skills for those tasks leads to greater efficiency of your work unit. To identify and capitalize on employee strengths, follow these guidelines.

1. Review employees' performance appraisals and list each employee's strengths and weaknesses.
2. Explain to your subordinates that you will delegate responsibilities to help them build on their strengths and overcome their weaknesses.
3. Analyze all tasks that come into your department in terms of the skills required. Then assign tasks in a way that allows subordinates to capitalize on their strengths. Also look for assignments that will help employees address their development needs.

4. From time to time, meet with individual employees to discuss the reasons for your delegation decisions and the effort you have made to match work assignments to employee needs. Remain open to feedback on the appropriateness of your task assignment.

Deciding When to Supervise and Coach Subordinates and When to Leave Them Alone

Subordinates of varying skill and experience levels need varying degrees of supervision. It is up to you to determine the development level of your subordinates in order to supervise them effectively.

The theory of Situational Leadership, developed by Hersey and Blanchard, asserts that the effective manager varies the amount of structure he or she provides based on the developmental level of the subordinate. Each time you delegate a task, ask yourself:

1. How skilled is the individual in the competencies necessary to perform this job successfully?
2. How willing is the individual to do this job?

Based on your answers to these two questions, determine how closely you must supervise the subordinate to ensure successful completion of the task. For instance, a new and enthusiastic employee will need a great deal more supervision than an experienced and reasonably motivated subordinate.

Providing Adequate Instructions and Guidance When Delegating

Valuable time can be wasted if subordinates receive inadequate or unclear instructions and guidance on the tasks they are to perform. In the worst cases, subordinates produce results that bear little or no resemblance to the desired outcome. Such experiences are frustrating to both the subordinates and the manager.

To avoid this problem, ensure that your instructions contain sufficient detail and that employees fully understand the instructions. The following procedure should help.

1. For each assignment, write a clear statement of the purpose and objectives of the task. Also specifically identify:
   - When the task is to be completed
   - Where it is to be performed

- How it should be accomplished
- Any interim progress reports required

A short-form memo that creates automatic copies is ideal for this purpose; the employee can be given one copy and a second copy can be retained in your follow-up file.

2. Discuss your instructions with the employee and answer any questions about the details of the assignment. Do not end the discussion until you are sure the employee fully understands what is expected. If additions to or clarification of the instructions arise during the discussion, add them to your written statement.

3. At the end of the review session, ask the employee to describe the assignment in his or her own words. This will help you determine whether the assignment is clear in the employee's mind.

4. Check with the employee periodically during the project to ensure that he or she is proceeding without difficulty. Sometimes, questions arise during the course of a project, and employees are reluctant to ask for assistance because they don't want to appear incompetent.

5. During the course of the project, keep track of any instances of unclear or inadequate instructions. Note the cause of each misunderstanding so that you can improve your instructions on future assignments. You may wish to initiate discussions with employees to obtain feedback on your instructions and guidance. Record employees' comments and consider these concerns when making future assignments.

Delegating the Appropriate Amount of Work

When delegating, it's easy to assign too much work to experienced workers and too little to those who require more assistance. It's important to remember that each employee needs sufficient responsibilities to challenge his or her abilities. You must help them strike a comfortable balance that leaves them neither overworked nor underchallenged.

To develop your skill in delegating the appropriate amount of work to each subordinate, follow these guidelines.

1. Arrange individual discussions with subordinates to solicit feedback on their workloads. Seek answers to the following questions.
   - Is the timing of delegated tasks compatible with employees' regular schedule of tasks?
   - Have delegated assignments been challenging without being overwhelming?

● Has the amount of delegated work been appropriate—neither too much nor too little?

Be sure to inform subordinates that the purpose of these discussions is for them to give feedback on your delegation practices, not for you to critique their ability to complete assignments.

2. Take notes of comments that indicate areas in which you can improve your delegation practices. Incorporate these comments into assignments you make in the future.

3. Continue to initiate discussions with subordinates at regular intervals to determine whether your skill level is increasing.

Monitoring Progress Toward Goals

An important part of delegation, especially in the beginning, is checking subordinates' progress. It is not enough to simply establish a final deadline; subordinates may not realize they are running behind until it's too late to finish the job by the final date. The following guidelines offer a good way to check subordinates' progress without creating more work for yourself than you save by delegating.

1. Ask subordinates to break their tasks into steps and to create progress reports based on these steps. Subordinates should give a copy of the reports to you and keep one for themselves; this ensures that both you and the subordinates always know what is expected. Depending on a subordinate's experience level, you may wish to become involved in the planning process to ensure that the progress reports are acceptable. This will also help to firmly establish and clarify mutual expectations regarding progress points within the assignment.

2. Working with your subordinates, establish dates for interim reports, and keep a file of these reports.

3. Set aside time to work with subordinates who require personal attention.

It is important to remember that subordinates have different requirements for attention depending on the difficulty of their assigned tasks and their experience levels.

Avoiding Upward Delegation

Upward delegation refers to cases in which an employee, with the manager's explicit or implicit acceptance, gives the manager a task to complete. For example, if an employee told his manager that he didn't know how to complete the last section of a report, the manager might be busy at the time and say, "Just leave it here. I'll finish it." Most likely, this subordinate will require help with his next report, too.

If a subordinate has problems doing a delegated task, talk about the assignment and make suggestions on how to accomplish the task. If it's obvious that the task is too difficult for the employee, assign it to someone else. Ordinarily, you should not take the task back. If you do, you're right back where you started in terms of your workload, with even less time to complete the task.

See the reference portion of this section for more sources of suggestions for avoiding upward delegation.

Developing Follow-up Systems

As was mentioned before, follow-up is a necessary element of delegation. These two follow-up systems work very well for both self and subordinate follow-up.

1. **The "1-31" filing system, also called a "tickler file."** This system involves a series of file folders numbered 1 through 31 (to correspond to the days of the month). When you identify an item that requires follow-up, place a reminder in the file corresponding to the date on which the follow-up action should occur. Then, at the beginning of each day, go through the items in the appropriate folder and note the items requiring follow-up on that day.

2. **Note follow-up dates on your calendar.** Many people note meeting dates on their calendars. It's far less common for managers to note follow-up and deadline dates. If a date for follow-up passes without action, be sure to move the follow-up item to a new date on the calendar. Get in the habit of using your calendar for noting these items.

If you have a secretary, you may wish to work as a team with that person to develop your own systems for follow-up control and organization of other delegation-related details.

Recommended Readings

Mackenzie, R. Alec. *The Time Trap.* New York, NY: McGraw-Hill, 1975.

In a chapter on delegating, Mackenzie identifies fourteen "barriers in the delegator," seven "barriers in the delegatee," and six "barriers in the situation." Barriers in the delegator include such traits as insecurity, lack of confidence in subordinates, perfectionism, and lack of experience in the job or in delegating. Barriers in the delegatee include lack of experience, disorganization, overload of work, or avoidance of responsibility. Barriers in the situation include confused responsibilities and authority, understaffing, no tolerance of mistakes, or a "one-man show" policy. Mackenzie's lists of barriers can be used to analyze the reader's own situation and barriers to delegation. This can be done alone or with input from others.

McConkey, D.D. *No-nonsense Delegation.* New York, NY: AMACOM, 1979.

This book presents a practical approach to delegation, with detailed instructions on how to delegate and a description of the benefits of delegation. This is one of the most comprehensive books written on the subject and includes the following chapters: 1) "What Is a Manager?," 2) "Why Delegate?," 3) "Symptoms of Poor Delegation," 4) "Causes of Poor Delegation," 5) "Building the Foundation for Delegation," 6) "The Truths of Delegation," 7) "The Role of the Delegatee," 8) "What Delegation Requires of the Job Description," 9) "Delegation by Levels," 10) "Authority That Gets Results," 11) "Establishing Dynamic Controls," 12) "Delegation and Decision Making," 13) "Developing Managers Through Delegation," 14) "Evaluation of Delegation," and 15) "The Demand for Accountability and Participation." McConkey takes a concrete approach to managing people and resources through delegation and control.

Oncken, W., Jr. *Managing Management Time: Who's Got the Monkey?* Englewood Cliffs, NJ: Prentice-Hall, 1984.

Based on Oncken's highly successful "Managing Management Time" seminars, this book outlines, in step-by-step detail, powerful time management strategies that can help managers at all levels achieve more visible, far-reaching results through others, both inside and outside one's own organization.

Suggested Seminars

The seminars listed here were selected for their appeal to a managerial audience and have received good to excellent ratings from managers attending them.

Because of the dynamic nature of the seminar marketplace, some seminars may have been added, upgraded, or replaced, and others may no longer be offered. Additional information about these seminars may be obtained by calling the vendor directly, or through Seminar Clearinghouse International, a subscriber organization located in St. Paul, Minnesota. Call 612/293-1004 for information.

BRYANT COLLEGE, The Center for Management Development, 450 Douglas Pike, Smithfield, RI 02917, 401/232-6200.

Delegating for Results. Defining delegation, the benefits of delegation, barriers to delegation, the process of delegation, what to delegate, what you cannot delegate, effective communication, and evaluation are the key topics included in this one-day seminar.
Length: 1 day
Cost: $295
Location: Farminton, CT.

CAREERTRACK INC., 1800 38th Street, Boulder, CO 80301, 303/447-2300, 800/334-6780 (outside Colo.).

Getting Things Done. Key topics in this program include: how to say no when you mean no (and not feel bad about it); how to overcome changing priorities; the start-stop syndrome, and incomplete work assignments; human "downtime" and how to make it productive; "team time"—why it's essential; and the delegator's checklist.
Length: 1 day
Cost: $49
Locations: Burlington, CA; Corte Madera, CA; Milpatas, CA; Atlanta, GA; Duluth, MN; Asheville, NC; Atlantic City, NJ; Cherry Hill, NJ; Binghamton, NY; Buffalo, NY; Chattanooga, TN; Johnson City, TN. For additional locations, contact the vendor.

How to Delegate Work and Ensure It's Done Right. This one-day seminar teaches participants when, what, and how to delegate. More specifically, the skills presented at this program enable managers to learn how and why to delegate tasks you know you can do better than anyone else, handling employee resistance to taking on a new assignment, getting

approval for hiring, what to do when you've delegated the wrong project to someone who can't handle it, and setting deadlines your people will keep.
Length: 1 day
Cost: $95
Locations: Washington, DC; Daytona Beach, FL; Deerfield Beach, FL; Ft. Lauderdale, FL; St. Louis, MO; Cincinnati, OH; Columbus, OH; Allentown, PA; Erie, PA; Dallas, TX; Ft. Worth, TX; Arlington, VA. For additional locations, contact the vendor.

CHARLES R. HOBBS CORPORATION, 2290 East 4500 South, Suite 220, Salt Lake City, UT 84117, 801/278-5381, 800/332-9929.
Insight on Time Management. Participants in this program will gain insight in the following areas: coping with impossible demands; handling priorities; retrieving important data; retaining every worthwhile idea; remembering every meeting; reducing crisis management; doing more in less time; delegating more effectively; dealing with interruptions; handling lengthy phone calls; and avoiding procrastination.
Length: 1 day
Cost: $145
Locations: Birmingham, AL; Ft. Lauderdale, FL; Jacksonville, FL; Tampa, FL; Louisville, KY; Baton Rouge, LA; Albuquerque, NM; Cincinnati, OH; Cleveland, OH; Columbus, OH; Columbia, SC. For additional locations, contact the vendor.

DUN & BRADSTREET BUSINESS EDUCATION SERVICES, P.O. Box 803, Church Street Station, New York, NY 10008, 212/312-6909.
Building Your Supervisory Skills. This two-day comprehensive seminar features how to set goals, communicate them to your employees, and follow them through to completion.
Length: 2 days
Cost: $295
Locations: Miami, FL; Tampa, FL; Albany, NY; Buffalo, NY; Cincinnati, OH; Columbus, OH.

FRED PRYOR SEMINARS, 2000 Johnson Drive, P.O. Box 2951, Shawnee Mission, KS 66201, 800/255-6139.
How to Get Things Done. This program focuses on how to waste less time; tips for digging out from under; how to produce more—better, faster & easier; delegating; and how to make the most of your work style.

Length: 1 day
Cost: $98
Locations: Hartford, CT; Arlington Heights, IL; Chicago, IL; Boston, MA; Framingham, MA; Detroit, MI; Grand Rapids, MI; Kalamazoo, MI; Morristown, NJ; Hempstead, NY; White Plains, NY; Allentown, PA. For additional locations, contact the vendor.

UNIVERSITY OF MICHIGAN, Executive Education Center, School of Business Administration, Ann Arbor, MI 48109, 313/763-1000, 313/763-1006.

Delegation and Team Effort: People and Performance. Participants in this program are introduced to the skills necessary for effective delegation. Individuals learn the need for delegation, overcoming roadblocks to effective delegation, developing employees through teamwork and delegation, the need for teamwork, and translating problems into solutions.
Length: 3 days
Cost: $1100
Location: Ann Arbor, MI.

VANDERBILT UNIVERSITY, Owen Graduate School of Management, Office of Executive Education, Nashville, TN 37203, 615/322-2513.

Effective Management Techniques. This two-day seminar focuses on the management technique of delegation—the art of motivating, developing, and challenging your staff into a finely tuned productive team.
Length: 2 days
Cost: Call vendor
Location: Nashville, TN.

WICHITA STATE UNIVERSITY, Center for Management Development, Campus Box 86, Wichita, KS 67208, 316/689-3118.

Art and Skill of Delegation. The topics in this program include: importance of delegation; reluctance to delegate; process of delegating effectively; and skill building practice.
Length: 1 day
Cost: $95
Location: Wichita, KS.

WILLIAM ONCKEN CORPORATION, 8344 East R. L. Thornton
Freeway, Suite 408, Dallas, TX 75228, 214/328-1867 (in Dallas),
612/473-2404 (in Minneapolis).

    Managing Management Time. Also known as "Get Them Monkeys Off
Your Back," this program goes beyond the "daily diary" approach—it
examines the causes and effects of time management problems and deals
with the realities of getting performance through other people.
Length: 2 days
Cost: $450
Locations: Washington, DC; Chicago, IL; New Orleans, LA;
Minneapolis, MN; Dallas, TX; Houston, TX; Seattle, WA.

Staffing, Coaching, and Developing People

Many managers fail to realize that most employee performance problems start before the employee is even hired! Too often, in the hurry to obtain a "warm body" for an urgent project, inappropriate candidates are selected. Once this occurs, the manager and the total organization have a difficult and expensive problem on their hands.

The guidelines presented in this four-part section are designed to help avoid this problem through effective staffing and coaching. In addition, because even the best manager must occasionally face employee performance problems, it also presents guidelines for effectively addressing these problems.

Part I: Recruiting Employees
- Evaluating the Effectiveness of Recruiting Efforts (p. 156)
- Improving the Interviewing Process (p. 156)
- Using Multiple Interviewers (p. 157)
- Increasing Your Interviewing Effectiveness (p. 158)

Part II: Developing Employees
- Improving Your Employee Orientation Program (p. 158)
- Training New Employees (p. 160)
- Evaluating Training Programs (p. 161)
- Encouraging Subordinates to Attend Courses or Training Programs for Further Development (p. 161)
- Matching Individuals to Jobs (p. 162)
- Providing Day-to-day Coaching (p. 163)
- Providing Feedback Regularly (p. 163)
- Recognizing and Acknowledging Subordinates' Good Performance (p. 164)
- Letting Subordinates Know When They Are Doing Things Well (p. 164)
- Giving Stretching and Challenging Assignments to Subordinates (p. 165)
- Accurately Understanding Subordinates' Strengths and Weaknesses (p. 166)
- Preparing Effective Development Plans (p. 166)
- Keeping Subordinates Up-to-date (p. 167)

Tips

- Develop selection interview questions to fit all areas of the job descriptions for positions reporting to you.

- Develop a reference check interview format to use with external candidates.

- Attend an interviewing workshop such as the **Selection Interviewing: Information Gathering** and **Information Interpretation** public workshops presented by PDI.

- Learn to interview candidates in a way which gets them to describe what they have done in the past in areas relevant to the job under consideration.

- Meet subordinates individually to identify what you can do to help them be more effective in their jobs.

- Use the PDI Wheel of Managerial Success in this Handbook to identify your subordinates' individual strengths and weaknesses. In individual discussions, use the Wheel for developmental purposes. Ask each subordinate to draft a development plan.

- Identify the positions that are key to the success of your organization. For each, decide whether the person in that position is a high potential, solid citizen or marginal performer. Next, identify the high potential persons not in key positions. Formulate a plan to replace marginal performers in key positions with the high potentials holding non-key positions.

- Develop job descriptions for each of the positions in your organization highlighting the knowledge, skills, and abilities required. Evaluate position incumbents against those requirements.

- Recognize the importance of sound staffing principles and decisions; devote personal time to its review.

- Have others in your organization conduct interviews and rate incumbents' predicted future performance on all areas of the job description. Then synthesize all independent ratings and discuss discrepancies.

- Attend seminar in Developing Managers such as the one offered by PDI.

- Look at performance appraisal and review as being a manager's only "individual contribution" work—i.e., it cannot be delegated. Then devote the hard work and analytical effort required to do it well.

- Maintain a file on each subordinate. Keep track of successes, failures, development needs, and how you have agreed to help.

- Practice observing the behavior of people in order to give good feedback. Learn to be more descriptive and less evaluative in your feedback.

- Remember that people grow by successive approximation. Help them to make small steps in their growth toward a larger change.

- Help your subordinates identify their strengths and limitations. Try to have each subordinate work on one limitation and enhance one strength at a time. Be specific on what steps he/she can take to meet his/her goal.

- Be alert to articles and development tips that could be of help to subordinates; pass them on to appropriate individuals.

- Create your own development handbook of ideas especially suited to your company and function in the organization.

- Ask subordinates to read this Handbook and identify one or two suggestions they'd like to tackle.

- Learn more about your organization's performance appraisal process so you can do a better job of it.

- Be certain every employee reporting to you knows you are willing to support him/her in his/her development process.

- Meet individually with subordinates to discuss their career goals and identify the skills they need to achieve these goals.

- Identify the one or two subordinates most likely to replace you and begin "grooming" them for your responsibilities.

- Identify the weakest performer on your staff. Decide whether you feel he or she has the ability to perform adequately. If so, develop a program to bring him/her up to speed.

- Do not be afraid to confront poor performance as soon as you notice it. Give feedback and begin constructive action to help.

- Learn how to do performance problem solving with employees who are performing below standard.

Part I: Recruiting Employees

Evaluating the Effectiveness of Recruiting Efforts

Recruiting plays a significant role in the success of your staffing program. If you are in a position that allows you to evaluate the effectiveness of your program, conduct or, if appropriate, ask your personnel organization to conduct the following analysis.

1. Gather the following types of information about the effectiveness of your program.
   - What is the cost per hire? (Find this figure by dividing the cost of each recruiting source by the number of hires. Also, divide the total cost of your entire recruiting program by the total number of hires. This analysis will tell you whether a given source is cost-effective.)
   - What is the time lapse from identification of need for candidates to hire date? (This analysis will tell you whether your recruiting process is efficient.)
   - How many hires are produced from each source? (This analysis, combined with cost information, will tell you whether a given recruiting source is productive.)
2. Analyze the data you've collected. Establish a rank order of recruiting sources based on overall effectiveness of the sources.
3. Concentrate your recruitment efforts on the sources that provide the best candidates at the lowest cost in the shortest time.

Continue to evaluate your program periodically to ensure that it remains effective.

Improving the Interviewing Process

Although the interview is often the primary mechanism for obtaining information about applicants, many interviewers spend more time telling applicants about the job than finding out about the applicants. As a result, many interviewers make hiring decisions that are based more on "gut feeling" than on objective data.

The following procedure will help you obtain more information during the interviewing process.

1. Before you interview, determine the specific requirements of the job to be filled, including the knowledge, skills, and other characteristics

needed to perform the job effectively. This information will ensure that you evaluate all candidates in relevant areas.

2. Prepare a standard interview outline. Include questions that you will ask all candidates applying for a position. Research has shown that the use of a standard outline improves the reliability and validity of hiring decisions.

   Be sure to emphasize questions that probe a candidate's past performance in areas related to the job for which you're interviewing. The answers to these questions can help you determine how that person will respond in similar situations.

   Avoid asking questions based on hypothetical circumstances, inquiring about the candidate's attitude, or relying too heavily on the candidate's stated goals.

3. Take notes during the interview to be sure that you can evaluate the candidate based on facts (rather than unclear recall) when the time comes to make the final hiring decision.

4. Try to get additional information about the candidate to confirm your conclusions. Reference checks and the conclusions of other interviewers can substantiate or contradict your own findings. If other interviewers disagree with your conclusions, consult with them and review the data they have collected. You may discover that you have obtained different information. You may also discover areas in your own questioning that could be improved.

Using Multiple Interviewers

Many companies have more than one person interview each candidate. The use of multiple interviews helps reduce individual biases and neutralizes the impact of rating errors. It also makes more efficient use of interviewer time and permits the collection of in-depth information.

The following guidelines can help make the multiple interviewing process more effective.

1. Assign responsibility for coordinating the process to one individual. Typically, this is someone from the personnel department.

2. If a job description exists for the position to be filled, give a copy to each interviewer. Otherwise, assign someone to document the specific requirements of the job. This will ensure that interviewers know what to look for when they interview.

3. Assign each interviewer a different dimension of the job so that each can focus on a limited area. For example, one person could obtain information on technical skills, another could assess people skills, and a third could investigate project-management skills.

    Each interviewer should use a standard outline containing questions that focus on the candidate's past performance and accomplishments in the area being evaluated.

    Also, decide which interviewer will tell the applicant about various aspects of the job and organization so interviewers don't repeat or contradict one another.
4. After the interview, each interviewer should rate the candidate on the dimension he or she was assigned.
5. The coordinator should then compare the independent ratings and look for a consensus. If there is a discrepancy among ratings or if the position being filled is very important, the interviewers should get together to discuss the candidate and arrive at a consensus.

Increasing Your Interviewing Effectiveness

Following are two additional methods for increasing your interviewing effectiveness.

-   Observe and take notes on the practices of effective interviewers during the interviewing process. After the interviews, evaluate the candidates and compare your conclusions with the interviewers' conclusions. Discuss any differences.
-   Save your interview notes and evaluations and review them at performance appraisal time. Look for areas in which your predictions are on target and areas in which you may need to develop more effective information-gathering techniques.

Part II: Developing Employees

Improving Your Employee Orientation Program

The orientation employees receive can have a significant impact on how well they perform on the job, how well they get along with their coworkers, their job satisfaction, and even their eventual career progress within the organization. To develop an effective orientation program, follow these guidelines.

1. Evaluate your current program. Orientation should provide employees with these three types of information:
   - General information about the day-to-day routine (location of restrooms and lunchrooms, how to use telephones and copy machines, obtaining supplies, and so forth)
   - A description of the organization's history, purpose, and products/services, and a discussion of how the employee's job contributes to the overall purpose
   - A detailed presentation or reference guide of the organization's policies, work rules, and employee benefits

   If your orientation program has not been formalized, you may wish to establish a task force to produce an orientation outline or package for new employees.
2. Take a poll of all employees to get suggestions on improving the company's employee orientation program. Ask them what they think

new employees need in order to function comfortably and effectively.

3. Ask new hires to help you evaluate the effectiveness of your program by providing feedback at designated points—such as two weeks, one month, and two months—after their hire dates.

4. Ensure that each new hire receives your orientation package. If you are too busy to provide orientation yourself, assign an experienced employee as a sponsor for each new employee. Let the new hire know that this person will be available to answer any questions.

Training New Employees

Too often, the training of new employees is forgotten in the day-to-day rush to get the job done. It's possible, however, to develop a program that takes a minimum of time to administer, yet effectively integrates the new employee into your department. To develop such a program, build the following elements into your training program for new hires.

- **Provide orientation.** A previous suggestion emphasized the importance of employee orientation, which should be viewed as the first step in the training program.

- **Establish a support network.** New employees should be told the names of more experienced employees who will provide assistance during your absence. Be sure to inform the experienced employees of their responsibilities in this area.

- **Establish an environment that is conducive to learning.** Newcomers usually have a variety of concerns. Let them know that you don't expect them to absorb everything the first time around, that you realize mistakes will be made, and that you encourage their questions.

- **Provide on-the-job training experiences.** A mix of on-the-job and formal training experiences will help new employees integrate their new knowledge and enable them to feel that they are contributing to the goals of the department.

- **Encourage feedback from new-hire monitors.** Feedback from experienced employees will help you determine the areas in which new employees require more training.

- **Create a manual of training materials.** Keep a record of the training procedures used to train new hires. After several employees have been trained, identify the procedures that have proven most effective and include them in a training manual. As the manual becomes more specific and complete, you will be able to delegate more and more training-related tasks to subordinates.

Evaluating Training Programs

An effective training program will offset the time and money spent on it by producing improved employee performance. To ensure that your training dollars are well spent, use the following procedure for evaluating the effectiveness of training programs attended by your employees.

- When an employee returns from a training experience, ask for a report of his or her impressions. Determine how the knowledge or skills learned in the program could improve performance on the job. Then ask for another report a few months later, when the employee has had time to incorporate the new skills. Determine if performance has actually improved.
- Ask for materials that describe the content of training programs your employees will attend. Many programs require management support of concepts that are to be incorporated into the employee's work routine.
- Observe employee performance yourself. People who participate in training programs are not always objective about the worth of their training experiences.

Encouraging Subordinates to Attend Courses or Training Programs for Further Development

The most powerful development opportunities by far occur on the job itself. Training programs, although at times costly, can be highly beneficial in certain situations, and there are a number of things you can do to maximize their impact and get the most from your training dollars.

- To select a training program for a subordinate, determine:
    - What are the specific developmental objectives?
    - What results do you hope to obtain?
- Share these ideas with your subordinate and discuss possible courses or seminars. Involving your subordinate in the decision will likely increase his or her interest in the seminar and willingness to participate.

You will find this Handbook to be a valuable reference for defining options. The most effective seminars and workshops are those that:

- Focus on specific skill areas (e.g., selection interviewing, appraising and developing employees, time management).
- Involve skills practice during the seminar.
- Provide feedback on participants' implementation of the skill. Videotaped role-playing can be an excellent vehicle for providing this feedback.

If the training objective is broader feedback on a greater number of skills, there are more extensive development programs designed to provide participants with in-depth feedback about their strengths and weaknesses as assessed over a two- to six-day period. Examples of these are PDI's **Leadership Development Program** and **Management Development Center.**

Having selected the appropriate program, you should now consider the optimum time to enroll your subordinate in the workshop. To assure transfer of skills to the job, your subordinate should attend the workshop or seminar just prior to performing the skill on the job. For example, if the skill is selection interviewing, your subordinate should attend the seminar just prior to doing some selection interviewing on the job.

More extensive feedback programs, such as PDI's **Leadership Development Program,** are most impactful about six months after a person has received a promotion or experienced a business setback.

Upon completion of the program, take time to debrief the participant on what he or she learned and what specifically will be done differently on the job to apply the skills. If appropriate, you may wish to have your subordinate make a presentation about the course to peers so that they can also benefit from his or her attendance of the program. You as a coach then need to assure that new skills are reinforced when your subordinate implements them so that the training results in lasting behavior change.

Matching Individuals to Jobs

The best performers are often those employees whose skills and interests closely match those required by the positions they hold. To improve your skills in matching individuals to jobs, take the following steps.

1. Identify the signals of poor matches in your department. Examples of these signals include resignations, terminations, substandard performance, excessive absenteeism, and excessive interpersonal conflict.
2. Review each situation that signaled a poor match over the past year. Try to isolate the reason for each mismatch. Were there skills an individual needed but did not have? Problematic personal characteristics? Skills that the individual had but didn't use?
3. As you analyze these situations, look for a pattern. For example, are your subordinates' skills consistently underutilized or consistently lacking in particular areas?

4. Develop strategies for avoiding employee-position mismatches by changing your selection or placement procedures. For example, if your past employees have been overqualified for their jobs, modify your selection standards.
5. When future mismatches appear, evaluate the reasons for them and, if possible, take steps to remedy them.

Providing Day-to-day Coaching

Coaching is one of the most powerful ways to help subordinates grow. Follow this procedure to establish an effective, ongoing coaching effort.

1. **Determine employee needs.** The most effective way to identify employee needs is to discuss with employees areas in which they would find coaching helpful. Typical developmental needs effectively addressed by coaching include needs for:
    - Increased assertiveness or decreased aggressiveness
    - Increased consideration for others
    - Increased professionalism
    - Improved communication and leadership skills, such as those used in leading formal presentations and conducting meetings
2. **Discuss methods for improvement.** Identify the behaviors that are effective and those to be avoided in the area to be addressed. When possible, use examples of the subordinate's past behaviors.
3. **Determine when the subordinate's behavior should be observed.** Decide upon the most appropriate situations or settings for observing the subordinate's behavior and set aside time for regular observation.
4. **Observe the subordinate's behavior.** Watch for effective and ineffective behaviors; people learn more quickly if you point out what they do right as well as what they do wrong. Take notes, including specific examples.
5. **Give immediate feedback whenever possible.** The more immediate the feedback, the more powerful it will be. Be sure to focus on specific, concrete behaviors. Whenever you point out an ineffective behavior, be sure to describe the correct behavior that should replace it.

Providing Feedback Regularly

Performance feedback is essential to employee development; it not only helps employees correct mistakes before they become habits, but also reinforces positive behaviors and encourages the development of desirable work habits.

As countless studies have shown, feedback must be timely to be effective. Thus, providing feedback on a regular basis is a key to developing subordinates' skills. To develop a habit of providing regular feedback, you may want to incorporate these tips into your routine over the next several months:

- Identify mechanisms that will help ensure that you review performance and provide feedback more frequently. For example, you might set a goal that you will review your subordinates' work at least once every two weeks and will provide feedback within 24 hours of review.
- Communicate the fact that you are willing to provide feedback. This encourages employees to consult you for advice before they make mistakes.
- Refer to the suggestion "Providing Feedback on Performance Problems" for methods of delivering negative feedback.

Recognizing and Acknowledging Subordinates' Good Performances

If subordinates are meeting their performance standards, it is likely that 80 percent of what they are doing is being done right. The proportion of feedback they receive, then, should reflect this ratio. This theory tends to oppose the theory of management by exception, which states that managers should give feedback only when subordinates are doing things wrong. To achieve the appropriate balance of positive vs. negative feedback, try the following:

1. Have your subordinates submit monthly achievement reports to help you focus on the positives and enable you to share in their successes.
2. Make it a point to give feedback, preferably face-to-face, based on what you see in your subordinates' monthly reports. Focus on the positives, but also address negative performance when necessary.

Letting Subordinates Know When They Are Doing Things Well

Positive feedback is a powerful motivator when it is specific and behavioral; global compliments, while encouraging, are too broad to be effective in maintaining or improving employees' performance.

To make your positive feedback specific and behavioral, try the following:

- Describe the behavior you are praising, such as meeting a deadline, surpassing productivity projections, or participating more fully in a meeting.

- Be specific so that the employee knows exactly what behavior to continue. For example, "I'm delighted that you found a solution to that design problem and beat the deadline by two days" is more effective than "You did a good job on this project."

Develop a habit of looking for and commending specific employee behaviors that are positive; such reinforcement will increase the incidence of those behaviors.

Giving Stretching and Challenging Assignments to Subordinates

One of the most powerful motivators for employees is the opportunity to accomplish challenging assignments and stretch their capabilities. It's tempting to always give the most challenging and crucial assignments to proven performers, but it's important to provide development opportunities for **all** employees.

To assess the way you currently assign projects, try the following process:
1. Examine current and past assignments in your department. For each project, ask yourself:
   - How difficult was this project to complete?
   - How crucial was this project?
   - Who was assigned to this project?
   - Why was this individual assigned?
2. Now look at each subordinate's project history, asking yourself:
   - Does this person often perform the same tasks repeatedly, or often take on new responsibilities?
   - Have I given this person opportunities to try new things and develop or enhance her or his skills?
   - Does this person ever indicate a desire for more challenging assignments?
   - Does this person appear to have the potential to handle more challenging work? If so, what skills, resources, or experience would help him or her tap this potential?
   - Do I tend to give the most challenging or crucial assignments to the same proven performers?
3. Now look at the overall picture of the group. If your analysis reveals that some subordinates are not being challenged by their current assignments, look for ways to provide the skills, resources, and experiences that will allow them to handle more challenging work—and then assign that work to them.

Accurately Understanding Subordinates' Strengths and Weaknesses

Recognizing your subordinates' areas of strength and weakness helps you coach and develop your staff more effectively. Try the following process to increase your understanding.

1. List the areas of competency that comprise the individual's job. You may want to select factors of performance and dimensions from the PDI Wheel and competencies stated on a job description, if available.

2. For each area, list the specific, behavioral actions that would demonstrate competency. For example, in the area of project management, you might list "Completes projects on schedule."

3. Now compare the individual's observable performance to the behaviors, using a rating scale from 1 (low) to 5 (high). (Keep in mind that the competencies should be defined differently at different levels of the organization. For example, your expectations for planning skills should be different for a vice-president than for a first-line manager; both, however, could receive a high rating.)

4. Discuss your ratings with your subordinate to ensure that you are in agreement about the person's skills. If you disagree on any ratings, negotiate differences until you reach agreement.

5. Focusing on the competencies that were rated low or high, create a plan for identifying activities that will help build on the person's strengths and overcome the limitations.

Preparing Effective Development Plans

Effective development plans help employees develop skills that benefit both the organization and themselves. When preparing development plans, check to ensure that you have considered the following eight features of a successful plan.

1. **Specificity.** Goals and activities should be stated specifically and concretely so that both you and the employee know when objectives have been attained. Be sure to describe the skills or knowledge to be gained as a result of the assigned activity.

2. **Limited focus.** Include no more than three major areas in the plan.

3. **Commitment.** Employees are more likely to be committed to plans they help develop, so encourage subordinates' input. In addition, management must be committed to providing the opportunities and resources needed by the subordinate to fulfill the plan; otherwise, development plans become another source of bureaucratic busywork.

4. **Small, reasonable steps.** Because people learn and improve in small steps, expecting too much too soon discourages progress. Developmental activities should be divided into small steps that lead to an ultimate goal.

5. **On-the-job opportunities.** The most powerful development occurs on the job. It's important that supervisors and subordinates use job responsibilities as opportunities for development.

6. **Support.** Management must provide support in the form of financial resources, time, feedback, reinforcement, encouragement, and other forms of coaching.

7. **Specified time frames for accomplishment.** Subordinates must have an established time frame for each task. Be sure to schedule target dates for completion and checkpoints for progress review.

8. **Adequate variety.** Employees will be more enthusiastic about their plans if the plans include a variety of activities. Take care to provide a mix of on-the-job activities, readings, coursework, evaluations, and other activities identified by the employee. (This Handbook is an excellent source of development suggestions.)

Keeping Subordinates Up-to-date

Subordinates will perform their work more effectively if their knowledge is up-to-date. The following activities will help you begin and maintain a program designed to keep subordinates informed.

1. Begin by increasing your own reading of publications in your specialty area. Route articles that would be helpful to subordinates.

2. Encourage subordinates to increase their reading and to share information with other employees.

3. Periodically meet with employees to discuss how new information can be applied to their work setting. If you don't have time to conduct these meetings, ask an assistant to do so.

Part III: Grooming Employees For Advancement

Identifying High Potential Performers

The identification of high potential performers is the first and perhaps most important step in developing a replacement for yourself or a key member of your staff. Subordinates who have already demonstrated aptitude in more advanced skill areas are usually easier to train and most likely to perform effectively.

The following guidelines and accompanying chart will help you improve your effectiveness in identifying high potential subordinates.

1. First, identify the standards to which you will compare your subordinates' capabilities. To do so:
   - Identify the positions in your organization to which your subordinates could advance.
   - Examine the job descriptions for these positions to determine the requirements for each.
   - Identify the achievers in these positions—the people who functioned most effectively in the past.
   - Determine the knowledge, abilities, skills, and personal characteristics that distinguish the achievers from their less productive colleagues.
   - Identify the achievers' behaviors that demonstrate the presence of the characteristics listed previously. For example, taking the initiative to suggest or implement new activities and showing enthusiasm when performing job duties are two behaviors that indicate high motivation.

Position	Job Requirements	Achievers	Knowledge, Abilities, Skills, Personal Characteristics	Behaviors

2. Compare the characteristics of your current employees to the requirements listed on your chart. First, look at the areas in which employees' current jobs overlap with potential future jobs. Next, consider past performance to predict whether employees are likely to be able to satisfy the requirements of future positions that are not yet required of them.

Your high potential performers are the employees whose characteristics most closely match the requirements of advanced positions.

Developing a Replacement

Grooming a replacement for your position is important because: 1) it will be difficult for you to advance in your organization if no one has been trained to replace you, and 2) a trained replacement can ensure continuity in the organization's work flow.

The best way to groom a replacement is to select an individual with high potential to serve as your assistant. This is the most effective way to help someone develop the knowledge, skills, and attitudes required. In addition, this person can serve as your stand-in when you are away.

Ideally, the person you select will possess the basic skills required to assume your position and have a position such as yours as a career goal.

Following are tips for helping to ensure the success of the individual you choose as your assistant.

- Transfer responsibilities gradually, adding one at a time and allowing time for that task to be mastered before another is added. Allow the individual to be completely responsible for assigned tasks; stay away from these responsibilities yourself. Encourage your assistant to ask for additional responsibilities as soon as he or she can handle them.
- Encourage your assistant to think things through alone. Insist that problems be thoroughly thought through before they are brought to you.
- Hold your assistant accountable for what you have delegated. Check on progress periodically and provide feedback. Ask for progress reports that include the current status of assignments, difficulties encountered, and methods used to solve problems and make decisions.
- Support your assistant's decisions. Consider orders issued by your assistant as important as your own and provide support if criticism arises. If it becomes necessary to reverse a decision your assistant has made, talk to the individual privately and let him or her announce the reversal.
- Let your assistant know that you expect a certain number of mistakes on new responsibilities but that the mistakes should be admitted and corrected promptly.
- Keep your assistant apprised of your plans so that he or she can make intelligent decisions during your absence.

These tips represent the ideal development situation. There will undoubtedly be times when you will find one or more of the guidelines impractical, inadvisable, or even impossible to follow. In general, however, adherence to these principles whenever possible will promote the successful growth of your successor.

You will have met your goal of developing a replacement when you can recommend your assistant as your successor with no major reservations.

Preparing Subordinates to Represent You at Meetings

By training subordinates to represent you at meetings, you accomplish two goals: 1) you expose your employees to a wider range of organizational activities, and 2) you free yourself to devote time to your own managerial growth.

The following procedure will help you prepare your subordinates to represent you.

1. Identify subordinates who possess the necessary skills to represent you at meetings. Look for qualities such as:
   - Knowledge of the subject areas typically addressed at meetings
   - The ability to participate in problem-solving and negotiation sessions
   - Maturity, in terms of projecting the appropriate managerial image
   - Interest in assuming managerial responsibilities

2. Over the next several months, determine, for each meeting, if it would be appropriate for one of your selected subordinates to accompany you. If so, prepare your subordinate for the meeting by explaining:
   - The purpose of the meeting
   - The personalities and politics involved
   - Your role in the meeting
   - Your expectations of him or her

3. After a meeting, discuss it with the subordinate. Carefully explain any unanticipated events or reactions to events.

4. After your subordinate has accompanied you to several meetings, send him or her as your replacement. Be sure that you provide appropriate coaching before the meeting and that your subordinate understands the degree of authority he or she has when acting as your representative.

5. After each meeting, discuss the events of the meeting with your subordinate and provide feedback when appropriate.

Whenever you delegate your responsibilities for leading meetings, it's important that you consider the needs of the others who will be attending the meetings. Take care that in sending a replacement, you don't negatively affect the outcome of the meeting.

Increasing Subordinates' Exposure to the Total Organization

By giving employees opportunities to be exposed to other areas within your organization, you accomplish several goals. Your employees:

- Become more versatile. If the need arises, they can assist in areas outside their specialties, including assisting you with your responsibilities.
- Better understand how their normal job duties contribute to the organization's overall goals.

• Gain increased awareness of career opportunities within the company, which allows them to participate in setting their career goals.

Use the following procedure and accompanying chart to begin a program for increasing an employee's exposure to the organization.

1. Meet with the individual to identify ways in which he or she can increase organizational exposure. Begin the session by listing several examples of opportunities, such as task forces, job rotation, attending organizational events, and acting as liaisons with other related departments.

   Then ask the individual to identify two or three ways in which he or she could increase contact with others outside the department and record them on the chart.

Ways to Increase Contact	Time Limits	Degree of Authority	Feedback Required
1.			
2.			
3.			

2. Next, work together to fill out the remaining boxes on the chart. Determine how much time the employee should spend on the activity, the degree of authority the employee will have in representing your department, and the feedback you expect from the employee.
3. Give the employee a completed copy of the chart and retain one for your records.
4. Periodically review the plans to determine if modifications—events added or removed, authority increased, and so forth—are necessary.

Providing Information to Subordinates on What They Need to Do to Advance Within the Company

A company that "grows" employees from one job into another is making powerful use of its human resources. When employees know **that** they have opportunities for advancement and **what** they must do to advance, their commitment to the oganization is enhanced and solidified. You can contribute to this commitment by providing appropriate advancement information to your subordinates. The following technique can help:

1. Encourage subordinates to share their career goals with you. When you know their goals, you can help them focus their plans and approaches.

2. Provide as much information as you can about positions within the organization that may be consistent with each employee's goals. Communicate skill requirements, additional education needs, and experiences that would help to qualify the individual for the new position. If you are unfamiliar with the requirements of a particular job, suggest that the employee interview individuals who either currently hold the job or know more about its requirements. Be sure to contact people to whom you refer a subordinate and ask for their cooperation.

3. Discuss with employees what they have learned about various positions and how their current skills and experience fit with the options they have identified.

4. If you agree that an employee has the potential to reach her or his goal, engage in development planning focused on that goal. (Refer to suggestions in this section to aid in this process.)

5. If you see a subordinate's goal as unrealistic given current skill levels, point out where you see discrepancies and suggest other more realistic alternatives. Make specific suggestions if you can; if not, refer the individual to others in the organization who can help.

Showing an Interest in Subordinates' Careers

Effective employee development depends in part on understanding employees' career goals. You can get a better idea of where to focus developmental activities by communicating with subordinates regularly about their careers.

Schedule periodic individual discussions with your subordinates to discuss their career goals. Address issues such as:

- What skills must they develop to reach their goals?
- Are their goals realistic considering their skill potential and position within the organization?
- Are their career goals challenging enough given their demonstrated potential?
- What can you and the organization do to help employees achieve their career goals?

Build development plans with employees that take the answers to these questions into consideration, and provide regular feedback on progress toward career goals.

Part IV: Addressing Performance Problems

Analyzing Performance Problems

Misdiagnosis of an employee performance problem can have serious consequences. To develop your ability to correctly determine the cause of a problem, use the following checklist the next several times a performance problem arises. The checklist addresses four of the most common causes of problem performance and will help you determine the most appropriate course of action.

Lack of Clear Communication	**Y/N**	**Comments**
1. Does the person know the problem exists? (If not, it may resolve itself when brought to the employee's attention.)	Y/N	
2. Have I clearly communicated my expectations concerning the employee's performance?	Y/N	
3. Did the employee clearly understand my expectations? (To answer this question, ask the person to state his or her interpretation.)	Y/N	

Situational Constraints

Do any of the following obstacles outside of the employee's control affect the employee's performance?
- Lack of resources   Y/N
- Lack of authority   Y/N
- Conflicting directives   Y/N
- Lack of time   Y/N
- Other (describe: _____) Y/N

Deficient Skills, Knowledge, or Ability	Y/N	Comments

1. Do I have evidence that this person has the necessary abilities, knowledge, and skills to do this job? **Y/N**

2. Has the employee performed this task adequately in the past? **Y/N**

3. Does the employee have the knowledge or aptitude required to improve performance? **Y/N**

4. Is training available for employees who have the required aptitude but not the required skills? **Y/N**

Inappropriate Consequences of Behavior

1. Do existing policies reward poor performance or punish good performance? **Y/N**

2. Have I done what is necessary to change policies that produce inappropriate consequences? **Y/N**

Tempering Premature Criticism

People learn by making mistakes. If you create an environment in which employees fear criticism whenever they try new tasks or skills, your department will soon become stagnant. Over the next several months, use the following tips to counteract a tendency to criticize prematurely.

- Become results oriented. Your subordinates may use methods that are different from yours but just as effective. Keep an open mind concerning new approaches.
- Stop yourself from jumping to conclusions. Gather and consider all of the facts before you criticize. Mistakes may be due to miscommunication or conditions outside of employees' control.
- Remember that your position as manager makes many employees extremely sensitive to your criticism. Your reaction to their work can make or break their careers. Thus, employees may overestimate the significance of offhand remarks or minor criticisms.
- Consider the sensitivity levels of employees before criticizing. A frown may be all it takes to let one employee know that he or she has made a

mistake, while another employee may require a blunt statement of the problem.

- If you become so personally involved with an employee that you can no longer be objective in your criticism, consider assigning a senior employee to assist in that employee's development. A different approach to solving the problem, rather than more criticism, may be the answer.

Providing Constructive Criticism

The way in which you provide criticism can make the difference between an employee whose performance continues to decline and one whose performance improves. If you find that employees often react defensively when you inform them of problems in their work, consider the following tips for providing constructive criticism.

- Respect the employee's need for privacy. Your reaction to an employee's performance should remain between you and the employee; any criticism should be made in private.
- Allow employees to present their side of the problem; avoid the tendency to lecture.
- Focus on the work, not the person. Avoid personal attack. The comment "You're getting lazy" is much more likely to arouse defensiveness than the comment "You've missed the last two deadlines."
- Make sure you are emotionally in control before criticizing an employee. Criticism offered when you are angry or upset may come out more harshly than you intended and have lasting negative effects.
- Avoid late-in-the-day criticism, especially on Friday.
- Try to provide a balance of positive and negative remarks. If you are too negative, the employee may see the situation as hopeless and stop trying to improve.
- Offer useful feedback. Along with informing the employee that a mistake has been made, offer suggestions for preventing similar mistakes in the future.

Providing Feedback on Performance Problems

It's usually easy to identify subordinates' performance problems, but it's not always as easy to communicate negative feedback effectively and constructively. The following guidelines can help:

- Describe the behavior in objective and specific terms. Focusing on the behavior rather than the person can help to defuse any defensiveness. Using phrases like "This type of situation requires more attention to detail" rather than "You should be more careful" can help.
- Express your observations calmly. Even if you're upset about the situation, avoid blaming or attacking the employee.
- Describe the behavioral change that is required specifically and concretely.
- Identify clearly what consequences will result if the desirable behavior emerges. This emphasizes the positive and helps motivate employees to work toward the behavior.
- Ask the employee to restate your directives to ensure understanding, and clarify if necessary.

Coaching Problem Employees

When employee performance requires improvement, the coaching you provide can make the difference between success and failure. The next time a performance problem arises, try the following procedure. When using this procedure, start with a minor problem, then when you're comfortable with the procedure, move on to more serious cases.

1. Get the employee's agreement that a problem exists. In some cases, this step is easy to accomplish; employees are already aware that there are problems with their work and are ready to take the steps necessary to resolve these problems. In other cases, however, this step may require a great deal of discussion. For example, an employee who is frequently late but who is able to get the work done on time may insist that his or her tardiness has no effect on performance and, therefore, is not a problem.

   In such cases, you must help employees see the effects of their actions, either on the department or on themselves. For example, an employee's frequent absence from work may affect the work schedules of others, cause schedules to slip, or cause increased costs. The personal effects of this behavior might be lack of sick time when a real need arises, demotion, or reduced raises.

   It's important to spend as much time as is needed on this step. Until the employee agrees that a problem exists, the problem cannot be solved.

2. Discuss alternate solutions. At this point, emphasize the quantity of solutions rather than the quality. Encourage the subordinate to generate alternatives; he or she will be more likely to accept a self-prescribed solution.
3. Mutually agree on the best action to be taken to solve the problem. Evaluate all of the alternatives generated to determine the best way to solve the problem. Agree on the steps to be taken and when each will be taken.
4. Follow up on employee performance. When monitoring the employee's actions, be sure to recognize and reinforce any improvements in behavior—especially in the beginning—until these improvements have been incorporated into the employee's routine.

Recommended Readings

Abbott, G. Patrick. "The Mystique of Counseling." *Supervision,* July 1984, pp. 7-8.

A procedure for problem solving and constructive criticism is set out in fifteen steps. Criticism should begin with bringing the problem to the employee's attention informally. If this does not bring results, a more formal critique including three stages (initial interview and two follow-up sessions) should follow.

Blanchard, Kenneth, and Johnson, Spencer. *The One-minute Manager.*
New York, NY: Berkley Publishing Group, 1987.

This book discusses how specific feedback in the form of short, one-minute praisings or reprimands can be used to increase productivity, profits, and job satisfaction. The authors describe studies that support the use of these techniques and explain how to apply them successfully.

Block, Peter. *The Empowered Manager: Positive Political Skills at Work.*
San Francisco, CA: Jossey-Bass, 1987.

In this book, Block shows managers how to break out of the bureaucratic mode of thinking and take more responsibility or the workings of their unit. He explains how managers can become empowered to make positive changes in their organizations and develop an entrepreneurial spirit in themselves and in members of their unit.

Dailey, Charles A., and Madsen, Ann M. *How to Evaluate People in Business: The Track Record Method of Making Correct Judgments.* New York, NY: McGraw-Hill, 1983.

A practical presentation on the effective evaluation of people in all business settings, this book argues that employees should be judged on the basis of a documented "track record" of results-producing performances, rather than on such criteria as good conduct, pleasing traits, or political pull. It covers writing accurate performance accounts for long and short timespans, replacing the traditional hiring interview with a "track record" inquiry, judging one's own potential to defend against unjust superiors, making experience work, and revising performance review via employee accountability.

Deegan, Arthur X., II. *Coaching: A Management Skill for Improving Individual Performance.* Reading, MA: Addison-Wesley, 1979.

This book discusses needs for technical growth, management growth, and total human growth. In addition, it identifies many day-to-day situations that provide opportunities for coaching. The author offers suggestions for development and evaluation interviews, and supplements his suggestions with ten cases the reader can use to practice communicating developmental ideas to subordinates.

Diffie-Couch, Priscilla. "How to Give Feedback." *Supervisory Management,* August 1983, pp. 27-31.

Most of this article is the author's summary of what research has found about the subject of performance feedback for employees (though she doesn't give citations). Some of the eleven points she makes are as follows:

"Immediate feedback is almost always more useful than delayed feedback."

"Negative feedback may be better than no feedback at all, but positive feedback produces the best results."

"Undeserved praise does not produce positive results."

Each of these points is discussed in a paragraph or two, and the author also includes a list of twelve "do's and don'ts" on giving feedback.

Ford, Robert C., and Jones, Charles W. "Effective Strategies for Matching Dynamic People with Dynamic Jobs." *Management Review,* September 1983, pp. 20-25.

When people keep developing but the jobs they are in are static, then morale and attitude problems are likely. To avoid this kind of situation and give people opportunities to keep developing in their jobs, this article proposes the notion of a "dynamic job," and suggests, in a fairly general way, how to make jobs dynamic.

Fossum, Merle A., and Mason, Marilyn J. *Facing Shame: Families in Recovery.* New York, NY: W.W. Norton & Company, 1986.

By integrating object relations and family systems theories, the authors show how trauma, the repeated abuse of physical and psychological boundaries, can lead the individual and the family to feel "bad" and worthless. Throughout this book, as the authors compare the shame-bound family system with the respectful family system, they reveal the goals of therapy and take the reader step-by-step through the stages of therapy.

Fournies, Ferdinand F. *Coaching for Improved Work Performance.* New York, NY: Van Nostrand Reinhold, 1978.

The author identifies popular but ineffective management concepts, explains why they are ineffective, and offers alternatives and usable theories based on research. The theories are translated into working techniques. The book also demonstrates, in dialogue form, coaching methods for handling some common problems, and includes numerous examples of real working problems from the personal experience of managers.

Gordon, Thomas. *Leader Effectiveness Training*. New York, NY: Bantam Books, 1980.

This is an excellent introduction to the interpersonal coaching and leadership aspects of management. It includes practical problem-solving techniques and communication skills necessary to: get people to work with you, not just for you; resolve conflicts between individuals; develop a work team that gets results; evaluate others without damaging their self-esteem; and make meetings more productive and enjoyable.

Grothe, Dr. Mardy, and Wylie, Dr. Peter. *Problem Bosses: Who They Are and How to Deal with Them*. New York, NY: Facts on File Publications, 1987.

A virtual survival guide to anyone who has a difficult working relationship with a boss. The authors—psychologists hailed by *Inc.* magazine as pioneers in the new field of business therapy—describe just about every type of problem boss imaginable, from ineffective to downright deviant. They also offer guides, tests, and exercises to help readers evaluate their particular situations.

Hersey, P., and Blanchard, K.H. *Management of Organizational Behavior: Utilizing Human Resources (4th ed.)*. Englewood Cliffs, NJ: Prentice-Hall, 1982.

This book examines the behavioral approach to management, develops an outline of change theory, and presents various strategies for planning and implementing change. Among the topics discussed are motivation and behavior, the motivating environment, leader behavior, determination of effectiveness, ways to diagnose the environment, and management for organizational effectiveness and planning.

Himes, Gary K. "Coaching: Turning a Group into an Effective Team." *Supervision,* January 1984, pp. 14, 16, 26.

This article introduces coaching as a technique for developing teamwork in a group, but most of Himes' discussion focuses on the objective of individual development. He contends that informal daily coaching between an employee and his/her supervisor is perhaps the single most important contribution to excellent job performance. A 12-point "coaching checklist" is included to remind the supervisor of important aspects of effective coaching.

Janz, Tom; Hellervik, Lowell; and Gilmore, David C. *Behavior Description Interviewing*. Newton, MA: Allyn and Bacon, 1986.

Behavior description interviewing improves on traditional approaches by systematically probing what applicants have done in the past in situations similar to those they will face on the job. This book is written for interviewers from many backgrounds who want to make the best, most scientific hiring decisions within the structure of an interview.

Johnson, Robert G. *The Appraisal Interview Guide.* New York, NY: AMACOM, 1979.

The first half of this book deals with understanding and planning for appraisal interviewing, and the second half explains how to effectively conduct the appraisal interview. Included in the first part are interesting, straightforward discussions of the problems inherent in most appraisal forms. Also offered are ways of conducting appraisals without a form (if you can sidestep the usual procedure) or minimizing the difficulties inherent in the form (if you must use a form).

Kaufman, Gershen. *Shame: The Power of Caring.* Cambridge, MA: Schenkman Books, Inc., 1985.

Writing in an informal style that permits the reader to join directly in the explanation, Dr. Kaufman carefully examines how shame so disturbs the functioning of the self that eventually distinct syndromes of shame can develop. These syndromes, rooted in significant interpersonal failure and governed by internalized scenes of shame, cripple self-identity with insecurity, inadequacy, mistrust, and inferiority.

Kaye, Beverly L. "Performance Appraisal and Career Development: A Shotgun Marriage." *Personnel,* March-April, 1984, pp. 57-66.

Both performance appraisal and career development are processes "aimed at maximizing employee resource utilization," says this author but, when the two processes are linked, they tend to reinforce each other. She discusses the specific favorable consequences of this linkage (e.g., greater motivation to improve performance and recognition of the learning value of the appraisal). Then she examines the two processes and their integration in terms of 1) preparation and 2) communication. A chart that accompanies the article highlights the roles of managers and employees in both career development and performance appraisal.

Kelley, Robert E. *The Gold-Collar Worker.* Reading, MA: Addison-Wesley, 1985.

Management consultant Robert Kelley maintains that a new breed of workers demanding a new kind of management has come into play. These he terms as the "gold-collar workers"—the brain power of American business. Intelligent, independent, and innovative, these employees are incredibly valuable. In this book, Kelley takes a close look at these new workers, examines their impact on corporations, and offers practical advice for the people who manage them.

King, Patricia A. *Performance Planning and Appraisal: A How-to Book for Managers.* New York, NY: McGraw-Hill, 1984.

Concentrating on practical, hands-on applications, this no-nonsense guide plots out a systematic way to improve performance and greater management control over employee productivity. It also covers what to do when your best efforts fail and you must fire someone legally and humanely.

Peters, Tom, and Austin, Nancy. *A Passion for Excellence.* New York, NY: Random House, 1985.

The chapter on coaching may be the best single chapter in this well-read, highly acclaimed book. Coaching is face-to-face leadership that pulls together people with diverse backgrounds, talents, experiences, and interests, encourages them to step up to responsibility and continued achievement. The chapter covers five coaching roles: educate, sponsor, coach, counsel, and confront; plus the most vital aspects of coaching: visibility, listening, limit-setting, value shaping, and skill stretching.

Raelin, Joseph A. *The Clash of Cultures.* Boston, MA: Harvard Business School Press, 1986.

This is the first book to fully analyze and attempt to resolve the conflict between managers and professionals by examining the corporate culture to which managers are committed and the professional culture through which professionals are socialized. The mediation strategies are designed to minimize and manage conflict before it erupts into a major managerial problem.

Roseman, E. *Confronting Nonpromotability: How to Manage a Stalled Career.* New York, NY: AMACOM, 1977.

Recognizing the warning signals and evaluating options open to persons who have reached this stage in their careers are discussed in this book. It also describes effective techniques for counseling individuals facing career impasses, revitalizing stale people and jobs, and creating a motivating work environment that will discourage turnover when employees become unpromotable.

Rosenbaum, Bernard L. *How to Motivate Today's Workers: Motivational Models for Managers and Supervisors.* New York, NY: McGraw-Hill, 1981.

This book provides ideas for dealing with specific coaching and motivating problems. It is a set of active skill-building exercises and models that show how to build improved behavior models for poor, average, and dissatisfied performers. Included are keys to: dealing with disciplinary action, resistance to change, conflict between employees, absenteeism, and unrest.

Sheard, James L.; Stalley, Rodney E.; and Williamson, David L. *Opening Doors to the Job Market.* Minneapolis, MN: Augsburg Publishing House, 1983.

This book by three professionals experienced in counseling individuals through job change answers questions related to facing unemployment, finding career direction, assessing abilities and interests, developing job searching skills, establishing a job search strategy, and finding fulfillment in work.

Smedes, Lewis B. *Forgive & Forget.* New York, NY: Pocket Books, 1984.

The author shows the reader how to move from hurting and hating to healing and reconciliation. With the lessons of forgiveness, one can establish healthier relationships, reclaim the happiness that should be yours, and achieve lasting peace of mind.

Smith, H.P., and Brouwer, P.J. *Performance Appraisal and Human Development.* Reading, MA: Addison-Wesley, 1977.

The argument that performance appraisal is a vital key to the development of human talent is the basis of this book. The authors tell how and why performance appraisal ideas and methods used by managers either impede or stimulate the growth of their subordinates. The authors believe that the company within which the individual can find personal fulfillment while achieving corporate goals is the company that accomplishes practical results.

Stowell, Steven J., and Starcevich, Matt M. *The Coach: Creating Partnerships for a Competitive Edge.* Center for Management and Organizational Effectiveness, 1987.

This book takes a look at leader/employee relationships in the context of partnerships. The contention of the authors is that there needs to be and will be a substantial change in the role of the traditional leader and his/her skills to interact on a one-to-one basis. The new job of the leader will be to coach, develop, train, delegate, etc., rather than directing from an authoritative base.

Notes:

Suggested Seminars

The seminars listed here were selected for their appeal to a managerial audience and have received good to excellent ratings from managers attending them.

Because of the dynamic nature of the seminar marketplace, some seminars may have been added, upgraded, or replaced, and others may no longer be offered. Additional information about these seminars may be obtained by calling the vendor directly, or through Seminar Clearinghouse International, a subscriber organization located in St. Paul, Minnesota. Call 612/293-1004 for information.

AMERICAN MANAGEMENT ASSOCIATIONS, P.O. Box 319, Saranac Lake, NY 12983, 518/891-0065.

Recruiting, Interviewing, and Selecting Employees. This is a basic course for those involved in the employee recruitment process. The key topics include: where to find the right people to fill your job needs; how to analyze job specifications and prepare and effectively utilize job descriptions; the role of planning in the interview and selection process; how to use proven selection tools to narrow down the choices; how to get the most out of an interview; how to avoid legal pitfalls in the interview and hiring process; and how pre-employment screening can help you avoid serious hiring mistakes.

Length: 3 days

Cost: $750

Locations: San Francisco, CA; Orlando, FL; Atlanta, GA; Chicago, IL; New York, NY; Philadelphia, PA; Dallas, TX.

COMMUNISPOND, INC., 485 Lexington Avenue, New York, NY 10017, 212/687-8040.

One-to-one Communication Skills. Two-day program with key topics that include: participating in listening exercises; learning to use the energy of the employees' emotions/perceptions; planning a supervisor-initiated meeting regarding employee conduct; practicing one-to-one communications skills to influence employees to change their behavior without resenting their managers; and applying those skills in working with outside suppliers, customers.

Length: 2 days

Cost: $950

Locations: Newport Beach, CA; Chicago, IL; New York, NY; Dallas, TX.

DISNEY SEMINARS, P.O. Box 3232, Anaheim, CA 92803, 714/999-4436.
  Starting Your Own Magic. A one-day program that includes the following topics: establishing the goals of an effective orientation program; creating the orientation environment; presenting company traditions, history and philosophy; designing audiovisual/media support for an orientation program; and developing the human element in an orientation program.
  Length: 1 day
  Cost: $375
  Location: Anaheim, CA.

PERSONNEL DECISIONS, INC., 2000 Plaza VII Tower, 45 South Seventh Street, Minneapolis, MN 55402, 612/339-0927, 800/633-4410, ext. 875 (outside Minn.).
  Selection Interviewing: Information Gathering. Two-day workshop designed for employment interviewers with less than one year of experience and those who interview for selection and promotion. Participants will learn how to structure and control the interview; ask comprehensive, open-end questions; probe for pertinent behavioral data.
  Length: 2 days
  Cost: $475
  Location: Minneapolis, MN.

  Selection Interviewing: Information Interpretation. Two-day workshop geared toward the more experienced employment interviewer or manager who interviews for selection and promotion as well as those who have attended the Information Gathering workshop. Participants learn to analyze job positions; interpret both subtle and obvious data from the interviewing; and structure a selection system to improve decision making.
  Length: 2 days
  Cost: $475
  Location: Minneapolis, MN.

PRACTICAL MANAGEMENT INCORPORATED, P.O. Box 8789, Calabasas, CA 91302, 800/423-5099, 800/874-8695 (in Calif.), 818/342-9101.
  Fundamentals of One-on-one Instruction. Participants in this program learn to develop skills in focusing on trainer rather than trainee, job/task analysis, writing objectives, sequence of one-on-one instruction, lesson plan for one-on-one, and putting the one-on-one instruction format together—insuring that results occur from the instruction.

Length: 1 day
Cost: $195
Locations: Phoenix, AZ; Anaheim, CA; Los Angeles, CA; Sacramento, CA; San Francisco, CA; Detroit, MI; Charlotte, NC; Winston-Salem, NC; Omaha, NE; Las Vegas, NV; Reno, NV; Salt Lake City, UT. For additional locations, contact the vendor.

TRAINING CLINIC. 645 Seabreeze Drive, Seal Beach, CA 90740, 213/430-2484.

Make New Employee Orientation a Success. This course provides participants an overview of orientation, plus gives them the tools necessary in developing and setting orientation objectives, selecting content and methods, taking into account special considerations—new company start-up, mergers, acquisitions, new departments, stores, etc.; and evaluating orientation efforts.
Length: 1 day
Cost: $195
Locations: Los Angeles, CA; San Francisco, CA.

UNIVERSITY OF MICHIGAN, School of Business Administration, Executive Education Center, Ann Arbor, MI 48109, 313/763-1000.

Advanced Selection Interviewing: A Systematic Approach to Assesing Technical/Professional Applicants. This program is designed for participants who wish to build a solid base of interviewing skills. Included in this three-day program are topics such as review and elaboration of interviewing fundamentals; evaluation of the applicant; building the skills of the professional interviewer; and evaluation of the interview.
Length: 3 days
Cost: $850
Location: Ann Arbor, MI.

Effective Managerial Coaching and Counseling. This program is designed for mid- to upper-level managers. Some of the key topics include: difference between coaching and counseling; identifying problems; structure and strategy of a counseling session; the session as seen through the subordinate's eyes; and evaluation of the coaching or counseling session.
Length: 3 days
Cost: $990
Location: Ann Arbor, MI.

UNIVERSITY OF WISCONSIN, Management Institute, 432 North Lake Street, Madison, WI 53706, 800/262-6243 (outside Wisc.), 800/362-3020 (in Wisc.).

Coaching and Counseling Skills. The program teaches participants how to identify their personal coaching-counseling styles. Class time is devoted to role-playing and practice sessions using videotape and playback along with critique and feedback.
Length: 3 days
Cost: $545
Location: Madison, WI.

Leadership Skills

Notes:

FACTOR 3

Interpersonal Skills

Today's successful, respected manager knows that "people" skills are as important as business skills in performing the overall management function. By forming working relationships in which you strive to enhance understanding and mutual respect, acknowledge the needs and feelings of others, and focus on the positive aspects of conflict, you can create a healthy, holistic environment for productivity. In addition, you can foster personal and professional growth in peers, subordinates, superiors, and yourself.

This section presents suggestions for improving your interpersonal skills in the following two major areas.

Human Relations Skills: showing awareness of and consideration for the opinions and feelings of others and developing and maintaining smooth, cooperative working relationships (with peers, subordinates, and superiors)

Conflict Management and Negotiating: bringing conflict into the open to arrive at constructive solutions while maintaining positive working relationships

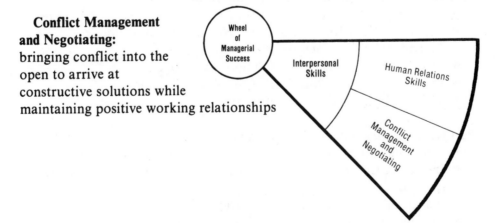

Human Relations Skills

Matt is a department manager who conscientiously reads the business journals and attends seminars on management-improvement techniques in an effort to excel at his job. His skills in delegating, planning, and financial management are outstanding. However, when asked to evaluate Matt's overall managerial ability, a trusted colleague informed Matt of his tendencies to dominate discussions at meetings and be somewhat intolerant of others' viewpoints. She suggested that Matt do some reading on the human relations component of management—maybe even sign up for a workshop on applying human relations skills in the work setting. Matt decided that he did need help in that area and took his coworker's advice.

This four-part section provides suggestions that can help managers who, like Matt, need practice in developing their human relations skills.

Part I: Social Skills
- Obtaining Feedback on Your Interpersonal Style (p. 196)
- Reducing Tendencies to Dominate (p. 196)
- Becoming More Relaxed and Open (p. 197)
- Developing a Sensitive Sense of Humor: Reducing Sarcasm (p. 198)
- Increasing Tolerance for Differing Points of View (p. 198)
- Increasing Your Sociability (p. 199)
- Experimenting With New Social Roles (p. 199)
- Making Small Talk (p. 200)

Part II: Improving Human Relations With Subordinates
- Becoming More Approachable (p. 201)
- Increasing Your Knowledge of the Needs and Motivations of Individual Subordinates (p. 202)
- Taking a Personal Interest in Subordinates (p. 203)
- Improving Relationships With Subordinates (p. 204)
- Treating Individuals Fairly (p. 205)

Part III: Improving Relationships With Peers
- Adopting a More Accepting View of Your Colleagues (p. 206)
- Increasing Communication With Colleagues in Other Departments (p. 206)
- Increasing the Quality of Peer Relationships (p. 207)
- Encouraging Feedback From Your Associates (p. 208)

Part IV: Improving Relationships With Superiors

Tips

- Be alert to **nonverbal** signals of rejection or withdrawal.

- Keep a calendar of birthdays, etc., and recognize people on significant dates through comments or sending cards or notes.

- Check your common courtesies to others, i.e., do you greet people in the morning, say hello in the halls, say thank you, especially with lower status persons?

- Have an occasional social event with coworkers such as golf or tennis. Get to know them outside the workplace.

- Listen to the input of your spouse or close friends. They often have insights about your style and personality which others may not share as openly.

- Try smiling more!

- Identify several people you take for granted and be sure to speak to them, take them to lunch, or otherwise extend yourself.

- Apologize to people you have hurt, ignored, or "stepped on" unintentionally.

- Pay more attention to people . . . even in small ways, like having better eye contact.

- Be aware of when coworkers are hurting in their personal life—death, illness, etc.—and express your interest and concern in words, by a visit, or with a gift or flowers.

- Develop more "human relations" orientation by accepting other persons and searching for their good qualities.

- Improve your human relations skills by undertaking a "group process training" experience and then a "team building laboratory."

- Try to be less judgmental and evaluative in your day-to-day dealings with people.

- Seek feedback from trusted others about your personal impact.

- When dealing with people, try out different strategies depending on the situation and the people involved.

- Temper your directives to others with statements that acknowledge that you hear and understand their comments.

- Make attempts to learn about others by asking them about their personal lives.

- Learn to be less abrasive and tactless in your interpersonal relations by confronting the **issue** instead of the **person.**

- Learn to become less sarcastic by having a trusted friend give you feedback whenever he/she hears you being sarcastic.

- In order to develop a more relaxed, less intense, more tentative approach to problem solving, focus more on problem analysis and less on gaining quick approval or "image-building."

- Be more friendly, positive, and optimistic when you first meet someone.

- Expand your circle of friends and become more active in the community.

- Directly inquire about how things are going for others or, more specifically, what they are seeking from a given situation.

- Make sure you are not giving off signals of manipulation or in other ways creating a climate of mistrust around you. Especially, don't use information unfairly to your advantage.

- Try "management by wandering around," i.e., get out in the work area and see what is going on. Do this frequently.

- Do not allow yourself to become so busy or self-centered that you fail to notice the needs and concerns of others.

- Look for small opportunities to build acquaintances with coworkers—coffee, lunch, etc.

- Reinforce coworkers' performance. State your pride to them **and others** for being part of such a team.

- Ask if you can be of help when you see a colleague "in a bind" on a project or assignment.

- Compliment your peers for comments, ideas, or successes you've noticed which you appreciated.

- In order to develop a more relaxed, less intense, more tentative approach, seek feedback from your working associates about your personal impact in this area.

- Seek feedback from your manager regarding instances when you may have reacted without due consideration of people's feelings.

- Seek feedback from your manager and trusted peers about instances when your dominance comes across as too self-serving.

Part I: Social Skills

Obtaining Feedback on Your Interpersonal Style

To improve your relationships with others, you must see yourself as others see you. But because few of us ever get direct feedback on how we come across, you'll need to arrange settings that will provide feedback on your interpersonal style. Begin by setting up two or three situations in which you could solicit feedback on a regular basis. Following are suggestions for accomplishing this.

1. Ask a respected colleague or superior with whom you regularly participate in one-to-one and group settings to serve as a feedback source. Ask for the person's impressions of your style and impact in a variety of situations.

2. When conducting performance appraisal interviews, encourage an exchange of information; that is, ask subordinates for feedback on your interpersonal style.

3. Seek feedback from others on the behaviors you are trying to change. If possible, record several discussions and review them with someone in a position to give you objective feedback. That person's feedback can help you determine which areas need improvement. An alternative is to obtain feedback on your interpersonal skills using an instrument called the Management Skills Profile available through Personnel Decisions, Inc.

Reducing Tendencies to Dominate

At times, a speaker's enthusiasm about his or her ideas or desire to ensure that those ideas are heard and accepted can be carried to the point where others in the discussion feel that the speaker is abrasive, overbearing, or domineering.

To determine if you dominate discussions, either intentionally or unintentionally, ask yourself the following questions after each of the next several discussions in which you participate.

- Did I interrupt frequently to interject my opinions?
- Did I restate my opinions more frequently than was necessary?
- Was I overly forceful in stating my opinions?
- Did I speak too often, thereby preventing others from obtaining equal discussion time?
- Was I overly critical of the opinions of others?

If you answered "yes" to any of these questions, consider the following suggestions when participating in future discussions.

- Make a conscious effort to eliminate interruptions.
- Set a limit on the number of times you will voice the same opinion; for example, decide that you will restate your opinion only if it is apparent that the group did not hear or understand it the first time or if you are asked to restate it.
- Concentrate on presenting your viewpoints using an approach that is less dogmatic or domineering.
- Develop an awareness of the proportion of discussion time you use; become sensitive to signals that indicate that others would like to speak.
- Consciously refrain from immediate judgment and criticism of others' ideas. If criticism is required, deliver it in a way that demonstrates sensitivity to the feelings of others.
- Ask open-ended questions that encourage others to provide their points of view.

In time, you will find that considering the value of others' contributions to the group will help you become more accepted by the group and make the group willing to consider your ideas more readily.

Becoming More Relaxed and Open

It's easier to work with people if they feel that you are comfortable with them. If you create an initial impression of extreme seriousness or intensity, people may be hesitant to open up and establish in-depth communication with you. Practice the following three steps to give the impression that you are relaxed and open in the presence of others.

1. When you are meeting someone for the first time, be quick to greet them, stand up, and shake hands.
2. Smile warmly at the person you are meeting.
3. Work on your ability to make small talk and use light humor in your initial conversation. (Later subsections in this section provide additional tips in these areas.)

You may feel more comfortable practicing these behaviors in informal settings at first. Then seek out work-related group situations, such as meetings and conferences, in which you can practice letting down some of your interpersonal guardedness.

Developing a Sensitive Sense of Humor: Reducing Sarcasm

Humor can be an effective group-leadership tool. Sarcasm, however, can hurt and alienate people who do not know you well enough to interpret your humor correctly. It may even cause you to lose the support of such people in meeting your objectives. The following guidelines can help you reduce your use of inappropriate or potentially hurtful sarcasm.

- Develop an awareness of the occasions on which you use sarcasm in a way that may offend others. After each group session over the next few weeks, analyze the way in which you used your wit in that session. Determine whether there were any instances in which your use of humor may have hurt others.
- If you notice a pattern of too many instances of inappropriate sarcasm, work to change this behavior. In each situation, analyze the personalities of the people present to determine the appropriate use of humor.
- Remind yourself that your goal is to retain your sense of humor while eliminating any tendencies to insult or hurt others.

Continue this development program until you feel comfortable with your use of humor.

Increasing Tolerance for Differing Points of View

When you feel strongly about an issue, objective consideration of others' viewpoints can be difficult. Yet it's important to recognize others' contributions and realize that their viewpoints are just as important to them as yours are to you. If you have determined that you have difficulty acknowledging and accepting others' ideas, try the following exercise to increase your tolerance.

1. Ask a trusted coworker or supervisor to accompany you to group situations to help you identify any patterns of rigid or intolerant behavior. Together, examine the probable effect of your words and actions on others. It's important that you remain as open and nondefensive as possible during these reviews.
2. Together with your "coach," analyze how the other group participants may have felt. Did they become angry, hurt, or obstinate? What made them feel that way, and what could you do in the future to minimize such negative reactions? Consider alternate approaches to these situations.
3. Consider role playing each situation—having your coach play the role of the "injured party" while you experiment with more tolerant

approaches. Ask for your coach's response to your new approaches.

4. When you are comfortable with your new style, apply it in actual group sessions. With practice, you will develop a more objective, less judgmental attitude concerning others' viewpoints.

Increasing Your Sociability

The ability to meet new people and feel comfortable in social situations can be important to career advancement. If you have difficulty in social situations, you may want to enroll in a program to develop your social skills. The following guidelines can also help.

- Over the next month, set goals to take the initiative in forming social contacts, particularly in informal settings. Make a conscious effort to become more involved; for example, you might set goals to speak up more frequently, attend more social functions, or meet more people at these functions. In setting your goals, avoid drastic changes; remember that you have plenty of time to develop your skills.

- Set a goal to broaden your circle of acquaintances. Introduce yourself to people you have wanted to meet but were too busy or too shy to talk to. Consider specifying a certain number of people with whom you would like to become acquainted per week.

- Make an effort to learn more about each of your acquaintances' interests. This is especially helpful if you have difficulty thinking of things to talk about; others' interests often provide excellent opportunities for small talk.

Don't expect to become comfortable in social situations immediately; changes like this don't happen overnight. As time passes, however, you should find that you are beginning to enjoy social situations more and that they have become less threatening.

Experimenting With New Social Roles

Experimentation with new social behaviors can be difficult in work settings, yet practice is important. To gain practice in nonthreatening situations, consider the following situations.

- Take an active role in a selected civic or community service activity. This type of volunteer activity allows you to work with new people under minimal pressure. Plus, you don't have to worry about the effects of your behavior or actions on your long-term career growth.

- Set specific goals for each type of behavior you plan to try. Keep a record of the new behaviors, your initial reactions to them, and your feelings about your progress over time.

As you become comfortable with your new behaviors, begin to practice them in the work setting.

Making Small Talk

The ability to make small talk can help you make others more comfortable and often helps establish cooperative relationships. Many people find it difficult to make small talk—to find something to say to people they don't know very well. Following are two simple methods for overcoming this problem.

- Listen for "free" information. Listen to people talk and notice the hints they give about their interests, likes, and dislikes. In a casual conversation about the weather, for example, people might mention that they can't wait to get home to the garden or out on the lake. You've learned two topics of interest to those people—gardening and boating.

  To practice using free information, follow these guidelines.
  - Over the next week, listen to a variety of conversations and note the information people give that could be used as a lead-in to small talk.
  - Use this information to formulate questions. For example, if a person mentioned that it's a great day for golf, you could find out about his or her interest in the game by asking such questions as, "How long have you played?" and "Do you play often?" You may want to practice this skill with a friend. Ask the friend to make a comment and then respond with a question.
  - Take care not to ask too many questions in rapid succession. Once you have asked some questions, reveal some information about yourself. Mention how you feel about the subject or offer some free information about your own interests.
- Prepare topics for discussion. Read through the newspaper or news magazines, or watch the news on television. Prepare a few opening and follow-up comments you could use in making small talk. Practice including these comments in your conversations with others.

Practice these methods for several weeks. You will probably feel awkward in the beginning, but as time passes, you should become increasingly comfortable about asking questions of others, revealing information about yourself, and discussing current events.

Part II: Improving Human Relations With Subordinates

Becoming More Approachable

Approachable managers are more likely to be informed of the events—both negative and positive—taking place within their organizations. This is an ideal position because it helps eliminate "surprises." Thus, becoming more approachable can help you manage more smoothly by preventing crises.

The following suggestions will help you increase your approachability.
- If employees currently view you as unapproachable, try to determine what it is that you do to give this impression. Is it that they never see

you? Do you appear uninterested in their problems? Do you become angry when informed of problems? Try to reverse roles and see yourself as your employees see you. Then make changes based on your analysis.

- Establish an open-door policy. This does not mean that you must be available at all times. It means setting aside regular blocks of time for discussing employee concerns and making sure that employees are informed of your new schedule.
- Be accessible. Consider moving closer to your employees' work area— their "turf"—to appear less remote and show your interest in day-to-day operations. Gradually increase the frequency of your informal, drop-in visits with subordinates. A drastic change may cause them to think that you are unhappy with their work and want to check up on them.
- Practice "management by walking around" as described in the book **In Search of Excellence** by Peters and Waterman.
- If you invite employees to discuss problems, make sure you are prepared to respond nondefensively. A "shoot the messenger" reaction will put you right back where you started, regardless of how much time you set aside for discussions.

Be prepared to stick with your program once you start it. Insincere attempts to appear approachable may make communication worse instead of better. For example, if you establish times when you will be available and then consistently schedule other events at these times, your employees may decide that you are not really interested in establishing communication and may view your efforts as a half-hearted experiment.

Increasing Your Knowledge of the Needs and Motivations of Individual Subordinates

Your subordinates have individual, personal needs and motivations that determine what they expect from their jobs. By discovering these needs and motivations and showing that you care about your employees as individuals, you can increase their loyalty and even improve their performance. To increase your knowledge of your subordinates, follow this two-step plan.

1. Set up individual, informal interviews with subordinates over the next several months. During these interviews, ask subordinates about their work history, goals, and expectations of their jobs. Practice using good listening skills during these discussions (see the section entitled

"Listening"). By listening, you show employees that you are interested in them.

2. As a follow-up to these sessions, prepare a career file for each subordinate, summarizing the information you have gathered about career goals, aspirations, and work-related likes and dislikes. Review these files periodically and use the information in making assignments to projects, task forces, and so forth.

Taking a Personal Interest in Subordinates

The preceding subsection discussed the benefits of becoming interested in employees' career aspirations. In addition to work-oriented concerns, it is often worthwhile to take an interest in employees' personal concerns when building a manager-employee relationship. It will help you understand why employees perform as they do and let employees know that you care about them as individuals, which can improve their performance.

Over the next few months, use the following guidelines to demonstrate a personal interest in subordinates. Keep in mind the importance of getting to know employees gradually. A sudden, intense expression of interest may make it seem as if you are prying into their personal lives.

- Take time for informal chats with employees in the hallways or during brief, unscheduled visits. Ask about their personal interests—family, hobbies, goals. Follow up by occasionally inquiring about their current concerns.
- Share some of your personal interests. Employees will feel more comfortable sharing their interests with you if they feel that you are willing to reveal information about yourself.
- Consider arranging occasional social events, such as lunches or department parties, where you can discuss mutual interests other than business.
- If employees wish to discuss personal problems, be willing to listen. Take care, however, not to take on roles for which you are not professionally trained, such as that of financial or family counselor.

Finally, respect the confidentiality of employees' personal concerns and avoid using shared personal information in a way that employees may see as traitorous. For example, if an employee is late to work, a comment such as, "I know you have small children that you must take care of in the morning, but it's essential that you get to work on time," can make the employee regret that he or she opened up to you and feel reluctant to supply personal information in the future.

Improving Relationships With Subordinates

You can improve your relationships with subordinates by soliciting their feedback on your performance. Because such a request can lead to awkward or otherwise uncomfortable communication, make sure to ask for the feedback in an informal, nonthreatening manner. Also, let subordinates know that your reason for requesting the information is to improve your working relationships with them. Following are guidelines for soliciting subordinates' feedback.

1. Arrange an individual, informal meeting with each subordinate to discuss your working relationship, and ask the person to think about the topic ahead of time. During the meeting, provide as nonthreatening an environment as possible. Hold the meeting on "neutral" territory— for example, in the employee's office or at an off-site location (anywhere but in your office). Ask for the subordinate's comments on things you do that help the working relationship and what you might do to improve it. Be careful not to dominate the conversation, and try to respond to the employee's remarks in a nondefensive, honest way. Don't promise more than you can deliver; remember, your follow-through will be the key to improving the relationship.

2. Explore other ways to solicit employees' feedback on your relationships with them. Some employees might favor a format that would provide anonymity.

3. Ask for the feedback of a trusted peer who is in a position to observe your relationships with subordinates. Whatever plan or procedure you use to obtain subordinates' feedback, your aim should be to generate goals for improving your working relationships with them. You may want to share your goals with your subordinates, either collectively or individually, and ask them to work on developing mutual goals that you would both have responsibility for meeting.

4. Ask your supervisors, subordinates, and peers to rate your skills using the Management Skills Profile available from Personnel Decisions, Inc.

After working toward your goals for a period of time, go through the feedback-solicitation process again to get your subordinates' impressions of how your relationships with them have changed.

Treating Individuals Fairly

How can you be sure you're being "fair" in the way you handle your subordinates? You can't—because fairness is such a subjective quality. For example, although you might decide it's fair to assign the most challenging and interesting tasks to your best performer, other staff members might see you as playing favorites.

You can't always do what's fair for each individual as you strive to do what's best for the department. You can, however, evaluate others' perceptions of your fairness—and perhaps create a little more equality—by seeking and responding to feedback from your subordinates and peers. Here are some suggestions:

- Schedule a "gripe session" on a regular basis to allow employees to air their frustrations and concerns. Be sure to use listening skills during these sessions and avoid responding defensively.
- Set up a suggestion box. Sometimes people who hesitate to air their complaints publicly can communicate their feelings anonymously.
- Seek feedback on your performance in this area, and be sure to discuss your reasons for doing things your subordinates may see as unfair.

Part III: Improving Relationships With Peers

Developing positive, productive relationships with your peers is important for keeping morale up and getting work done efficiently. Following are tips for improving your relationships with peers.

1. Prepare a list of the peers with whom you work on a daily or weekly basis.
2. Using the following scale, rate the quality of your working relationship with each peer on your list.
   - 1 = Work poorly together
   - 2 = Have an adequate working relationship
   - 3 = Work together reasonably well (room for improvement)
   - 4 = Work together very well
3. Develop a plan for improving your readings in the area of human relations (see recommended readings later in this section) or discussions with colleagues, friends, or your superior.

4. Set a date by which you can reasonably accomplish your goal of improving your working relationships with peers.

5. After this date, reevaluate each peer relationship.

If your improvement plans are effective, the quality of your peer relationships—even those rated poorly in the beginning of this exercise—will have improved by the time you reach the reevaluation stage.

Adopting a More Accepting View of Your Colleagues

Tolerance of others requires insight into their strengths and weaknesses. This insight enables you to respond to both their "good" and "bad" points. Follow these tips for developing a more accepting view of colleagues who "rub you the wrong way."

1. Identify two or three peers with whom you find it difficult to work. Over the next few weeks, concentrate on the positive aspects of working with them. Try to come up with a list of at least five positive characteristics of each individual.

2. As you observe each person, be attentive to what others see as his or her positive traits—the qualities that make that person likeable to his or her associates and friends.

3. Whenever you work with these peers, concentrate on the strengths you've identified. Give compliments on the strong points, when appropriate. As you learn to focus on and appreciate your peers' strengths, you will find yourself more tolerant of their weaknesses. You may also find that the cooperative interaction that develops has a positive impact on their work areas. Eventually, you'll find it easier to overlook the qualities that once made it difficult for you to work with these individuals.

Increasing Communication With Colleagues in Other Departments

It's often difficult to work effectively with people you don't know well. Therefore, it's important to establish some type of contact with your associates in other units. The following guidelines provide suggestions for getting to know your peers in other units well enough to feel comfortable working with them.

1. Compile a list of the names of employees from other units/departments with whom you have contact.

2. Identify the individuals you don't know well.

3. Arrange an introductory meeting with each of these people. A lunch or coffee break would offer the desired relaxed, informal atmosphere.
4. Make an effort to maintain contact with your peers in other units or departments. Pursue joint interests with them or simply call them periodically to stay in touch.
5. Update your list of contacts on a regular basis—say, every few months. As time permits, arrange informal get-togethers with these new colleagues as well as those you've already met.

Increasing the Quality of Peer Relationships

The interaction style based on "winning by intimidation" holds few benefits for anyone and almost always produces a hostile, uncooperative environment. Therefore, the following guidelines are provided to help you pave the way for a cooperative work environment by increasing the amount of positive reinforcement you give your peers. (The following chart can help you structure your information.)

1. Over the next three weeks, keep track of the number of times you give positive feedback to each of your colleagues. Also monitor the number of positive comments you get from others on your accomplishments.
2. After determining your current use of positive comments, try to increase the number of positive comments you make to peers.

Colleague's Name	No. of Positive Comments Given	No. of Positive Comments Received	Positive Feedback Goal	Reinforcing Comments Received in Return

Whenever you can honestly commend them on good jobs they've done, do so. Be especially careful to reinforce any actions that have positively affected you or your work area. Set goals for a specific number of positive, rewarding comments you will make each week for each colleague. (Pace yourself; don't make them all on Friday!)

3. Keep track of how many reinforcing comments you get in return and note if that number increases as your positive comments increase.

4. Be particularly careful, when chairing a task force or other meeting, to give positive feedback to members who make contributions. These people increase the group's success and make your task easier.

5. Look for chances to work on projects where cooperative efforts are likely to result in win-win outcomes, which benefit everyone involved.

Encouraging Feedback From Your Associates

If you want to increase the amount of feedback you get from your peers on your ideas or personal impact, you must come across as a team member, not a competitor. This requires that you spend time on the peer relationship itself, not just on tasks to be accomplished. A good way to do this is to foster relationships in which you are attentive to and interested in others. This will encourage them to open up to you, volunteer information, and discuss issues. The following procedure is designed to help you initiate this mutual reinforcement.

1. As you work with peers over the next week, ask yourself if you're emphasizing your tasks and opinions at the expense of team relationships. Take notes on your behaviors, and, at the end of the week, write a goal for yourself based on your self-assessment.

2. As you become more relaxed, less intense, and more attentive to your peer relationships, monitor your peers' new willingness to volunteer information, provide feedback on your ideas and impact, and discuss issues with you. You'll know you're making progress when you start getting feedback from peers who have never offered it in the past.

Part IV: Improving Relationships With Superiors

Minimizing Defensiveness in Interactions With Your Superior

Defensiveness (the tendency to be protective when others give us feedback) is an obstacle to be reckoned with in almost all instances of interpersonal communication. It's an especially difficult barrier when it affects your ability to open yourself up to your superior and accept helpful feedback. Learning to think of negative feedback as suggestions for dealing with particular situations—rather than as personal criticism—will increase your effectiveness and make you open to receiving valuable information. The guidelines that follow can help you learn how to use your superior's feedback to your advantage.

1. Make a conscious attempt to check your response patterns for phrases like "Yes, but . . .," and eliminate them from your speech. Whenever you catch yourself assuming this defensive posture, stop talking, and **listen** rather than **justify**.

2. Be aware of your emotional response the next several times you receive negative feedback. Rate each response on a scale of 1-10, with 1 standing for "virtually no emotion" and 10 representing "intense anger."

3. Try to paraphrase the feedback and demonstrate in other ways your understanding of what was said.

4. Try asking yourself a fixed set of rational/analytical questions like the following ones to help diminish your defensiveness.
    - Do I understand exactly what is being said?
    - Is the criticism about a topic or behavior I could do something about if I wanted to?
    - What would happen if I acted on the feedback?
5. Act on the advice given. If your superior simply made a judgment, ask for coaching. Devise a plan and timetable for implementing his or her suggestions.
6. Think of additional instances in which others' advice helped you improve your work performance. In cases in which the advice included criticism, did the benefits of your improvement outweigh the unpleasantness of the criticism?

As your resistance to it diminishes, you will come to think of criticism less as a sign of defeat than as a tool for improving your interactions with others.

Increasing the Amount of Feedback From Your Superior

Your superior is a valuable source of the feedback you need for self-improvement. Unfortunately, many people's fear of criticism causes them to miss opportunities to receive their superiors' evaluation. The following guidelines can help you actively seek feedback.

1. Select an area in which you feel you need improvement—preferably, one in which you've received criticism in the past.
2. Prepare a plan for increasing your proficiency in that area. This Handbook offers valuable suggestions for your plan. Other sources of information include readings in the area of skill development and friends and colleagues who are reasonably familiar with your work skills and habits.
3. Present your plan to your superior, informing him or her that you will be devoting time to it over the next month. Ask for comments or suggestions on the plan and request feedback on the area you're seeking to improve.
4. At the end of the month, review your progress with your superior. Show your appreciation for his or her input by pointing to specific outcomes that resulted from it.

Increasing Support For Your Superior's Management Objectives

Supporting your superior's management objectives can do more than improve your working relationship with your superior; it can also be a means of increasing your professional expertise. This procedure can help you show support for your superior's objectives.

1. Identify three to five ideas for providing additional assistance to your superior. You can do this by:
   - Analyzing the scope of his or her responsibilities and listing all of the projects and activity areas in which he or she is involved
   - Generating at least one way in which you could assist your superior in each area on your list
2. Present your ideas to your superior and ask which forms of assistance would best support his or her management objectives.
3. Together with your superior, clarify:
   - The types of assistance that would be appreciated
   - The exact nature of your assistance in each area
   - Time frames for each form of assistance
   - A method for receiving feedback on your progress in providing assistance

Voicing Disagreement With Your Superior

Many people find disagreeing with their superiors to be one of the most unpleasant and difficult parts of their jobs. If you are hesitant to express disagreement with your superior or to deliver "bad news," follow these guidelines for developing a plan to voice disagreement in a confident, straightforward manner.

1. Talk to your superior about how disagreement between the two of you, in general, could best be handled. Work on identifying the amount and type of disagreement you both can tolerate.
2. Before going to your boss with a topic that may produce disagreement, think through your reasons for your position. Be prepared to logically and calmly state them during the discussion. Think of ways to resist becoming defensive about your position or quickly deferring to your superior's position. Try to vividly picture the disagreement scene in your mind, imagining both your manager's expression of his or her opinion and your statement of your case. Doing this can help you take a more positive, unwavering stand during the actual disagreement situation.

3. Remember that your superior's position does not make his or her ideas inherently better than yours. You may do yourself and your superior a disservice by not pushing for what may prove to be a better idea or at least pointing out alternate ways of looking at a problem or a situation.

4. Be open to your superior's point of view and be willing to accept his or her points. Always remember that your supervisor is the boss and is the final authority.

Increasing the Information You Provide to Your Superior

Most managers frown on surprises—and not only unpleasant ones. Whatever the situation, they want to be informed in advance so they know what to expect and have a chance to prepare for it. Therefore, keeping your boss informed about your activities and major factors or occurrences that might affect him or her is an important part of your job. The following guidelines can help you ensure that you are providing enough information to your superior.

1. Meet with your boss to identify the kinds of information he or she is most interested in receiving from you. Also ask about areas in which your boss wants **immediate** updates after you've taken action.
2. Try to prevent surprises by giving your superior information that may have negative implications for your work unit or important items that he or she is likely to hear from someone else if you don't pass it along.
3. As you attempt to increase the information you provide to your boss, check to ensure that you are providing the desirable amount of information—not too much or too little—in each of the identified critical areas.

Recommended Readings

Anthony, William P. *Managing Your Boss.* New York, NY: AMACOM, 1983.

The author attempts to show the reader that, as a subordinate, he/she has more power than he/she thinks. Anthony provides tips on how to understand one's role and one's boss's role, how to shape expectations, and how to shape one's own image. Anthony also discusses how to communicate with one's boss and how to be a problem solver rather than a problem creator. This book also contains over thirty exercises to help the reader learn more about him/herself and how to exert the power he/she has.

Baskin, O.W., and Aronoff, C.E. *Interpersonal Communication in Organizations.* Santa Monica, CA: Goodyear Publishing Company, 1979.

Differentiating between interpersonal communication and business and organizational communication, this book focuses on the person-to-person, manager-to-subordinate, and subordinate-to-manager relationships.

Bennett, Dudley. *TA and the Manager.* New York, NY: AMA, 1976.

This book shows how transactional analysis can help managers work more effectively and improve personal growth and interpersonal skills. Simple techniques are featured.

Blicq, Ron. *On the Move: Communication for Employees.* Englewood Cliffs, NJ: Prentice-Hall, 1976.

This book traces the employee-as-communicator through four stages: job applicant, new employee, junior supervisor, and small business owner. Each stage shows different relationships existing between the individual and his or her employer, employees, peers, and customers. Exercises are fully developed; many can be used as discussion topics or communications assignments.

Bolton, Robert. *People Skills.* New York, NY: Touchstone Books, 1986.

This practical communications skills handbook focuses on how more effective communication can help the reader strengthen family ties, increase the warmth in friendships, and make work relationships more productive. It includes skills in listening, asserting viewpoints, resolving conflicts, and working out problems with others.

Bolton, Robert, and Bolton, Dorothy Grover. *Social Style/Management Style.* New York, NY: AMACOM, 1984.

Based on the authors' feelings that "the best managers excel at being what they are rather than at trying to be about what they are not," the Boltons take a business-oriented approach to interpersonal relationships. They attempt to show the reader how to assess various behavior patterns in him/herself and others and use that knowledge to predict how others will react in specific situations. Based on the Boltons' extensive research, four basic social styles are identified, and the authors attempt to show the reader how to use his/her style to manage others more effectively, set appropriate life goals and career paths, and more.

Costley, Dan L., and Todd, Ralph. *Human Relations in Organizations (3rd ed.).* St. Paul, MN: West Publishing Co., 1987.

This book focuses on the behavior of individuals in organizations. Its emphasis is on the skills needed for effective leadership, including the abilities to communicate, understand human needs, cope with conflict and frustration, motivate others, use authority, and increase group productivity.

Davis, George, and Watson, Glegg. *Black Life in Corporate America: Swimming in the Mainstream.* New York, NY: Van Nostrand Reinhold, 1979.

This book, which deals with the human issues that concern all managers, black or white, male or female, and what these managers have experienced and revealed, has profound implications for the future of American motivation, productivity, and bottom-line profitability. It is the first in-depth look at men and women trying to "make it" in a world created by and for white males.

DuBrin, Andrew J. *Winning at Office Politics.* New York, NY: Van Nostrand Reinhold, 1980.

This book concentrates on what is done, rather than what should be done, to gain advantage in the office. It explains how to become attuned to the political climate in the office, how to learn the political strategies that can be useful there, and how to practice sensible office politics.

Gabarro, John, and Kotter, John. "Managing Your Boss." *Harvard Business Review,* January/February 1980, p. 92.

This article points out the importance of managing your relationship with your boss. Coming to understand both yourself and your boss will help both of you be more effective.

Garner, Alan. *Conversationally Speaking: Tested New Ways to Increase Your Personal and Social Effectiveness.* New York, NY: McGraw-Hill, 1980.

This practical book teaches the reader techniques and skills for making contact with others, turning acquaintances into friends, and putting greater warmth into long-term relationships. It shows the reader how to: ask the kind of questions that promote conversation, avoid rejection-producing behavior, issue invitations that are likely to be accepted, achieve deeper levels of understanding and intimacy, handle criticism constructively, resist manipulation, become far more confident in social situations, and listen so others will be encouraged to talk to you.

Hegarty, Christopher. *How to Manage Your Boss.* New York, NY: Ballantine, 1985.

This book shows the reader how to identify the real needs of his/her boss and select the strategies needed to transform the typical boss/subordinate adversary relationship into one of creative teamwork and mutual benefit. The author shows the reader how to make teamwork really work through clarity, communication, and commitment.

Neilsen, E.H., and Gypen, J. "The Subordinate's Predicaments." *Harvard Business Review,* September/October 1979, pp. 133-143.

The superior-subordinate relationship is often tense and threatening to the subordinate, which can result in behavior that is damaging to the organization. The authors apply Erik Erikson's theory of stages in human development to a subordinate's growth in the workplace. They claim that management awareness of the stages can make subordinates more manageable, and they offer suggestions on ways to help subordinates in handling their growth.

Ritti, R., and Funkhauser, G. *The Ropes to Skip and the Ropes to Know: Studies in Organizational Behavior (3rd ed.).* New York, NY: John Wiley & Sons, 1987.

The aim of this book is to help the reader become aware of the complexities of organizational behavior and recognize some of the moves of some typical corporate characters. Each chapter is a striking occasion that demonstrates some fundamental fact of organizational life. It is designed to get the reader thinking about why people in organizations behave the way they do.

Swets, Paul W. *The Art of Talking So That People Will Listen.* Englewood Cliffs, NJ: Prentice-Hall, 1983.

This guide provides practical techniques for mastering the art of effective, persuasive communication. It identifies communication goals and strategies for meeting those goals which allow the reader to: gain control of the complexities of the communication process; discover what builds communications barriers between people and what one can do to tear them down; win the attention and cooperation of friends and business associates; and present oneself clearly and effectively in social situations.

Suggested Seminars

The seminars listed here were selected for their appeal to a managerial audience and have received good to excellent ratings from managers attending them.

Because of the dynamic nature of the seminar marketplace, some seminars may have been added, upgraded, or replaced, and others may no longer be offered. Additional information about these seminars may be obtained by calling the vendor directly, or through Seminar Clearinghouse International, a subscriber organization located in St. Paul, Minnesota. Call 612/293-1004 for information.

AMERICAN MANAGEMENT ASSOCIATIONS, P.O. Box 319, Saranac Lake, NY 12983, 518/891-0065.

Executive Effectiveness Course. This two-part laboratory experience is directed at middle management people. Unit 1 focuses on how to see yourself as others see you. Unit 2 focuses on how well you work as a member of a group. Cost quoted is for both programs.
Length: 5 days
Cost: $2175
Locations: Carmel, CA; San Diego, CA; Tarpon Springs, FL; Bolton Landing, NY; Hamilton, NY; Hilton Head Island, SC; Williamsburg, VA.

CENTER FOR CREATIVE LEADERSHIP, 5000 Laurinda Drive, P.O. Box P-1, Greensboro, NC 27402, 919/277-7210.

Managing For Commitment. The program topics offered in this workshop include: manager as motivator and facilitator; role of manager in producing decisions; performance development; interpersonal awareness and effectiveness; and setting goals for application.
Length: 4 days
Cost: $1400
Locations: San Diego, CA; College Park, MD; Greensboro, NC.

LEADERSHIP DEVELOPMENT CENTER, 4541 N. Prospect Road, #1, Peoria, IL 61614, 309/685-1900.

Working With Others: A Management Process. A three-day seminar with content focusing on situational leadership, getting the most from groups, productive feedback, awareness of interpersonal approach, setting goals for further development. This is a Center for Creative Leadership licensed program.

Length: 3 days
Cost: $895
Locations: Chicago, IL; Peoria, IL; Louisville, KY.

LEARNING INTERNATIONAL, 200 First Stamford Place, P.O. Box 10211, Stamford, CT 06904, 203/965-8400.
Interpersonal Managing Skills. The new interpersonal managing skills system prepares professionals for the demands of today's changing organizations. Participants learn how to encourage subordinates and peers to contribute the best work they have to offer, as well as giving constructive criticism, crediting good performance, clarifying and confirming understanding, acknowledging the value of other people's contributions, and managing differences.
Length: 3 days
Cost: Call vendor
Locations: Marina Del Rey, CA; San Francisco, CA; Atlanta, GA; Chicago, IL; Schaumburg, IL; Boston, MA; Bloomington, MN; New York, NY; Pittsburgh, PA; Dallas, TX; Houston, TX; Bellevue, WA. For additional locations, contact the vendor.

MENNINGER FOUNDATION, Box 829, Topeka, KS 66601, 913/273-7500.
Executive Seminar: Toward Understanding Human Behavior and Motivation. Participants in this workshop gain a new understanding of human behavior and motivation, take a critical look at their own strengths and weaknesses as executives, and evolve plans to putting what they learn to work in their professional and personal lives.
Length: 1 week
Cost: $2500
Locations: Colorado Springs, CO; Topeka, KS.

NTL INSTITUTE, P.O. Box 9155, Rosslyn Station, Arlington, VA 22209, 703/527-1500.
Management Work Conference in Interpersonal Competence. This seminar will improve abilities to lead and manage task groups, foster group problem-solving and decision-making process, and assess management style effectiveness in others.
Length: 7 days
Cost: $895
Locations: San Diego, CA; San Francisco, CA; Colorado Springs, CO; Ponte Vedra, FL; Safety Harbor, FL; Bethel, ME.

Senior Managers' Conference in Interpersonal Competence. This seminar will strengthen abilities to sustain a supportive climate for human

resource development in their organization, mediate conflicts, negotiate positively within conflicting priorities, improve communication, and build incentive for cooperation among organizational subunits.
Length: 7 days
Cost: $1135
Locations: Colorado Springs, CO; Kiawah Island, FL; Safety Harbor, FL.

RIDGE ASSOCIATES INC., 5 Ledyard Avenue, Cazenovia, NY 13035, 315/655-3393.

People Skills for Managers. Topics included in this four-day program are skill selection, listening, positive reinforcement, assertion, conflict resolution, and cooperative problem solving.
Length: 4 days
Cost: $900
Locations: San Francisco, CA; Cazenovia, NY.

UNIVERSITY OF WISCONSIN, Management Institute, 432 North Lake Street Madison, WI 53706, 800/262-6243 (outside Wisc.), 800/362-3020 (in Wisc.).

How To Work More Effectively With People. In this seminar participants learn the secrets of positive relationship building. You learn how to tune in to the needs of others, and discover how to understand and manage frustration and defensiveness in yourself and others. As participants you will become better managers of yourself and your relationships with others.
Length: 2 days
Cost: $395
Location: Madison, WI.

Notes:

Conflict Management and Negotiating

In a dynamic organization, conflict can't be avoided. Your goal should be to ensure that the outcomes of conflict are productive rather than destructive.

The suggestions in this section are divided into two parts.
Part I: Conflict Management, provides suggestions for:
- Improving Your Conflict Management Style (p. 225)
- Determining Your Approach to Conflict Situations (p. 225)
- Using Listening Skills to Reduce Conflict (p. 226)
- Addressing Conflict and Discussing the Real Reasons Underlying the Problem (p. 227)
- Resolving Conflicting Demands Among Subordinates (p. 228)
- Resolving Conflict Through Equitable Assignment Distribution (p. 228)
- Minimizing Recurrent Conflict (p. 229)

Part II: Negotiating, deals with the more specialized skills required for productive negotiation sessions:
- Developing a "Win-win" Negotiating Style (p. 230)
- Preparing Negotiation Strategies (p. 231)
- Incorporating the Techniques of Skilled Negotiators Into Your Negotiation Style (p. 232)
- Clarifying Points of View When Negotiating (p. 233)

Tips

- Use active listening skills to restate the position held on each side of the conflict. Make sure the conflict is not simply misunderstanding.

- Look for ways of reorganizing to reduce conflict. Don't assume it's an interpersonal conflict.

- Don't try to gloss over genuine differences in point of view. Clarify the differences and attempt to understand the **goals** that each party is trying to reach. Ask each party if they could help in assisting the other party to achieve its **goals** in a different way than has thus far been discussed.

- Encourage people to depersonalize the conflict; look at it as a conflict of ideas/approaches rather than people.

- **Talk about** your frustration over the conflict rather than **showing** it.

- Place yourself in the other person's situation and imagine how you would feel and react. Try to see their side before defending your own.

- Be willing to confront others when you feel they have made an error or oversight.

- With your manager, develop job coaching situations where you can test your ideas against others—and challenge other's ideas—without antagonizing them.

- When a conflict situation arises, discuss it with your manager. When you have handled it, seek feedback from him or her about how successful you were.

- In order to learn to confront rather than avoid conflict, have your manager urge you into conflict situations where you would be supported by your manager and where you would be on solid ground in opposing someone else's position.

- Bring conflict out into the open without feeling that your leadership is threatened by it. When people disagree with you, analyze the reasons for their positions.

CONFLICT MANAGEMENT
AND NEGOTIATING

- Seek feedback from peers in both formal and informal situations about your effectiveness in handling interpersonal conflict.

- Try to identify and spell out the best mutual incentives available to the parties in conflict for solving the problem. Look for solutions where both sides can win.

- At times, one party must acquiesce to the other side. If so, make the acquiescing party (yourself or others) feel worthwhile and respected rather than defeated.

- Find ways for a "win-win" rather than "win-lose" solution. Often that attitude produces surprising results.

- Ask a neutral third party to help you and the conflicting party to talk through the problem.

- Do not back down so readily that you feel others are taking advantage of you.

- Read *Getting to Yes* by Fischer and Ury.

Part I: Conflict Management

Improving Your Conflict Management Style

To improve the effectiveness of your conflict management style, you can implement the following plan.

1. Over the next few weeks, keep track of situations involving interpersonal conflict or tension, both on and off the job. Record your observations in a notebook, indicating the cause of the conflict, what occurred during the conflict situation, and the outcome of the conflict.
2. At the end of this period, analyze your observations to determine if they form a pattern. Which of the following describes you in a typical conflict situation?
   - Withdrawn—you avoid conflict altogether.
   - Agreeable—you usually allow the other party to win.
   - Disagreeable or aggressive—you promote win-lose situations.
   - Constructive—you work toward compromise.
3. Based on your analysis, decide whether you want to change your conflict resolution style and, if you do, prepare a plan of action. The suggestions in the remainder of this section provide ideas. Readings in the area of conflict management (such as those in this section) and discussions with friends, respected colleagues, and family members can provide additional ideas.
4. Implement your plan. Read it over frequently to reinforce your intentions.
5. After you have incorporated your plan into your conflict resolution style, record conflict situations you encounter for several more weeks. Compare the results of your new style to those of your old style to determine if you are able to reach satisfactory agreements with fewer negative repercussions.

Determining Your Approach to Conflict Situations

When a conflict seems likely to reduce the overall effectiveness of the organization, consider mediating the conflict. You must remember, however, that there are no guarantees that you will be successful in your undertaking and that becoming directly involved in such conflict situations carries a certain risk.

The first step is to consider whether you are able to and ought to remove the source of the conflict. For example, if conflicts arise from work flow problems, you might consider whether restructuring the work would remove the source of the conflict. Likewise, competition for supplies or resources can be alleviated by strictly allocating these commodities or establishing an additional buffering supply.

At times, however, it will not be feasible to remove the root of the problem. It will then be necessary to try to reduce the negative emotional charge of the situation.

Using Listening Skills to Reduce Conflict

Too often, the parties involved in an argument spend most of their time talking instead of listening. When one party is speaking, the other is busy preparing a rebuttal or thinking of additional ways to support his or her viewpoint rather than listening to what is being said.

In addition, most people have been conditioned to immediately judge the statements of others—to either agree or disagree. Frequently, a statement is judged from one point of view; the other person's perspective is not considered. Thus, true listening is not occurring; the parties hear what they expect or want to hear rather than what the speaker means to communicate.

Both of these types of behavior encourage disagreements to escalate into arguments. When neither person stops to listen, there is a good chance that agreement or compromise will be delayed or prevented. In addition, when emotions run high, people may say or do things they later regret.

Over the next month, each time you sense that an argument is about to begin, mentally switch from a defensive position to the listening mode. To accomplish this switch, try a technique called **active listening.** It involves the following steps.

1. Listen carefully to what the speaker is saying. Give the speaker your full attention, without thinking about how you are going to respond, and without judging the speaker's statements. Show that you are really listening through the use of nonverbal behavior such as leaning forward, raising your eyebrows, nodding your head, etc.
2. Ask the speaker to clarify his or her position using open-end questions starting with phrases such as:
   - Tell me about . . .
   - Explain . . .
   - How do you feel about . . .

- Describe . . .
- What . . .
- Why . . .

Avoid closed-end questions that can be answered **yes** or **no**— questions that start with words such as **is, are, could, would, do, did, and should.**

3. Periodically paraphrase what the speaker has said to ensure that you understand what was meant and to let the speaker know that you are really listening. In doing so, try to reflect the feeling as well as the content of the message. Use phrases like, "What I hear you saying is that . . . " or "It sounds like you think . . . " If the speaker disagrees with your restatement, ask him or her to clarify the statement.

4. Determine whether your interpretations are becoming more accurate as the discussion progresses. Good listening should be rewarded with comments such as, "That's exactly what I meant" and "That's right! I think you understand my problem."

5. Make a conscious effort to avoid interrupting the speaker. Mentally tally the number of times you interrupt a speaker and try to eliminate such interruptions by the end of the month.

If you are effectively applying active listening skills, your conflict situations should become less intense, and people should become more reasonable and open to listening to your point of view and compromising. You will find that you are involved in more constructive debates and fewer destructive arguments.

Addressing Conflict and Discussing the Real Reasons Underlying the Problem

If you tend to avoid conflict situations, it may be because you lack a procedure for getting to the root of the problem. The following steps will help you structure your discussion the next time you find yourself in a conflict situation:

1. Ask to talk with the other party in a nonthreatening meeting place such as his or her office or a conference room.

2. Begin the session with a statement defining the purpose of the meeting. Something like, "Jim, I asked to meet with you today to discuss the disagreement you and I are having over the Fox contract," is all you need.

3. Use active listening skills to draw out information from the other person to help pinpoint the real source of the disagreement. Active listening is discussed on pages 259-274A in the Listening section of this Handbook.

4. Once the problem is pinpointed, investigate alternative solutions to the problem, remaining nonjudgmental and entertaining all possibilities.
5. Together, evaluate the possibilities you've both generated, listing pros and cons. Remember the goal is to work *with* the other party to find the best solution for you both.
6. Once you've evaluated the alternatives, commit to a solution with the other person.
7. At this point, you should each state what the solution is and develop a plan to execute it. List out the specific action steps, assign responsibility, and set specific completion dates for each step. It is important that the execution plan be specific and that each step be measurable and attainable.
8. Develop a plan for future follow-up meetings or discussions to evaluate how things are going.

By working together with the other person to find the source of the problem and how to best resolve it, you will find it easier to address conflicts you encounter on the job.

Resolving Conflicting Demands Among Subordinates

Handling conflicts between subordinates is a sensitive issue. It's important to keep from interfering too much, but there may be times when intervention on your part is necessary. Following is a process that will help you become involved in conflict resolution without becoming overinvolved.

1. Get feedback from your subordinates on your level of involvement in their conflicts. Are you involved too much? Not enough?
2. When a conflict does arise that requires intervention, do the following:
   - Help the individuals involved to define the problem in specific, observable terms.
   - Ask the subordinates involved to meet on their own to propose solutions.
   - Then, meet with them to create a problem resolution plan. If they are unable to do this cooperatively, it may be necessary for you to step in and determine the best course of action.
   - Set up future meetings during which you will discuss how things are going and whether the chosen approach is working.

Resolving Conflict Through Equitable Assignment Distribution

If assignments are not equitably distributed, you will notice interpersonal problems developing among your employees. Workers will begin to compare their work situations, and there is likely to be increased buck-passing, quarreling, complaining, and rivalry. Following are suggestions for ensuring equitable distribution of work assignments.

1. Make a list of each employee's assignments. Then analyze the distribution of assignments considering the:
   - **Amount of work assigned to an employee.** Is it too much or too little when compared with the amount assigned to other employees?
   - **Level of the tasks.** What is the proportion of "dirty work" to challenging work, and how does it compare to that of other employees?
   - **Importance of the tasks.** What is the proportion of important, visible tasks to less important, mundane tasks, and how does it compare to that of other employees?
   - **Way in which assignments are made.** Are some employees allowed to become more involved in determining the distribution of work assignments than others are?
2. Ask subordinates for their reactions to the current distribution of assignments, considering the factors mentioned above.

If your analysis reveals any inequities in work distribution, consider shifting the current work load to alleviate the situation or make plans to assign future work in a way that evens the distribution.

Minimizing Recurrent Conflict

Recurrent conflict can have damaging repercussions on a work unit's efforts. To minimize this type of conflict, follow these guidelines.

1. List the two or three people or departments who tend to "lock horns" on the job.
2. For each source of conflict, try to determine the cause of the conflict. For example, does the conflict arise because people require the same resources at the same time? Or because people have different philosophies about how the operation should be conducted?
3. Next, analyze the problem from both parties' perspectives. Be as objective as possible, and try to understand the other parties' reasons for behaving as they do.
4. Decide if it is necessary to meet. Start the discussion by stating your goal—to reduce the conflict so that work can be accomplished more efficiently. Then ask the other parties to describe the problems from their perspectives.

Because you initiated the conflict resolution process, it is important that you take steps to manage any tension that arises.

5. Once both parties have stated their problems, move into the problem solving mode to determine ways to work together to minimize conflict in the future. In this phase, it is important that both parties remain open to compromise.

6. If the parties are able to reach agreements on ways to reduce conflict, get an agreement from them to get together periodically in the future to discuss progress and any problems that arise. Face-to-face discussions will keep conflict from escalating.

Part II: Negotiating

Developing a "Win-win" Negotiating Style

Successful negotiation, especially between parties that have ongoing interaction, involves seeking and identifying a solution that is satisfactory to both parties. This means that both parties should be open to winning on some points, compromising or losing on others, with a goal of arriving at a solution that both parties can accept and support. If a clear winner and a clear loser emerge from a negotiation session, it is possible that no one will "win" in the long run. Long-lasting hard feelings are likely to result, and the "loser" may undermine the chosen solution.

To develop a win-win style of negotiation, follow these guidelines.

1. In your next several negotiation meetings, carefully monitor any tendency to win. Look for positions proposed by the other party that you could live with. Seek an outcome that includes some of the items you want and some of the items the other party desires.

2. After each session, write down your analysis of what took place during the session. Recall both parties' initial positions and compare them to the outcome. Note the extent to which both sides compromised and the extent to which both sides "won."

Continue to strive for win-win resolutions to problems. Analyze and improve your negotiation style until you are comfortable that you no longer contribute to a win-lose attitude in negotiation sessions.

Preparing Negotiation Strategies

Professional negotiators spend a great deal of time preparing for negotiating sessions. In addition to developing their own personal strategies, they also anticipate the strategies of the other parties.

The following guidelines will help you prepare strategies for your future negotiating sessions.

1. Before attending the next situation where you are involved in negotiating, gather as much information as you can about the other party—past positions taken and indications of what his or her other viewpoint will be on the current problem. Anticipate the party's strategy and use this information to build a tentative strategy of your own.

   When you begin the negotiation session, remember that, despite your data gathering and preparation, negotiations seldom proceed as planned; therefore, it's important to remain flexible and to adapt to unforeseen circumstances.

2. After the session is over, analyze how well you anticipated the other party's strategy and adapted to unanticipated occurrences.

As your ability to anticipate the other party's strategy increases, you will note that you are better prepared for, more comfortable with, and more successful in negotiating situations.

Incorporating the Techniques of Skilled Negotiators Into Your Negotiation Style

One method of improving your negotiation skills is to observe skilled negotiators and incorporate their techniques into your own negotiation style. To use this development method, follow these guidelines.

1. Identify skilled negotiators within your organization and arrange to accompany them to several meetings involving negotiations.
2. If possible, discuss how the individuals have prepared for the sessions and what their strategies are before the sessions begin.
3. Attend the sessions and carefully observe each negotiator's approach. Meetings in which conflict is likely to occur may be particularly helpful, because they require the use of more negotiation skills. Take notes on what happens during the sessions.
4. If possible, discuss the strategies used during the meetings and the outcomes of the meetings with the individuals you accompanied.
5. Incorporate any useful techniques you discover into your own negotiation style.

Clarifying Points of View When Negotiating

If each party clearly understands the other party's point of view, the effectiveness of a negotiation session is greatly increased. Clarification during negotiation is beneficial because it:

- Improves the accuracy of your interpretations so that you and the other party spend your time debating the actual issues
- Helps you guard against emotional reactions to issues
- "Buys you time" to think through your responses

To employ clarification skills, follow these guidelines.
1. The next time you're in a negotiation situation, listen carefully to what the other person is saying.
2. Restate the speaker's message.
3. Wait for the speaker to indicate whether you have accurately interpreted the message. If not, give the speaker an opportunity to clarify the statement before moving on.

Practice this clarification exercise in your next several negotiation sessions and observe whether it results in smoother, less emotional, more productive negotiations.

Recommended Readings

Blake, Robert R., and Mouton, Jane Srygley. *Solving Costly Organizational Conflict.* San Francisco, CA: Jossey-Bass, 1985.

In this book, the authors describe a practical, tested method for reducing tensions, resolving conflicts, and establishing trust and cooperation among groups, departments, and divisions that must work together to achieve organizational goals.

Bolton, Robert. *People Skills.* New York, NY: Touchstone Books, 1986.

This communications skills handbook provides practical ideas for asserting yourself, listening to others, resolving conflicts, and working out problems with others. Chapters 8-11 cover assertion, including: developing assertiveness; impacting; submissive/assertive/aggressive communications; and effective ways of confronting defensiveness. Chapters 12-15 deal with conflict management (conflict prevention and control, handling the emotional components of conflict, and collaborative problem solving).

Bower, Sharon Anthony, and Bower, Gordon. *Asserting Yourself: A Practical Guide for Positive Change.* Reading, MA: Addison-Wesley, 1976.

A complete program for positive change is presented in this book. Using new techniques of behavior modification, readers can acquire important skills for finding out how assertive they are, improving self-esteem, coping with stress, and making more friends. The book also describes new techniques for dealing with conflict and provides useful exercises for easy practice.

Donaldson, Les. *Behavorial Supervision: Practical Ways to Change Unsatisfactory Behavior and Increase Productivity.* Reading, MA: Addison-Wesley, 1980.

This book describes how supervisors and managers on any level can deal with and correct subordinates' behavioral problems. It explains how techniques of behavioral change can be used to deal with uncooperative subordinates.

Fink, Steven. *Crisis Managment: Planning for the Inevitable.* New York, NY: AMACOM, 1986.

The author uses actual crises drawn from his own extensive hands-on management experience to vividly demonstrate how to identify, isolate, and manage a crisis; how managers can forecast their next crises and develop critical contingency plans; and how any individual at any rung of the management ladder can strive to create achievement out of adversity. The book gives four examples of actual mega-crises and the unfolding of each crisis.

Fisher, Roger, and Ury, William. *Getting to Yes: Negotiating Agreement Without Giving In.* New York, NY: Penguin Books, 1983.

A straightforward, universally applicable method for negotiating personal and professional disputes without getting taken—and without getting nasty. This book offers the reader a concise, step-by-step, proven strategy for coming to mutually acceptable agreements in every sort of conflict.

Hauck, Paul A. *Overcoming Frustration and Anger.* New York, NY: Institute for Advanced Study in Rational Psychotherapy, 1977.

Hauck illustrates the dynamics of anger with short case histories and offers specific techniques for being firm without being aggressive or hostile.

Jakubowski, Patricia, and Lange, Arthur J. *The Assertive Option: Your Rights and Responsibilities.* Champaign, IL: Research Press, 1978.

The reader is given specific techniques that can be put into practice to change the thoughts, feelings, and behaviors that support nonassertiveness and aggressiveness to those which are more assertive. Major emphasis in the book is on providing a process or a collection of new skills which can be used in those situations the reader does not handle as effectively as he/she would like.

Judson, Arnold S. *A Manager's Guide to Making Changes.* New York, NY: John Wiley & Sons, 1966.

This book is designed to help every manager and administrator develop a better understanding of the problems created by the introduction of change. It combines a practical consideration and analysis of the problems of instituting changes within organizations with some of the useful insights into these problems and some of their possible solutions.

Kotter, J.P., and Schlesinger, L.A. "Choosing Strategies for Change." *Harvard Business Review,* March/April 1979, pp. 106-114.

Organizations by their very nature must change; but many people, especially at work, feel threatened by any alteration in the status quo. Therefore, while the manager is implementing the change, he or she must also overcome the resistance to it. In this article, the authors list four reasons that people resist change, suggest ways of dealing with that resistance, and present a guide to the kinds of approaches that work best with different types of opposition.

Likert, Rensis, and Likert, Jane G. *New Ways of Managing Conflict Between Groups*. New York, NY: McGraw-Hill, 1976.

The authors of this seminal work apply modern organizational theory to the management of the kind of conflict which occurs within or between organizations. They examine the different ways the conflict arises and analyze how it can be minimized and controlled. The kinds of conflict that arise between line and staff, research and development, and engineering, manufacturing, sales, union, and management personnel are covered, with the characteristics of each fully described.

Turner, Steve, and Weed, Frank. *Conflict in Organizations: Practical Solutions Any Manager Can Use*. Englewood Cliffs, NJ: Prentice-Hall, 1983.

This practical guidebook offers managers a new method for eliminating organizational conflict—effectively! It gives the basic tools, including worksheets, needed to effectively think through conflict problems and provides step-by-step guidelines for developing and implementing truly workable solutions.

Suggested Seminars

The seminars listed here were selected for their appeal to a managerial audience and have received good to excellent ratings from managers attending them.

Because of the dynamic nature of the seminar marketplace, some seminars may have been added, upgraded, or replaced, and others may no longer be offered. Additional information about these seminars may be obtained by calling the vendor directly, or through Seminar Clearinghouse International, a subscriber organization located in St. Paul, Minnesota. Call 612/293-1004 for information.

DESIGNED LEARNING, 1009 Park Avenue, Plainfield, NJ 07060, 201/754-5100.

Managing Differences & Agreement. Program topics include: diagnosing the causes of conflict; developing commitment to an agreement through assertiveness, confrontation, negotiation, listening.
Length: 3 days
Cost: $775
Location: Plainfield, NJ.

INTERSKILL INCORPORATED, 256 1st Avenue North, #400, Minneapolis, MN 55401, 612/545-9158.

Negotiating Agreement. Participants attending this seminar learn standard negotiating strategies and why they don't always work, why negotiating agreement is different and why it works, four basic tools for negotiating agreements, and stages of a negotiation and what to do in each stage.
Length: 3 days
Cost: $695
Locations: San Francisco, CA; Washington, DC.

KARRASS SEMINARS, 1633 Stanford Street, Santa Monica, CA 90404, 213/453-1806.

Effective Negotiating. A two-day program that includes: using hidden leverage; strengths and weaknesses; what your opponent really wants; long-term relationships versus one shot deals; better agreements right now!—both sides win; one win, do well for yourself; personal negotiating; how to set and achieve your targets; using your strength in business, legal conflicts, engineering specifications, personal needs and transactions; how other cultures negotiate; traps and tactics; countermeasures; dealing with deadlocks; guarding against tricks; and more subtleties—more skills.

Length: 2 days
Cost: $550
Locations: Irvine, CA; Los Angeles, CA; San Francisco, CA; Miami, FL; Kansas City, MO; Atlantic City, NJ; Buffalo, NY; New York, NY; Cincinnati, OH; Cleveland, OH; Dallas, TX; Houston, TX. For additional locations, contact the vendor.

LMA INC., 365 Melendy Road, P.O. Box 140, Milford, NH 03055, 603/672-0355.

Positive Negotiation. Participants learn how to work most effectively in formal and informal, internal and external situations—where there are common conflicting interests. Emphasis is on how to plan and manage the negotiation and how to best influence based on skills used by the most effective negotiators.
Length: 5 days
Cost: $950
Locations: Manchester, NH; Merrimack, NH; Nashua, NH.

NEGOTIATION INSTITUTE, 230 Park Avenue, New York, NY 10169, 212/986-5555.

Art of Negotiating. Participants in this program will gain valuable insight into the "Art of Negotiating." Topics include: getting ready to negotiate; using and countering the major strategies; learning the strategies of your specialized field; negotiation "climates"—how they control negotiations; non-verbal negotiating; making the agreement stick; how to get what you want—Nierenberg's need theory of negotiation; function of questions; and other methods for preparing creatively.
Length: 2 days
Cost: $595
Locations: San Francisco, CA; Denver, CO; Washington, DC; Atlanta, GA; Chicago, IL; Boston, MA; St. Louis, MO; New York, NY; Philadelphia, PA; Dallas, TX; Seattle, WA.

POWER NEGOTIATIONS INSTITUTE, 633 Skokie Boulevard, Northbrook, IL 60062, 312/564-9155.

New Perspectives on Negotiating. This program covers the architectural design for satisfying outcomes, dimensional negotiating strategies, and the optimal strategic negotiator.
Length: 1 day
Cost: $295
Locations: Chicago, IL; New York, NY.

UNIVERSITY OF WISCONSIN, Management Institute, 432 North Lake Street, Madison, WI 53706, 800/262-6243 (outside Wisc.), 800/362-3020 (in Wisc.).

How to Manage by Negotiation. In this three-day program, participants learn to understand themselves in conflict situations. Case materials give hands-on experience in analyzing conflict situations and in developing negotiation techniques.

Length: 3 days
Cost: $495
Location: Madison, WI.

Interpersonal Skills

Notes:

Notes:

FACTOR 4

Communications Skills

Employees frequently complain that their managers are poor communicators. This is not surprising, because many managers are promoted due to their technical rather than communications skills. Yet the majority of a manager's day is spent communicating or interpreting the communications of others.

Effective communication is a challenge in this age of information. Yet the manager who masters communications skills harnesses a great deal of power—the power to get things done through others.

This power is gained by:
- Knowing who needs what information and communicating that information in a concise, timely way
- Knowing when and how to listen, to ensure that you are informed of your organization's problem as well as its successes
- Choosing and effectively using the most appropriate communications medium— oral or written—depending on who will receive the information and how it will be used
- Helping others communicate effectively, to ensure that information is sent and received at all organizational levels

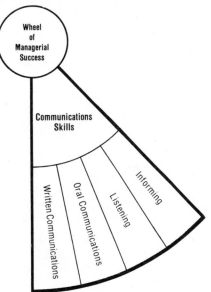

Communications Skills

This section presents communications development activities in the following four communications areas.

Informing: passing on decisions, changes, and other relevant information to the right people at the right times

Listening: actively attending to and demonstrating understanding of the comments and questions of others

Oral Communications: using effective verbal communications in one-to-one and group settings

Written Communications: writing clearly and concisely, using appropriate style, format, grammar, and tone in formal and informal business communications

Informing

Suppose you received a memo that contained information you felt would be of interest to your subordinates. Would you:
   a. Route the memo as written, including parts you felt weren't suitable for the subordinates?
   b. Have the relevant portions retyped and routed?
   c. Refrain from routing the memo because of the unsuitable content?

If you chose **b,** you show an awareness of subordinates' need to be informed about issues and topics that concern them. Whether the information appears in a memo, a piece of technical literature, or a policy statement, find a way—either written or oral—to make it known to those who could benefit from it. The same holds true for keeping other departments and your supervisor informed of activities and plans that are likely to affect them.

This section contains three parts.

Part I: Keeping Subordinates Informed

Part II: Keeping Other Departments Informed

Part III: Keeping Your Superior Informed

Tips

- Institute a departmental bulletin board to keep people up-to-date on both personal and professional items of interest.

- Hold periodic staff meetings to share information about recent developments in the organization.

- For the purpose of informal communication, hold monthly breakfast meetings which have no agenda.

- Talk to subordinates about what additional information they need to perform their roles effectively.

- Keep your boss and subordinates up-to-date by submitting a monthly activity report for your area.

- Ask your manager and subordinates for feedback on the information you pass along. Is it too much, not enough, just right? What changes do they request?

- Alert your manager to possible implications of events occurring either inside or outside of the organization. Don't assume that your manager is aware of those implications.

- Make a list of the key organizational people upon whom your success depends, and make a special effort to keep them informed.

- Ask your boss which key people you should keep informed.

- Copy your boss on all correspondence to managers in the organization at his or her level or higher.

- Ask what are specific key indicators of which your boss wants to be kept abreast.

- Inform your manager about any deviations from plan.

- Ask your manager about any perceived "surprises" in your area and then look for ways to avoid any recurrences.

- Don't gloss over anything that goes wrong in your area. Report the situation as accurately as possible.

- Talk with peers or people in other departments about "communications breakdowns." Devise ways to avoid them.

- Always double check all written communications before mailing; also, ask yourself, "Who else should know about this?"

- For one month, copy **someone** on every document you write.

- Use the "informal organization" as a way of keeping others informed. "Wander around," have coffee with people, ask them questions, etc.

- At the beginning of a project, specify preparation dates for interim reports and then deliver them on time to the appropriate people.

- Keep a note pad by your telephone and, during calls, take notes to be routed to others.

- At the end of every day ask yourself what occurred that should be reported to other people.

- Make a point of updating the appropriate people even when nothing new has developed.

- Ask your secretary to suggest who should be copied on documents you produce.

- Appoint a "recorder" for every meeting you conduct and have the minutes distributed to the appropriate people.

- Respond promptly to notes, letters, and other requests so people know what you are doing about their communications.

Part I: Keeping Subordinates Informed

Conveying a Lot of Information to Others

The flow of information in an organization is its life force; to maintain and improve the vitality of the organization, information must flow freely upward, laterally, and downward.

The following information flow checklist can help you keep in mind the many types of information that should "keep moving" in all three directions.

Your Boss

_____ Monthly status reports
_____ Project progress reports
_____ Work items behind schedule
_____ Department/organization problems or concerns
_____ Possible staffing changes
_____ Communications with your boss's peers and superiors
_____ Vacation or travel plans

Your Peers

_____ Procedural or technical changes or innovations
_____ Upcoming projects affecting them
_____ Reorganizations within your department
_____ Your department's objectives

Your Subordinates

_____ Company policy changes
_____ Upcoming projects
_____ Organizational events
_____ Development opportunities

You may wish to add to this checklist if you have additional communication needs specific to your department or organization.

Informing Subordinates by Sharing Information

For subordinates who don't have access to organizational correspondence, a program to disseminate such information can contribute a great deal to their development and awareness of the organization.

Following are suggestions for sharing written information that you receive or find through research.

- When you receive an informational memo, consider whether the information would be useful to your subordinates. If so, route the memo as is or change it to fit the circumstances. For example, if parts of a memo are appropriate for subordinates but other parts are not, highlight the appropriate parts and have them retyped and routed. This will help increase subordinates' awareness of organizational events and decisions.
- As you read technical, professional, or community literature, think of others who may be interested in the information. You may want to route articles or post clippings on the bulletin board.
- If you route policy memos generated by someone else in the organization, you can help your employees understand the policies by:
    - Attaching a note that explains the thrust of the policies
    - Highlighting the parts of the policies most relevant to them
    - Explaining why the policies are being made (if you don't know the reasons for the policies, find out before routing the policy memos to your department)
- Consider establishing a departmental bulletin board. Encourage people to post items of interest to others. Also use the bulletin board to announce personal or company events and activities.

    Ask someone to volunteer to be in charge of the bulletin board to ensure that the items posted are current and that the board doesn't become cluttered.

Informing Subordinates Through Oral Communications

Some information is best passed on to subordinates orally, especially if employees are likely to have questions about the information or a need to discuss their concerns or reactions. Following are methods for using oral communications to keep employees informed.

- Make yourself available to employees. Let them know that you support them in asking questions about the department, the organization, and their own jobs.
- Consider holding department-/division-wide informational meetings periodically. Invite your entire staff, including clerical and support personnel. Use this meeting to inform your employees of the organization's plans and goals and the progress they are making in helping to attain these goals. Ask your staff to comment on the organization and to offer suggestions for improvement.

This process helps employees understand the impact of their work and allows you to make full use of your resources as you search for innovative methods for attaining your goals.

Informing Subordinates of Organizational Events

Lack of information often causes anxiety. By keeping subordinates apprised of what is happening within the organization and the reasons for these occurrences, you minimize the time employees spend trying to discover this information for themselves. Following are guidelines for two specific situations.

- If you must delegate an "action item," a task with rigid time constraints, explain the reason for the deadline and the urgency of performing the task. Taking a moment to explain the rationale helps reduce the time the employee spends wondering what the big rush is about.

- If a major change in another department will impact your department, keep rumors to a minimum by providing information to your employees before the grapevine does. Let them know what the change is and how it will affect your department. Encourage employees to come to you with their questions and concerns.

Part II: Keeping Other Departments Informed

Informing Other Departments of Your Department's Activities and Plans

Frequently, managers make the mistake of assuming that what happens in their own area has little impact on activities in other areas of the business. Although it is possible for a department to function relatively independently, departments that do so are usually not functioning with maximum effectiveness and efficiency.

By facilitating the flow of information between departments, you help coordinate your department's activities with those of other departments. This is one of the first steps in assuming a broader perspective of the organization and its functions—a view that is necessary for managerial advancement.

To open communications channels, get to know people in other departments. Find out about their current priorities and problems and the directions they foresee for their groups. Look for areas in which your responsibilities overlap with theirs. Then discuss how you might establish a process for communicating with each other. Following are three suggestions for establishing communications.

- When you write or receive a memo, ask yourself whether the contents would be of interest to someone in another department. If so, route the memo. Get in the habit of writing "FYI" (For Your Information) at the top of memos you route; this indicates that the memo is being routed for informational purposes rather than action.
- Analyze the coordination and communications problems you encounter. Determine whether some of these might be solved by an interdepartmental work group. If so, take the initiative to form the group. Bring the idea to the attention of your superior, volunteering

yourself or someone else in the department as chairperson, or, if appropriate, call the meeting yourself.

- If you find yourself saying, "This is not my responsibility," remind yourself that you are in the process of developing a broader organizational perspective. Managers who do not concern themselves with matters beyond their assigned duties are forfeiting opportunities to prepare for advancement.

Part III: Keeping Your Superior Informed

Evaluating Your Communications With Your Superior

Superiors differ in the amount of information they wish to receive from subordinates and the degree to which they wish to be consulted on decisions. The following exercise will help you determine the degree of upward communication you have established with your superior.

Does one or more of the following statements describe your communications with your superior?
1. You assume your superior is uninterested in most of what goes on in your department.
2. You avoid giving your superior bad news.
3. You tend to wait for your superior's decision instead of voicing recommendations of your own.

If any of these statements are true, your superior is probably uninformed about many activities at your level and lower. Such blocks in communications can impede an organization's progress toward its goals. The remaining guidelines in this section are provided to help you break down these communications blocks.

Establishing Communications With a New Boss

Adjusting to a new boss, whether because of a corporate reorganization or a move to a different company, takes some energy and effort on your part. The following procedure will help you establish communications guidelines for your new relationship.

1. Request a meeting to discuss your mutual expectations. Of course, timing is important here. If a reorganization has just occurred, wait until your new boss is settled in and is somewhat familiar with the new organization. If you've changed companies or departments, you'll want to become familiar with your new responsibilities before requesting this meeting. (If communication is a priority for your new boss, he or she may initiate the meeting.)

2. Clarify the amount of authority your boss expects you to assume for your various responsibilities—whether you are to proceed on your own, proceed but inform your boss of what you are doing, or seek approval before proceeding.

3. Determine how your boss wants you to submit information (in writing, orally, with what frequency, etc.).

4. Starting with this meeting, work to establish a relationship in which you feel free to go to your boss with both positive and negative information. Although it is important that you be able to act independently, let your superior know when you are working on a major problem. For example, most superiors would rather know that sales are falling below forecast—and that you are trying to increase them—than find out after the fact. Follow the rule of "no surprises" when communicating with your boss.

Supplying the Appropriate Amount of Detail

Although most managers make the mistake of supplying too little information to their superiors, some have the opposite problem; they supply too much information. Their reasons for doing so include:

- Assuming that the superior needs every technical detail to understand why a decision was made
- Assuming that details will impress the superior
- Excitement about the project, including the technical details

Because superiors must manage their time just as you must in order to accomplish their tasks, it is important to use your judgment in deciding what information you should pass on. The suggestions in the "Handling Detail" section of this Handbook provide numerous tips on determining and supplying the appropriate amount of detail.

Informing Your Superior of the Effects of Decisions Made By Upper Management

If your superior or other upper-level managers are considering a decision that will have negative effects on your area, it's important that you inform your superior of the possible ramifications. Your superior's decision may not change, but it should be made with full knowledge of the consequences. It's possible that a lack of information from lower levels may be the reason that the decision is being considered.

Recommended Readings

To date we have not located readings on this topic that we feel comfortable recommending. We welcome any inputs you may have in this area.

Suggested Seminars

The seminars listed here were selected for their appeal to a managerial audience and have received good to excellent ratings from managers attending them.

Because of the dynamic nature of the seminar marketplace, some seminars may have been added, upgraded, or replaced, and others may no longer be offered. Additional information about these seminars may be obtained by calling the vendor directly, or through Seminar Clearinghouse International, a subscriber organization located in St. Paul, Minnesota. Call 612/293-1004 for information.

COLORADO STATE UNIVERSITY, Office of Special Programs, E-106 Rockwell Hall, Fort Collins, CO 80523, 303/491-7571.

Effective On-the-job Communication: How To Work More Successfully With Others. Some of the key topics included in this one-day program are: how effective communication works; developing rapport and a "common language" with anyone; assumptions can trap you; how to be clear; make the most of difficult communication situations; managing conflict; and maintaining positive relationships.
Length: 1 day
Cost: $95
Location: Northglenn, CO.

GAVIN-HODGES ASSOCIATES, P.O. Box 332, Glenside, PA 19038, 215/247-7420.

Planning Communications To Support Organizational Objectives. This two-day program enables participants to analyze and increase conceptual understanding of planned communications process, and it provides training in specific skills needed to implement communication plans.
Length: 2 days
Cost: $495
Locations: San Diego, CA; Chicago, IL; New York, NY; Dallas, TX.

NTL INSTITUTE, P.O. Box 9155, Rosslyn Station, Arlington, VA 22209, 703/527-1500.

Communication Workshop: Learning By Doing. The purpose of this seven-day program is to provide participants an opportunity to learn how to improve communication, practice skills involved in communicating and listening, understand problems of organizational communication, explore the effect of stress on interpersonal communication, practice giving and receiving feedback, experience communication that leads to

feeling understood, and gain greater awareness of your own communication style and your impact on others.
Length: 7 days
Cost: $795
Location: Bethel, ME.

UNIVERSITY OF WISCONSIN, Management Institute, 432 North Lake Street, Madison, WI 53706 800/262-6243 (outside Wisc.), 800/362-3020 (in Wisc.).

Improving Communication Skills. The topics covered in this three-day program include barriers to communications, written communication, one-on-one, giving a talk, and conducting meetings.
Length: 3 days
Cost: $495
Locations: Madison, WI; Milwaukee, WI.

VANDERBILT UNIVERSITY, Owen Graduate School of Management, Executive Programs, Nashville, TN 37203, 615/322-2513.

Effective Communication Skills: Written and Face-to-Face. Three-day program emphasizing building communication rapport skills, establishing successful business relationships, listening skills, what makes writing work, and developing a personal action plan.
Length: 3 days
Cost: $725
Location: Nashville, TN.

Listening

*A good listener is not only popular everywhere, but after
a while he knows something.*

—Wilson Mizner

Listening is indeed an effective learning tool, and a skill that managers must develop for maximum competence. In your conversations with subordinates, superiors, groups, and colleagues, your listening skills play as important a role as your decision-making and problem-solving abilities do.

As used in this Handbook, the term **listening** means not only hearing a speaker's words but also interpreting his or her nonverbal messages (crossed arms, drumming fingers, and so on). **Active listening** is a kind of listening that involves interpreting the speaker's verbal and nonverbal messages and asking clarifying questions throughout the conversation.

Other aspects of active listening covered in this section include:

- Evaluating Your Listening Skills (p. 263)
- Listening for the Total Message (p. 264)
- Interpreting Nonverbal Messages (p. 264)
- Using Nonverbal Attending (p. 264)
- Using Open-end Probes to Encourage Communications (p. 265)
- Using Paraphrasing to Improve Communications (p. 266)
- Using Reflective Statements to Open Communications Channels (p. 267)
- Using Summary Statements to Increase Understanding (p. 268)
- Listening to People Without Interrupting (p. 269)
- Listening Willingly to Subordinates' Concerns (p. 269)
- Listening Willingly to Subordinates' Disagreements (p. 270)

Tips

- Ask for feedback from others about your listening skills and how you could improve them.

- Practice using your listening skills at home and with friends.

- Take a course in active listening.

- Avoid answering the phone or sorting through your in-basket when talking with others.

- Reschedule a conversation if you cannot give your undivided attention.

- Avoid reacting emotionally to positions with which you disagree.

- Read and apply the suggestions made in the chapters on active listening in *People Skills* by Robert Bolton.

- Always follow the order "hear, understand, interpret, respond"; don't jump from "hear" to "respond" without making **sure** you understand.

- Try to pick up on the feeling as well as the content of the message.

- Focus your attention on getting and understanding someone's meaning instead of formulating your response.

- Avoid thinking about what you are going to say next while others are speaking.

- Avoid interrupting people until they have finished making their points.

- When disagreeing with someone, summarize what you think their position is before responding.

- Ask open-end questions to draw out a person's thoughts and feelings by using phrases beginning with what, how, why, describe, explain, etc.

- In meetings, paraphrase what others have said when clarification becomes necessary.

- Avoid closed-end questions that can be answered with a "yes" or a "no."

- Reflect what you think is needed to assure the speaker that the message is being received.

- Use nonverbal behavior to show that you are listening.

- Attend to nonverbal behavior to assess how a person is feeling.

- Maintain good eye contact without staring.

- Sit or stand squarely facing the other person. Lean forward to show interest.

Evaluating Your Listening Skills

How well do you listen when someone else speaks? Complete the following evaluation exercise after a:

- Conversation with a subordinate who has a problem
- Conversation with a subordinate who is passing on information
- Conversation with your superior
- Group problem-solving session in which you are very concerned about the decisions being made
- Negotiation session
- Casual conversation
- Discussion with a colleague

Evaluation Checklist

Did you frequently *(circle appropriate response):*

Interrupt?	**Yes/No**
Show impatience as you waited for the person to finish speaking?	**Yes/No**
Suggest solutions before the problem was fully explained?	**Yes/No**
Misinterpret what was said (hear what you wanted or expected to hear rather than what was meant) such that the speaker corrected your interpretation?	**Yes/No**
Demonstrate by your gestures (leaning back, looking bored, and so forth) that you were interested in what was being said?	**Yes/No**
Spend a great deal more time talking than listening?	**Yes/No**
Find that your mind often wandered to other subjects, causing you to miss what was being said?	**Yes/No**
Think about what you would say next rather than about what the speaker was saying?	**Yes/No**

Listening for the Total Message

Effective listening goes beyond hearing the words and facts the speaker communicates. It also includes processing the information to determine the total message. The following techniques can help you process a speaker's words.

- Listen for main thoughts or ideas. This is especially important with people who include a great deal of extraneous detail in their messages or who tend to ramble.
- Attempt to determine the speaker's frame of reference for what is said. What information forms the basis for the ideas?
- Try to view the thoughts and ideas from the speaker's perspective. Why does that person think the way he or she does about a subject?
- To increase your empathy for a speaker, try to feel the same feelings the speaker has about the subject.

Interpreting Nonverbal Messages

When listening, make a habit of paying attention to speakers' nonverbal messages as well their verbal messages. This will help you understand the total message. Nonverbal messages are conveyed by:

- Clenched fists (anger)
- Crossed arms (distance, resistance to negotiation)
- Hand on chin (thinking)
- Facial expressions (a variety of emotions, depending on the expression)
- Drumming fingers (impatience)

Using Nonverbal Attending

Nonverbal attending is nonverbal behavior that lets the other person know you are listening. It is important because it:

- Sets a comfortable tone
- Encourages the other person to keep talking
- Shows concern and interest
- Signals the speaker that you are following the conversation

To improve your nonverbal attending, try to increase your use of the following behaviors when listening to others:

- Move from behind the desk
- Maintain eye contact
- Lean forward slightly
- Allow pauses—don't feel you must speak when the other person pauses to collect his or her thoughts
- Raise your eyebrows when the speaker makes significant points
- Smile when the speaker uses humor
- Nod to indicate that you understand or agree

Using Open-end Probes to Encourage Communications

The open-end probe is a question that allows the other person to talk at length; it can't be answered yes or no. An open-end probe begins with words such as: Tell me about, why, how, explain, and describe. This type of question:

- Provides an invitation to talk
- Encourages the other person to "open up"
- Allows the other person to expand on a topic in a comprehensive way

- Lets the other person know that his or her thinking matters to you
- "Loosens up" quiet or reticent people
- Helps the other person vent anger and other negative emotions

The following are examples of open-end probes.

> **Subordinate:** I think it was a mistake to give Harry
>   the assignment.
> **Manager:** Tell me why you believe Harry can't do
>   the job.

> **Peer:** That's the craziest thing I've ever heard! If
>   you think that plan will work, you must be
>   out of your mind!
> **Peer:** What makes you say that?

To increase your use of open-end probes:
1. For a day, keep track of the number of open-end probes you use in your discussions with others.
2. Over the next month, consciously work to increase the number of open-end probes you use. If you are uncomfortable with this technique at first, you might want to begin by working with a peer or subordinate with whom you have a good working relationship. Then, when you have gained confidence, try the technique with others.

Using Paraphrasing to Improve Communications

A paraphrase is a brief rephrasing of information given by the other person. It states the essence of the content in the listener's own words. Generally, paraphrases differ from reflective statements in that reflective statements involve emotions and feelings, while paraphrases involve information, ideas, facts, and opinions.

Paraphrasing is important because it:
- Shows that you are listening and that you understand what the speaker is saying
- Helps you ensure that your interpretation of the message is correct
- Allows the speaker to explore the issue more fully

Following is an example of paraphrasing:

Manager: I can't figure out what to do with Pierce. He's bright, but he thinks he has the answer to everything. Usually he suggests something very different from what we're doing, or an idea that would require us to change our methods or work up some new gadget or form that would take time and money.

Peer: You think his ideas are too novel and would require too much deviation from what you're used to doing.

To increase your use of paraphrasing:
1. For a week, keep track of the number of times you use paraphrasing each day during discussions with other people.
2. Over the next three months, consciously work to increase the number of times you paraphrase speakers' comments. If you are uncomfortable with this technique at first, you might want to begin by working with a peer or subordinate with whom you have a good working relationship. Then, when you have gained confidence, try the technique with others.

Using Reflective Statements to Open Communications Channels

Reflective statements are short, declarative statements that repeat the speaker's emotions or feelings without indicating agreement or disagreement. These statements help open communications channels by:
- Creating strong rapport
- Causing the speaker to feel understood
- Helping the speaker further explore the issue or topic
- Helping the speaker vent emotions or "let off steam"

Following are examples of the effective use of reflective statements:

Manager: Since I've become a unit manager, I'm not sure how I'm doing. I don't know if I'm really in control. Sometimes I think I made the wrong decision in accepting this promotion.

Peer: You're worried about making it in your new position.

Subordinate: I'm stuck on the budget report, and I'll tell you why. I can't get any of the information from Thompson. I've asked him for the figures I need several times, but he keeps putting me off. I don't know if he's trying to sabotage me or what, but he's doing everything he can to create problems.

Manager: You're pretty ticked off at Thompson.

To increase your use of reflective statements:

1. For a week, keep track of the number of statements you use each day when other people discuss subjects involving emotions and feelings with you.

2. Over the next three months, consciously work to increase the number of reflective statements you use. If you are uncomfortable with this technique at first, you might want to begin by working with a peer or subordinate with whom you have a good working relationship. Then, when you have gained confidence, try the technique with others.

Using Summary Statements to Increase Understanding

A summary statement is a brief restatement of the core themes and feelings the speaker has expressed during a long conversation. The statement should not imply evaluation or agreement.

Summary statements increase understanding because they:

- Help the speaker identify the key elements of his or her situation
- Show that you are making an effort to understand the speaker's point of view
- Promote further discussion of the problem

Following are examples of summary statements:

- "It sounds like your main concern is lack of cooperation from quality control."
- "As I understand it, Charlie, you think the problem with the first line supervisors is their perception that they do not have enough responsibility and authority."

To develop your skill in using summary statements:

1. Practice by developing statements for discussions and speeches you see on TV or hear on the radio.

2. When you are comfortable that you can restate core themes and feelings in a natural manner, move on to use summary statements during meetings and discussions at work. Increase your use of these statements until you feel you use them regularly and appropriately.

Listening to People Without Interrupting

One of the keys to being a good listener is to allow the other person to make his or her point before presenting your own. If you find that you tend to interrupt others when they are speaking, try these guidelines:

- Over the next month, ask others from time to time to count the number of times you interrupt them in various conversations, both one-to-one and in group settings.
- Analyze each incident, asking yourself the following questions:
  - Who were you talking to?
  - What was the situation?
  - What was the topic of discussion?
- If your analysis reveals that you tend to interrupt others only in certain situations (you tend to interrupt when talking with a certain individual or about a certain issue, for example), make an effort each time you are in that situation to curb your tendency to interrupt.
- If no pattern develops, just be aware that you need to become more patient with others, allowing them to finish speaking before asserting your point of view.

As you implement your new behaviors, seek feedback from others on whether or not your interrupting has decreased.

Listening Willingly to Subordinates' Concerns

The last time you talked to a friend or colleague about work frustrations, were you looking for advice or just a willing listener? Chances are, you wanted a sounding board—someone to hear what you were saying and understand—not someone who would try to solve all your problems for you.

Subordinates, too, occasionally need to express their concerns or frustrations about their workloads, specific projects, coworkers, or other job-related matters. They're likely to be looking for a sounding board, not someone to solve their problems.

On such occasions, you can be most helpful by simply listening and showing empathy, understanding, and encouragement through the use of reflective statements. (See the suggestions in this section.)

In addition, you may want to analyze the balance between the amount of time you spend talking and the amount you spend listening. Although it feels great to command the attention of others, too much talking can isolate you from the communication you need to function in your role.

To analyze your talking-listening balance, try this technique:
1. Over the next two weeks, monitor your talking-listening ratio during conversations with subordinates. You may want to use a tape recorder in meetings or discussions to determine your ratio.
2. Review your data and determine the trend. If you find that you talk more than 50 percent of the time, you will probably want to improve the ratio.
3. Use the listening techniques described in this section to decrease your percentage of talking time and increase your percentage of listening time.
4. Continue to monitor your talking-listening ratio for an additional two weeks by spot-checking conversations or meetings to make certain that you are talking less than 50 percent of the time.

Listening Willingly to Subordinates' Disagreements

How do you react when a subordinate disagrees with your point of view? It can be tempting to assume that you've heard that argument before and counter it before the employee has finished explaining. A subordinate who can express disagreement with management demonstrates the valuable quality of independent thinking. You can encourage this quality by listening willingly when your subordinates disagree with you.

A good way to show willingness to listen to disagreements is to use summary statements. (Refer to the suggestion on summary statements in this section for examples.) Next time a subordinate disagrees with you, try this approach:
1. Wait until the person has finished speaking, even if you're sure you understand the argument.
2. Restate the main points of the employee's argument.
3. Ask the employee to verify the accuracy of your statement and to clarify it if necessary.
4. Then—and only then—state specifically which points you disagree with and why.

While you may not change your position any more frequently using this technique, subordinates will feel that you have considered their input and understand their point of view.

Recommended Readings

Atwater, Eastwood. *I Hear You: Listening Skills to Make You a Better Manager.* Englewood Cliffs, NJ: Prentice-Hall, 1982.

This book explains the attitudes and techniques required for effective listening and provides suggestions and exercises for improving listening habits. Areas discussed include distinguishing between hearing and listening, nonreflective listening, reflective listening, nonverbal communication, remembering what you hear, and the do's and don'ts of listening.

Bolton, Robert. *People Skills.* New York, NY: Touchstone Books, 1986.

Chapters 3 through 7 of this communications skills handbook explain how communications can be improved through effective listening. They describe skills such as attending, paraphrasing, reflecting, and reading body language. They also give practical suggestions on how to incorporate these skills into everyday communications.

Burley-Allen, Madelyn. *Listening: The Forgotten Skill.* New York, NY: John Wiley & Sons, 1982.

This book describes a program to help you acquire and use active and productive listening skills. It makes extensive use of examples and exercises and explains how to deal with conflict, prevent misunderstandings, solve problems, and confront others effectively. Among the topics addressed are projecting interest, overcoming language barriers, interpreting body language, asking constructive and nonthreatening questions, and getting others to listen to you.

Garner, Alan. *Conversationally Speaking.* New York, NY: McGraw-Hill, 1981.

Chapter 1 of this book discusses asking effective questions. It covers closed versus open questions as well as mistakes commonly made in asking questions. Chapter 3 gives suggestions on how to listen so others will talk and focuses on active listening techniques.

Glatthorn, Allan A., and Adams, Herbert R. *Listening Your Way to Management Success.* Glenview, IL: Scott, Foresman, and Company, 1984.

This book focuses on how to listen critically, analytically, and creatively in both individual and group interaction. Among the topics addressed are comprehending the message, listening and responding to criticism and praise, listening during meetings, and listening to persuasive messages.

Gordon, Thomas. *Leader Effectiveness Training*. New York, NY: Bantam Books, 1980.

Chapters 4 and 5 of this book describe the art of effective listening. Passive and active listening and acknowledgement responses are discussed and illustrated through the use of clear examples. Road blocks to effective listening are also explained. The author gives helpful suggestions on how to develop and implement effective listening skills.

McKay, Matthew; David, Martha; and Fanning, Patrick. *Messages: The Communication Skills Book*. Oakland, CA: New Harbinger Press, 1983.

This book gathers the most essential communications skills into one volume, with many examples and exercises. It begins with basic skills such as listening and expressing, followed by advanced skills such as body language and paralanguage. Also included are conflict skills (i.e., assertiveness, negotiating), social skills (making contact), and public skills such as public speaking.

Suggested Seminars

The seminars listed here were selected for their appeal to a managerial audience and have received good to excellent ratings from managers attending them.

Because of the dynamic nature of the seminar marketplace, some seminars may have been added, upgraded, or replaced, and others may no longer be offered. Additional information about these seminars may be obtained by calling the vendor directly, or through Seminar Clearinghouse International, a subscriber organization located in St. Paul, Minnesota. Call 612/293-1004 for information.

COLLEGE OF ST. THOMAS, The Management Center, 2115 Summit Avenue, St. Paul, MN 55105, 612/647-5219.

Effective Listening Skills. This one-day seminar includes topics such as: listening to what your employees really are saying; four critical blocks to effective listening and how to eliminate them; non-verbal clues; negotiating for mutual comprehension; when to listen, when to talk; and what to do when passivity and dependency are masked as listening.
Length: 1 day
Cost: $90
Location: Minneapolis, MN.

COMMUNISPOND, INC., 485 Lexington Avenue, New York, NY 10017, 212/687-8040

One-to-one Communication Skills. Participants in this program identify and practice communication skills. Program topics include: participating in listening exercises; learning to use the energy of the employees' emotions/perceptions; planning a supervisor-initiated meeting regarding employee conduct; practicing one-to-one communications skills to influence employees to change their behavior without resenting their managers; and applying those skills in working with outside suppliers, customers.
Length: 2 days
Cost: $950
Locations: Newport Beach, CA; Chicago, IL; New York, NY; Dallas, TX.

PARTRAINING CORPORATION, 4936 President's Way, Tucker, GA 30084, 404/493-7188.

Listening: The Key To Teamwork. This two-day workshop includes the following agenda: determining others' motivation; recognizing others'

points of view; establishing credibility and rapport; clarifying problems/opportunities; and on-the-job applications.
Length: 2 days
Cost: $195
Location: Atlanta, GA.

PERSONNEL DECISIONS, INC., 2000 Plaza VII Tower, 45 South Seventh Street, Minneapolis, MN 55402, 612/339-0927; 800/633-4410, ext. 875 (outside Minn.).

The Emerging Manager: Skills & Strategies For Success. The Emerging Manager is a week-long (40-hour) program presenting a full range of management and leadership skills for first level managers at an early stage in their careers. Participants not only gain knowledge but also build skills and self-awareness in the following areas: interpersonal skills, adaptability skills, cognitive (thinking) skills, communication skills, personal motivation skills, administrative skills, and leadership skills.
Length: 5 days
Cost: $1750
Location: Minneapolis, MN

UNIVERSITY OF WISCONSIN, Management Institute, 432 North Lake Street, Madison, WI 53706, 800/262-6243 (outside Wisc.), 800/362-3020 (in Wisc.).

Improving Communication Skills. The content covered in this three-day seminar includes: barriers to communications, written communication, one-to-one, giving a talk, and conducting meetings.
Length: 3 days
Cost: $495
Locations: Madison, WI; Milwaukee, WI.

Interpersonal Nonverbal and Listening Communication Techniques for Managers. In this program you will explore listening in depth and come to understand the hidden messages, known as nonverbals, that your body sends. You will also practice chairing a meeting and learn how the proper meeting attitude, conduct, and choice of words can encourage involvement of others.
Length: 3 days
Cost: $595
Location: Madison, WI.

VANDERBILT UNIVERSITY, Owen Graduate School of Management, Executive Programs, Nashville, TN 37203, 615/322-2513.

Effective Communication Skills: Written and Face-To-Face. A three-day workshop providing participants an opportunity to build communication rapport skills, establish successful business relationships, develop listening skills, identify what makes writing work, and develop a personal action plan.
Length: 3 days
Cost: $725
Location: Nashville, TN.

Notes:

Oral Communications

Following are examples of four managers' oral communications habits.

- Arnold likes to use the words he learned in a college linguistics course to impress his subordinates at meetings.
- When giving formal presentations, Claire provides a minimum of background information to avoid boring any higher level employees who might be in attendance.
- Dirk avoids holding meetings because he claims he's "better at putting things in writing."
- Kari assumes that employees whose eyes dart around the room during her meetings are shy or otherwise uncomfortable with maintaining eye contact.

Each of these managers is considered highly competent by superiors and subordinates alike. Yet each needs improvement in at least one facet of oral communications. Without the ability to communicate effectively, clearly, and dynamically using the spoken word, even the most competent leader falls short of managerial excellence.

This section provides guidelines for improving your oral communications skills. It includes suggestions for:

Tips

- Develop a flash card system to record new words and their meanings as you come across them in your daily reading. Try for five words a day and review them periodically.

- To prevent rambling, outline in your mind what you are trying to say and then stick to it.

- Ask the listener if you are being clear.

- Paraphrase questions you are asked, both to be certain of the meaning and to give yourself time to think.

- Get a coworker to provide you with immediate feedback through a prearranged signal on a behavior you are trying to improve.

- Learn "lead-in phrases" such as "that's a good question," to give you time to organize what you want to say when asked a question.

- Eliminate annoying speech habits such as talking too slowly, too rapidly, or too hesitatingly.

- For increased impact, learn to breathe from your diaphragm in order to project your voice.

- Deliberately try to use a new word every day in your discussions.

- If you have trouble with basic English usage, such as subject-verb agreement, have your spouse or a personal friend give you frequent feedback on it.

- When asked a tough question, allow yourself to pause for a moment to compose your answer instead of "shooting from the hip."

- Seek feedback on your communications ability from a friend or trusted peer.

- Try to become more animated in your style by using appropriate gestures and body language to "punctuate" your discussion.

- Work at varying your volume, pitch, and pace to emphasize your major points in discussions.

- Watch for nonverbal cues of disinterest or nonunderstanding in others so you can clarify your point.

- Lean forward to show more intensity and commitment when presenting your point of view.

- Tape-record a talk or speech and review it critically by yourself or with a friend.

- If you have an important presentation, rehearse it on videotape to see how you are coming across.

- Look for opportunities to make presentations with your boss and get feedback on your progress.

- Before making a formal presentation, anticipate and prepare for doubts and questions.

- Seek feedback and suggestions from your supervisor regarding appropriate hand gestures, grammar, delivery, use of visual aids, etc. when preparing for a formal presentation.

- Seek opportunities to make more presentations, either on behalf of or to your supervisor.

- Seek speaking assignments on behalf of your company through organizations in your community such as the Chamber of Commerce.

- Join groups in which you have to make regular presentations.

- Take a Dale Carnegie course.

- Take a formal evening course in speech or public speaking at a local college.

- Join a local Toastmasters club to become more comfortable speaking in front of groups.

- To polish your presentation skills, take a seminar with videotaped feedback.

Analyzing Miscommunication Problems

Being misunderstood is a common problem. If you feel people misunderstand you more often than seems reasonable, you can take steps to reduce instances of miscommunication.

During the next month, when you discover that you have been misunderstood, analyze the situation by taking the following steps.

1. Determine what you intended to communicate.
2. Determine what the other person involved understood you to say. You may already have found out, depending on how you learned of the communication problem. If not, ask the person to tell you what he or she heard you say.
3. Identify the reason for the miscommunication by asking yourself the following questions:
   - Did I provide sufficient information?
   - Was my information accurate?
   - Did I provide unnecessary information so that the main points were obscured?
   - Were the other person and I simply operating on "different wavelengths"? In other words, did the other person, for whatever reason, simply not get my intended message?
4. Under what circumstances did the miscommunication occur? Who was the other person involved? What topic were you discussing? Where did the conversation take place?

After you have analyzed a number of instances of miscommunication, you will probably discover a pattern. For example, you may find that insufficient information is often a factor. Or, miscommunications may occur most often when you talk to a specific individual, discuss a specific topic, or communicate with a specific department. By analyzing the situations and the causes of the misunderstandings, you can determine which behaviors you need to change to prevent miscommunication in the future.

Getting Your Point Across When Talking

If you frequently find that people are missing the point you are trying to make, you may need to invest more effort in thinking about and organizing what you want to communicate. Following are some tips to help you ensure that your message is communicated.

- Decide on the major theme or idea you are trying to express. Work it into a concise statement that is clear and understandable.

- Organize your supporting thoughts into a logical flow leading up to the point you are trying to make. Write these down initially until you gain practice.
- Once you have made your point, ask the listener to paraphrase the main idea to ensure that it is clear to him or her.
- Make it a point to practice these skills, even in casual conversation, to develop finesse in getting your point across more efficiently.

Becoming Aware of How You Sound to Others

Do you have trouble convincing people of the soundness of your ideas and feel that customers or colleagues don't give your opinions enough consideration? Because your speaking style directly affects your ability to be convincing, it could be that the manner in which you present your ideas needs improvement.

One way of discovering how you sound to others is to record yourself and analyze how you sound. During the next two weeks, try the following procedures.

1. Record several conversations, perhaps one with a friend away from work and another one or two with a colleague at work. Choose conversations that are long enough to allow you to become comfortable with the tape recorder's presence, thus ensuring that you use your typical speech patterns.
2. Don't listen to the recordings immediately; set the tapes aside for at least one week.
3. After a week, listen to the recordings and answer the following questions.
   - Did your tone of voice and inflection accurately reflect the meaning of your words?
   - Did the speed of your speech hamper your ability to communicate effectively?
   - Was your level of enthusiasm appropriate for the topic and setting?
   - Did you express yourself clearly enough for the other person to understand what you were saying?
   - Was your vocabulary appropriate for the topic and setting?
   - How many times did you interrupt the other person?
   - How many times did the other person interrupt you?
4. Based on your answers to these questions, determine areas in which you were dissatisfied with your communications style. Identify

differences in your style for each type of conversation you recorded (business and personal).

5. Design a development plan to improve areas with which you're dissatisfied. For example, you may decide you need to speak more rapidly, lower your enthusiasm level to match the topic, interrupt less frequently, be more assertive, use less jargon, express yourself more clearly, or change your style in some other way.

6. If possible, ask a friend or colleague to review your taped conversations and to suggest ways of improving your communications style. Add these suggestions to your development plan.

During the next several months, make a conscious effort to incorporate the suggestions in your development plan into your conversations. You may want to work on one suggestion at a time, but try to follow all of them. Eventually, the changes will become habitual, and you won't need to concentrate on them so much.

Becoming More Concise

One barrier to effective communications is verbosity. Some people believe that wordiness is a sign of knowledge or power, but it actually obscures the meaning of your key points and distracts the listener. In addition, many people are annoyed by verbosity and tend to tune out speakers whose speech is overly wordy.

If you believe or have been told that you tend to be wordy, there are several steps you can take to change that pattern. Some people only need to remind themselves regularly to be more concise. For many people, however, wordiness is a habit that can be difficult to break without assistance from others. During the next several months, use the following methods in your effort to become more concise.

- Ask a trusted coworker or your manager to tell you, during your discussions, if you are being redundant or if you have wandered off the topic. In addition, for group discussions or formal presentations, ask someone to use a predetermined signal to let you know if you are becoming too wordy. When you get the signal, make an effort to condense what you are saying and get back on track.

- Pay attention to how others are reacting to your speech during discussions and meetings. If they begin to lose eye contact with you or get restless, assume that you are straying from the topic or that your communication has grown redundant. Pause to ask yourself if you are

being too wordy; if so, sum up what you are saying and end your speech or go on to your next point.

- To determine whether your key points are clear, ask people to summarize what you have told them. This will give you an opportunity to find out if you are being wordy and restate your points if others have misunderstood you.
- Ask your colleagues to let you know when you are speaking concisely as well as when you are being verbose.

Being More Concise in Meetings

People who are concise during meetings often have more influence than those who are redundant and go off on tangents. People don't like their time to be wasted by the ramblings of a wordy speaker and tend to react negatively to that person. If you would like to improve your ability to be concise during meetings, the following activities will help you achieve that goal.

1. Begin using the following procedures; make them part of your meeting preparation and performance from now on.
   - Before a meeting, write down the main points you want to bring up; then, unless the agenda changes, limit your discussion to those points.
   - During the meeting, try to limit the expression of each point to two or three sentences. If necessary, write down these sentences before the meeting to help you stick to your plan.
2. During the next few months, perform the following activities.
   - Immediately after each meeting, ask yourself:
     - Did I present all of the points I wanted to?
     - Did I limit myself to the important points?
     - Did I stick to two or three sentences per point?
     - Did I avoid talking about irrelevant information?
     - Did the others at the meeting seem interested in what I was saying?
     - Did I avoid straying from the topics being discussed?
     - Did I avoid repeating myself unnecessarily?
   - For every "no" answer, try to determine what happened and why it happened. Then, at the next meeting, make a conscious effort to change. When you get to the point where you can answer "yes" to most of the questions, you've accomplished your goal.
   - If possible, and with the permission of those present, record one of your next meetings. After the meeting, listen to the tape and evaluate your performance. Try to rephrase your remarks to make them more concise; this practice will improve your performance.
3. Consider attending an oral communications seminar that features extensive feedback from instructor or peers, or uses videotaped sessions, to let you see how you act and talk. Ask your human resources department to check out seminar resources available in your area.

Developing a More Informal Style of Oral Communications

Often, the good ideas suggested in a presentation go unnoticed because of the presenter's stiff, formal style. People find it much easier to understand ideas when they are presented in the natural, informal style that they are accustomed to hearing in their daily lives.

Here are some tips for developing a more informal speaking style—particularly when you are making formal presentations. Follow these suggestions closely for the next three months.

- When you plan a presentation, imagine yourself talking to one person. Consider how you would organize the presentation, the topics you would discuss, and the examples you would use if you were to make the presentation to this individual in private. Adopt the same style for the actual presentation.
- Use examples and analogies to liven up your speech. Also, make sure the presentation is applicable to your listeners, particularly when discussing highly abstract or technical topics.
- Try to be natural and to use a conversational style.
- Use relaxation techniques to become as comfortable as you can.
- Enjoy yourself and the speaking process. Your listeners will pick up your sense of satisfaction and will enjoy themselves more, too.
- Follow recommendations on effective use of language, including the use of:
    - Active rather than passive voice ("the committee debated the issue" rather than "the issue was debated by the committee")
    - Verbs that describe action rather than existence ("jump," "run," and "fly" rather than "is")
    - Short, simple words rather than complex words or jargon
    - Short, clear sentences rather than long, rambling ones

Improving Formal Presentations

Your effectiveness as a speaker in all kinds of situations can be improved by making formal group presentations. During the next several months, take every opportunity to give a formal presentation; actively seek out such encounters. For each presentation, carefully follow the steps outlined here to make the most of the developmental opportunity that a speech offers.

1. Find out what you can about the members of the audience.
    - What is their knowledge of the topic of the presentation?
    - What is their background? Do they share similar experiences and beliefs, or do they come from a wide variety of backgrounds?
    - What are they expecting from this presentation?
2. Based on your research of the audience, determine the approach you will take. Decide how much background information you need to provide, what questions your presentation should answer, and the tone you should adopt (persuasive, informational, or other). One word of caution: Don't pretend you are familiar with an area if you're not.

When speaking on or in unfamiliar topics, admit your lack of expertise up front.

3. Outline your presentation, write down all of the key points you wish to make, and then organize them in the most effective way.

4. Now, write down every word. Although you may never need to refer to the script during your presentation, you'll be glad you have it there. When deciding on the content of your presentation, consider the following points:

   - Choose explanations and examples that are appropriate for your audience. If you're speaking about highly technical subjects to an audience with little knowledge of these areas, be sure to provide clear, simple explanations and examples. If there's no way to determine the audience's knowledge of the topic being discussed, be prepared to present background information at the start of the presentation. If you're still in doubt at the time of the speech, ask the audience members what they know about the topic.

   - Use phrases such as "there are five methods of" or "the four most popular approaches are" to maintain a clear and logical flow to your speech.

   - Present your opinions forcefully and directly. Eliminate phrases like "It seems to me" and "It is likely," which tend to lessen the impact of what you have to say.

- Illustrate your key points with specific, "real life" examples from your own work.

5. Determine whether your presentation would benefit from the use of black or white boards, flip charts, overhead projection sheets, handouts, or other audiovisual aids. If you decide it would, organize these aids and work their use into your speech.

6. Rehearse each presentation—particularly the first several ones. Taping your rehearsal allows you to critique your speaking style and make adjustments before the presentation. Rehearsing in front of a mirror enables you to see whether your gestures and facial expressions are appropriate.

7. Try to predict which topics in your presentation might draw questions and/or opposing views from members of the audience. Be prepared to answer the questions, defend your points, and cite your sources of information, if necessary. If you don't know the answer to a question, admit it and go on; don't pretend that you know the answer.

8. Keep a resource file of items you come across that could potentially be used in your presentations. Newspaper clippings, facts, thoughts, and ideas can be stored for future reference.

Improving Your Oral Communications Through Practice

The best way to continue to develop your speaking abilities is to look for occasions to practice your skills. Consider the following suggestions.

- Seek out assignments that require you to make presentations to groups.
- Volunteer for membership on committees, task forces, and interdepartmental projects; these usually involve speaking opportunities.
- Whenever possible, offer to represent your superior at meetings. This will ensure that you are called on often to speak before the group.
- Pursue speaking opportunities in your community. You may wish to volunteer to speak as a representative of your company at meetings of community organizations.
- Assist other people in developing their speaking skills; often the "teacher" learns as much as the "pupil" does.
- Join an organization such as Toastmasters or Toastmistresses that encourages the development of speaking abilities.

Improving Your Awareness of Nonverbal Communications

Consider all of the ways people say "no." The speaker of that one word can make the listener feel rejected, sad, happy, hopeful, or any of a range of feelings in between. That's because it's not just **what** we say but **how** we say it that determines what we've communicated. We all send nonverbal messages through gestures, body posture, and facial expressions as we talk and listen. A good communicator picks up the nonverbal messages sent by listeners and responds accordingly.

To improve your awareness of nonverbal communications, spend some time during the next several months performing the following activities.

1. During the next week, carefully notice the nonverbal messages being sent by listeners in a variety of speaking situations—casual conversations, group discussions, and formal meetings or presentations—in which you are just an observer. Look for nonverbal indications of the listeners' feelings, such as:
   - Whether listeners maintain eye contact with the speaker
   - The listeners' postures (relaxed, tense, leaning toward or away from the speaker)
   - The listeners' facial expressions
   - The listeners' hand motions (drumming, fidgeting, etc.)
2. After each situation, write down the examples of nonverbal messages you've observed and indicate whether you received a positive or negative feeling from them. (Try to find both positive and negative behaviors.) The chart that follows can help you structure your information.

Behavior Noted	Positive or Negative Feeling?

3. Now observe the nonverbal messages sent by the people to whom you are talking. After each speaking situation, write down the behaviors you noticed, and whether they were positive or negative, what you said that might have caused the behavior, and what you did or should have done in response to the nonverbal message. This analysis will help you become more aware of the messages others send you, which in turn will increase your ability to respond quickly to such messages. The following chart can help you with this analysis.

Behavior	Negative	Positive or Possible Cause	Response

Recommended Readings

Baskin, O.W., and Aronoff, C.E. *Interpersonal Communication in Organizations.* Santa Monica, CA: Goodyear Publishing Co., 1979.

Differentiating between interpersonal communication and business and organizational communication, this book focuses on the person-to-person, manager-to-subordinate, and subordinate-to-manager relationships.

Garner, Alan. *Conversationally Speaking: Tested New Ways to Increase Your Personal and Social Effectiveness.* New York, NY: McGraw-Hill, 1981.

This practical, concise book outlines strategies which teach the reader to: start conversations, ask the kind of questions that promote conversation, avoid rejection-producing behavior, issue invitations that are likely to be accepted, achieve deeper levels of understanding, handle criticism constructively, resist manipulation, become more confident in social situations, and listen so others will be encouraged to talk to you.

Guth, C.K., and Shaw, S.S. *How to Put on Dynamic Meetings.* Englewood Cliffs, NJ: Reston, 1980.

This book deals with the details that may seem obvious but are too often overlooked in the planning of meetings. They include: combining oral and visual communication techniques, speaking effectively, and forming an agenda. The first half of the book defines and offers advice on different kinds of meetings; the second half deals with visual aids and presentation techniques.

Hasling, J. *The Message, the Speaker, the Audience (3rd ed.).* New York, NY: McGraw-Hill, 1982.

Focusing exclusively on the public speaker, this book provides basic methods and techniques necessary for successful presentations.

Hunt, G.T. *Communication Skills in the Organization.* Englewood Cliffs, NJ: Prentice-Hall, 1980.

While many books about communication focus on theory, this book emphasizes practical applications. It examines the individual's role in organizational communication and shows how to communicate in various organizational settings. It discusses such essentials as listening skills, mutual understanding in interviews, group participation skills, leadership skills, and an examination of both oral and written communications.

Lazarus, S. *Loud and Clear: A Guide to Effective Communication.*
New York, NY: AMACOM, 1975.

This book is a practical guide to mastering or improving both verbal and nonverbal communication. It could be useful to those who often wonder if people really understood what they said or wrote.

McKay, Matthew; David, Martha; and Fanning, Patrick. *Messages: The Communication Skills Book.* Oakland, CA: New Harbinger Press, 1983.

This book gathers the most essential communications skills into one volume, with many examples and exercises. It begins with basic skills such as listening and expressing, followed by advanced skills such as body language and paralanguage. Also included are conflict skills (i.e., assertiveness, negotiating), social skills (making contact), and public skills such as public speaking.

Montgomery, Robert L. *A Master Guide to Public Speaking.* New York, NY: Harper & Row, 1979.

This book addresses fears about facing a group. It presents the methods professional speakers use to prepare presentations, organize talks, prepare audiovisual aids, deliver masterful speeches, and give impromptu and off-the-cuff speeches. It also discusses how to handle questions and face the media, handle special occasions, and be effective before groups or one person. The book includes an index of professional resource materials.

Morris, James A. *The Art of Conversation: Magic Key to Personal and Social Popularity.* Englewood Cliffs, NJ: Prentice-Hall, 1976.

This book reveals everything you need to know about good conversation—from breaking the ice with a stranger to enjoying a long, close talk with an old friend. Dozens of sample conversations demonstrate methods to help you improve your ability as a conversationalist.

Nirenberg, J. *How to Sell Your Ideas.* New York, NY: McGraw-Hill, 1984.

This guide is designed to improve the reader's effectiveness in getting ideas and thoughts across to others—and getting them accepted. Included are methods for: dealing with resistance, guarding credibility, getting the other person to listen, taking apart and countering objectives, constructing creative solutions, and negotiating.

Swets, Paul W. *The Art of Talking So That People Will Listen: Getting Through to Family, Friends, and Associates.* Englewood Cliffs, NJ: Prentice-Hall, 1983.

This guide provides practical techniques for mastering the art of effective, persuasive communication. It identifies communications goals and strategies for meeting those goals which allow the reader to: gain control of complexities of the communications process, discover what builds communications barriers between people and what one can do to tear them down, win the attention and cooperation of friends and business associates, and present oneself clearly and effectively in social situations.

Visual Education Corp. *Vocabulary Made Easy.* New York, NY: McGraw-Hill, 1983.

This text-workbook emphasizes the vocabulary readers must master to succeed on the job. Each lesson is four pages long, with two pages of text instruction followed by two pages of exercises.

Suggested Seminars

The seminars listed here were selected for their appeal to a managerial audience and have received good to excellent ratings from managers attending them.

Because of the dynamic nature of the seminar marketplace, some seminars may have been added, upgraded, or replaced, and others may no longer be offered. Additional information about these seminars may be obtained by calling the vendor directly, or through Seminar Clearinghouse International, a subscriber organization located in St. Paul, Minnesota. Call 612/293-1004 for information.

AMERICAN MANAGEMENT ASSOCIATIONS, P.O. Box 319, Saranac Lake, NY 12983, 518/891-0065.

Effective Executive Speaking. Participants in this program are actively involved in evaluating their pluses and minuses, making an impromptu talk, building ideas, using visual aids, answering questions, and speaking on special occasions. This program includes videotaping.
Length: 3 days
Cost: $895
Locations: Los Angeles, CA; San Francisco, CA; Washington, DC; Atlanta, GA; Chicago, IL; New York, NY.

CALIFORNIA INSTITUTE OF TECHNOLOGY, The Industrial Relations Center, Pasadena, CA 91125, 818/356-4041.

Vocal Communication and Effective Presentation Techniques. During this three-day program, participants learn how to analyze audience needs and set presentation objectives. The program includes nonverbal presentation techniques, vocal impact, projecting a positive image, overcoming inhibitions and fear of failure, interpreting the material, off-stage preparation, making different types of presentations, using visual aids effectively, and effective handling of questions and answers.
Length: 3 days
Cost: $695
Location: Pasadena, CA.

COLORADO STATE UNIVERSITY, Office of Special Programs, E-106 Rockwell Hall, Fort Collins, CO 80523, 303/491-7571.

Effective On-the-job Communication: How To Work More Successfully With Others. Some of the key topics included in this one-day seminar are: how effective communication works; developing rapport and a "common language" with anyone; assumptions can trap you; how to be clear;

making the most of difficult communication situations; managing
conflict; and maintaining positive relationships.
Length: 1 day
Cost: $95
Location: Northglenn, CO.

COMMUNISPOND, INC., 485 Lexington Avenue, New York, NY 10017,
212/687-8040.

Executive Communications. A two-day program based on the premise that
the participants are mature and professionally competent people who are
reasonably articulate but who would be more effective if they could
overcome nervousness, inhibition, and the loss of contact with their
audiences and subject matter.
Length: 2 days
Cost: $950
Locations: Los Angeles, CA; Newport Beach, CA; San Francisco, CA;
Chicago, IL; Boston, MA; Detroit, MI; Minneapolis, MN; New York,
NY; Dallas, TX; Houston, TX.

EXECUTIVE TECHNIQUE, 716 North Rush Street, Chicago, IL 60611,
312/266-0001.

Executive Speaking. A two-day seminar designed to help participants give
effective presentations. This program includes: physical skills, energy
expansion and control, organization/visual aids, persuasiveness,
questions and answers, slide presentations, handling the overhead
projector, videotaping, and critiques.
Length: 2 days
Cost: Call vendor
Location: Chicago, IL.

NTL INSTITUTE, P.O. Box 9155, Rosslyn Station, Arlington, VA 22209,
703/527-1500.

Communication Workshop. Through structured practice, participants
learn how to improve communication, practice skills involved in
communicating and listening, understand problems of organizational
communication, explore the effect of stress on interpersonal
communication, practice giving and receiving feedback, experience
communication that leads to feeling understood, and gain greater
awareness of one's own communication style and impact on others.
Length: 7 days
Cost: $795
Location: Bethel, ME.

OTHER THAN CONSCIOUS COMMUNICATIONS, P.O. Box 697, Friday Harbor, WA 98250, 206/378-5393.

Other Than Conscious Communication. An interesting array of topics including: how to better appreciate 80% of every communication; reappraisal of the phenomenon labeled "hypnosis"; how to get more of what you want; reappraisal of "learned" concepts of psychology; importance of "patterns" and how to direct them. An outcome of the program is learning to appreciate and effectively communicate with the parts of us that are outside our normal awareness.
Length: 2 days
Cost: $250
Locations: San Francisco, CA; Friday Harbor, WA.

SPEAKEASY SERVICES, Monarch Plaza/Suite 830, 3414 Peachtree Road, N.E., Atlanta, GA 30326, 404/261-4029.

How To Talk So People Listen. This course helps participants develop a more effective speaking style and feel more in control of both formal and routine speaking situations through extensive videotaping and individualized critique.
Length: 3 days
Cost: $995
Locations: San Francisco, CA; Atlanta, GA.

UNIVERSITY OF MICHIGAN, School of Business Administration, Executive Education Center, Ann Arbor, MI 48109, 313/763-1000.

Executive Communication: Improving Speaking and Writing Skills. This week-long program includes such key topics as analyzing your audience, organizing your material, structuring the communication, written communication issues, oral communication issues, and managing the communications of your subordinates.
Length: 5 days
Cost: $2850 (includes accommodations, meals, materials)
Location: Ann Arbor, MI.

Communications Skills

Notes:

Written Communications

Following is an example of a memo sent by a division manager.

TO: ALL DIVISION A EMPLOYEES
RE: RESTRUCTURIZATION OF THE DEPARTMENTS IN
     DIVISION A
The negative interface that transpired after the meeting held last
Wednesday on our division's restructurization has caused an
operational delay in the conversion of our facilities as desegnated.
Conseqently, future perimeters concerning the extensive
redevelopement of the work force of Division A will be determined by
those functionaly responsible for the implementation of the type of
tasks discussed. The inclusion of input by other individuals will be at
the sole desgretion of the aformentioned management personel.

The manager who wrote this had a message he wanted to get across to the
employees in Division A. Did this memo succeed in conveying it?

Documents like this one—confusing, wordy, and full of typos,
misspellings, and grammatical errors—are common in the business world.
So is confusion on the part of their recipients, who can only scratch their
heads and guess at the sender's meaning. Unfortunately, confusion resulting
from written documents is less likely to be cleared up than are
misunderstandings resulting from in-person communications. The need for
clarity, simplicity, and accuracy in written communications, then, is
obvious. This section can help you improve the effectiveness of your written
communications skills. It includes suggestions on:

Part I: Writing
- Writing Clearly and Concisely (p. 299)
- Improving Your Grammar, Sentence Structure, Spelling, and
  Punctuation (p. 300)
- Using Technical Terms and Jargon Appropriately (p. 301)
- Improving Your Report-writing Skills (p. 301)
- Writing Expressively (p. 302)
- Avoiding Miscommunication in Written Documents (p. 303)
- Creating Effective Visual Aids (p. 303)
- Reducing Procrastination When Writing Reports (p. 304)

- Combining the Techniques of Organization and Brainstorming (p. 305)
- Improving Your Business Letters and Memos (p. 305)

Part II: Reading
- Increasing Your Vocabulary (p. 306)

Tips

- When writing, consider the people in your audience. What do they know? What can you tell them?

- Outline your memos and letters before beginning to write.

- Whenever possible, limit letters or memos to one page.

- When writing reports, summarize key points or conclusions on the first page and document them with more information on subsequent pages.

- Write like you speak as much as possible to make documents highly readable.

- Learn the writing style of your organization and follow it. For example, don't use "flowery" language (many adjectives and adverbs) where it is inappropriate.

- Have your secretary edit and proof your correspondence for sentence structure and grammatical errors.

- Refer to the *Little English Handbook* when in doubt about grammar.

- Keep a dictionary or thesaurus on hand to check quickly on spelling for word usage.

- Use a variety of sentence structures—simple, complex, and compound—without "forcing" them.

- Read and keep at your fingertips a copy of *The Elements of Style* by Strunk and White.

- When writing for a nontechnical audience, have a nontechnical person (such as a spouse or a secretary) identify jargon. Then either eliminate it or include a glossary defining the terms.

- Use charts and tables wherever possible to present numerical information.

- Use "action verbs" when appropriate to add punch to your message.

- Eliminate "weak words" such as very, interesting, often, and other bland adjectives or adverbs.

- Keep paragraphs short. Make sure the content of a paragraph revolves on only one thought—the topic sentence.

- If you do a large amount of routine correspondence, try to standardize it as much as possible.

- If procrastination is a problem, start writing a rough draft early so you have the time to revise it at least once.

- When allocating blocks of time for writing, set aside periods of 1–1½ hours rather than trying to do it in segments of 5–15 minutes.

- Write legibly whenever others must read your handwriting.

- Develop a flash card system to work on your own common misspellings.

- Ask your boss to critique your writing occasionally.

- Dictate correspondence, memos, etc. to save time.

- Find a quiet, regular time to do your dictation.

- Seek immediate and specific feedback on reports you write.

- Be more sensitive in your written communications. Take a second or third look at your memos before sending them.

Part I: Writing

Writing Clearly and Concisely

One of the keystones of good written communications is the clear, concise expression of ideas or information. The guidelines provided here can help you achieve clarity and conciseness from the very start of the writing process.

1. Before you start writing, compile an outline of the key points or ideas you want to address in the order you want to present them.
2. Start your document by identifying the main topic of the piece and any supporting concepts you will be discussing. For example, you might begin by saying, "In summarizing the main points of the meeting, I will describe how they relate to our planning process."
3. In addition to introducing your topic before discussing it, be sure to end your document with a summary statement that capsulizes the ideas and facts you've presented.
4. Consider the reader's needs. How much detail is needed? Is the entire piece likely to be read? (If not, open with an "executive summary" a

page or less in length. This frees the reader from wading through unessential details before getting to the "meat" of the document.)

5. If time permits, write a first draft of your document, then review and revise it before composing the final version.

6. Feedback on one's writing is also helpful. Ask someone else for feedback on your writing. Give a superior, peer, or friend the letter or report to read. Ask them, "What did you think I was trying to convey?" and "What parts don't you understand?" You will know your writing is improving when your reader's understanding of your ideas matches your intent.

Improving Your Grammar, Sentence Structure, Spelling, and Punctuation

Following is an excerpt from a memo written by a department manager.
"We are checking into the feesability of the program for it's aplicability to our purposes. Upon reaching a decision you will be notified."

You probably understood what this manager was trying to say. However, the errors in spelling, punctuation, and sentence structure greatly reduce the impact and effectiveness of the message.

Correct use of the technical components of the English language—including grammar, spelling, punctuation, and sentence structure—is essential for producing effective written communications. Following are guidelines for improving your use of these components.

1. Choose a grammar/style book that you will use as a guide in working on your written communications skills. (Corbett's **The Little English Handbook,** which addresses 50 areas that commonly cause problems for adult writers, is recommended.) Set a schedule for completing the book, and get in the habit of writing a summary of each section's key points as you finish it. You might want to mark the sections that focus on your problem areas and check your documents against the guidelines offered in those sections.

2. If your secretary edits your memos and reports, ask to have the next few typed verbatim (exactly as you dictate or write them). Examine these copies for errors you typically make—grammatical errors, poor structure, and so on. You might also ask your secretary to compile a list of your most common writing errors. This list can help you pinpoint areas in which you need improvement.

Using Technical Terms and Jargon Appropriately

What were your feelings as you read the sample memo in the introduction to this section? Did the buzzwords and complex terminology affect your comprehension? Memos that contain technical terms and jargon may seem perfectly clear to employees in technical positions, but they are likely to confuse and frustrate nontechnical employees.

When writing a memo to a diverse group of individuals, be sure to keep technical language to a minimum. The following guidelines will help you determine the appropriate, effective use of technical terminology and jargon.

1. Define the document's audience. If it consists primarily of individuals with technical expertise, the use of technical terms and concepts may be appropriate, even desirable. The more diverse the group, however, the fewer technical terms you should use.

2. When preparing a document for wide distribution, have a colleague from another department read it before you send it. Ask the person to review it for its use of technical terms and the clarity of its overall message.

3. If the use of technical terms is unavoidable in a document intended for wide distribution, you may want to:
   - Define the terms
   - Use the terms in a context that makes their meaning apparent

4. If you communicate with specific departments on a regular basis, learn their jargon. You might get a list of the terms commonly used by those groups and occasionally use those words in your correspondence to them.

Improving Your Report-writing Skills

Some of the guidelines that follow overlap with those presented earlier. Keep in mind that these are specifically designed to help you improve your skill in writing reports that need to convey more information than the average letter or memo.

1. First, create an outline. Check to see that each section flows logically to the next. You might experiment with several outlines, selecting the one that is likely to have the greatest impact on and be clearest to the reader.

2. Use headings and subheadings to indicate to the reader when a new idea begins. Examples of headings include "Background Information,"

"Conclusions," and "Recommendations." A table of contents listing the headings is recommended for reports that are longer than 10 pages.

3. When you're ready to begin writing, make sure you have everything you'll need—your outline, resource notes, and any other information sources. Interrupting your writing to locate an article or notes from a meeting will break your train of thought.

4. Whenever possible, start your reports well in advance of their due dates. Give yourself time to write at least one rough draft and one preliminary final draft per report. Most good writers produce quality pieces because they've taken the time to rewrite and revise their documents.

5. Ask a superior or qualified colleague to review your preliminary final draft and offer feedback. The factors needing attention include organization (order and flow of sections), transitions, suitability of language for the audience, and overall clarity.

Writing Expressively

The preceding guidelines will assist you in improving the organization, clarity, and grammatical accuracy of your written documents. When you've mastered those skills, you're ready to work on putting "pizzazz" into your writing—to develop a style that's **expressive**. This touch is what compels the reader to keep reading. The following guidelines will help you develop a more expressive style of writing.

1. Use the active voice whenever possible. This means substituting action verbs for passive ("being") verbs. The active voice infuses your sentences with a lively tone. See if you can tell the difference between the following two versions of the same thought.
   - "Kraftco's marketing strategy is innovative."
   - "Kraftco implements an innovative marketing strategy."
   Notice how changing "is" to "implements" changes the tone of the sentence. You can make this type of change with any sentence written in the passive voice.

2. Avoid opening your sentences with bland phrases like "It is" and "There is." Starting a sentence with the subject is a good way to ensure that it ends up in the active voice.

3. Get in the habit of writing shorter sentences and paragraphs. Short sentences pack a stronger punch than long, convoluted ones do.

Avoiding Miscommunication in Written Documents

Communications problems that result from written documents can serve a useful purpose. They can enable the writers to identify and correct errors and be more concise in the future. When you learn that one of your written documents has missed its mark, follow this procedure.

1. Ask the recipient of the document to summarize its message, as he or she perceived it.
2. Identify the reason for the miscommunication by asking yourself the following questions:
   - Was insufficient information communicated?
   - Was inaccurate information communicated?
   - Was unnecessary detail communicated?
   - Did the reader simply misinterpret the message?
3. After evaluating a number of written documents, pinpoint any problem areas. Devote special attention to reducing errors in these areas in the future.

Creating Effective Visual Aids

Visual aids can help you illustrate and add impact to the key points in your written documents. Be sure, however, that the pictorial representation of your message is accurate and relevant. Following are guidelines for preparing effective visual aids.

1. Define the function of the visual aid.
2. Prepare samples of the various formats (tables, graphs, charts, and slides) to determine which one would most effectively support your written document.
3. Determine the general message you want to convey using the visual aid, then jot down the specific key points to be addressed.
4. Develop the visual aid, referring to your notes to ensure accuracy and consistency.
5. Ask a superior or skilled colleague to evaluate the usefulness and accuracy of your visual aid prior to its distribution with your document.
6. Solicit feedback on your visual aid and ask for suggestions on how you might improve it.

Reducing Procrastination When Writing Reports

Many people put off writing the first draft of a report because they can't decide on logical organizational structure. If you're one of these people, the following guidelines will give you some tips for getting started.

1. Think about the topic at hand and try dictating or jotting down ideas as they come to you. Creating an outline—detailed or general—can also help you decide on a basic structure for your material.
2. Write your first draft by developing the ideas or the outline points you identified in the preceding step.
3. Begin organizing the sections of your draft by isolating the lead-off idea (this is likely to be near the beginning of your draft).
4. Edit your report by deleting any unnecessary or redundant parts and simplifying wordy or unclear passages.
5. Write a brief (two- or three-sentence) foreword that conveys the main message of your report.

Combining the Techniques of Organization and Brainstorming

Even a well written, organized report won't make its point if it doesn't keep the needs and perspective of its audience in mind. The guidelines provided here emphasize the importance of remembering the purpose of your document throughout the writing cycle. Also provided are suggestions for using brainstorming to generate ideas and produce a document that clearly conveys your message.

1. Consider the needs and purposes of your audience throughout the writing cycle. Ask yourself what the reader should learn from the report, what he or she will do with the information, and what he or she already knows about the subject. This information will help you make decisions about the background data, terminology, and definitions you should include in your report.

2. Begin the writing process by brainstorming, or coming up with as many ideas as possible about the subject at hand. Don't judge ideas or worry about organization during this step.

3. Review the list of ideas you compiled while brainstorming, then set it aside for a while. Taking a "breather" at this point will help you develop a fresh perspective.

4. Reexamine the purpose of your written document. Write it down, keeping your audience in mind.

5. Review your brainstorming list, looking for key ideas and topics that support or relate to your document's purpose. Identify the major ideas, then group the subpoints under those headings.

6. Develop a rough but inclusive outline from the groups formed in the preceding step. Check to see that each major category relates to your purpose and the needs of your audience.

7. Decide on format for organizing the sections of your report. Select headings and subheadings that clearly indicate the content of the sections.

Improving Your Business Letters and Memos

Most people will do just about anything to avoid reading a rambling, aimless business letter or memo. Clarity, organization, and a sense of purpose are vital to getting and keeping the reader's attention. Following are guidelines for writing letters and memos that will be read and understood.

1. Open your letter or memo with a description of your subject and your purpose in writing about it.

2. Offer your conclusions, decisions, and recommendations. (If you anticipate a negative response to your conclusions, you may want to give the facts first and your conclusions later.)

3. Elaborate on the subject, providing only the details that are relevant to the purpose of your report. If you must include additional data or statistics to support your conclusions, use them to construct an easy-to-read table or graph that you will include in an appendix section.

4. End your letter or memo with an offer to provide additional information or to take appropriate action if the reader wishes.

Part II: Reading

Increasing Your Vocabulary

Increasing your vocabulary will help you to get through complex written material more quickly.

- Keep both a thesaurus and a dictionary at your desk for easy reference.
- Note unfamiliar words that you come across in your work and in outside reading. Write each word on one side of an index card. After looking the word up in the dictionary, write its meaning on the reverse side.
- Prepare 10 or 15 of these cards.
- Check yourself on the meanings of these words once a day. When you have correctly identified the meaning of a particular word for three days in succession, take the card out and add a new vocabulary card to your pile.
- Incorporate these new words into memos or reports you prepare on the job whenever possible. However, be careful not to use words that may be too difficult for your readers to understand.
- Keep the vocabulary cards you have mastered in a separate file. At the end of a month, ask a colleague or a family member to test you out on all of the accumulated vocabulary cards. If you have forgotten any of these, add them once again to the pile of cards you are reviewing daily.
- Increase your exposure to new words by reading business-oriented publications such as *Business Week* or *Harvard Business Review*.
- Use the word-building section of *Reader's Digest* for the next few months.

Recommended Readings

Anastasi, Thomas E. *Desk Guide to Communication (2nd ed.).* New York:
NY: Van Nostrand Reinhold, 1981.

This text offers the basic skills of business communication in a
reference-handbook format. It is a useful, up-to-date guide to the
pronunciation, use, and spelling of words often needed in business. It
also discusses when to write and when to speak, and contains a brief
guide to editing and dictating.

Carr-Ruffino, N. *Writing Short Business Reports.* New York, NY:
McGraw-Hill, 1979.

This book introduces the PREP outline—a simple-to-use approach to
preparing and writing short, effective reports. For anyone who needs to
brush up on their writing skills, the book employs case studies to illustrate
report writing in the business, industry, and government environments.

Corbett, E.P.J. *The Little English Handbook: Choices and Conventions.*
New York, NY: John Wiley & Sons, 1987.

This edition of Corbett's handbook discusses fifty areas of grammar, style,
paragraphing, and sentence mechanics that cause problems for many adult
writers. Those who are distressed by their ignorance of the correct formats
for business letters will find this guide useful.

Holtz, H. *Persuasive Writing: Communicating Effectively in Business.*
New York, NY: McGraw-Hill, 1983.

This book is designed for business people and focuses on methods of
persuading people through the written word. The principles provided apply
to a wide range of communications forms including: proposals, brochures,
reports, speeches, letters, memos, and newsletters.

Lazarus, S. *Loud and Clear: A Guide to Effective Communication.*
New York, NY: AMACOM, 1981.

This book is a practical guide to mastering or improving both verbal and
nonverbal communication. It can be useful to those who often wonder if
people really understood what they said or wrote.

Pauley, S.E. *Technical Report Writing Today (2nd ed.).* Boston, MA:
Houghton-Mifflin, 1979.

Exercises dealing with the special demands of technical writing are
provided. Assignments are applicable to all technical disciplines.

Poe, R.W. *The McGraw-Hill Handbook of Business Letters*. New York, NY: McGraw-Hill, 1983.

This is a widely varied collection of model letters representing over 160 common communications situations that face today's business writers. Ten broad letter categories are covered, including requests, confirmations, sales and customer correspondence, public relations, and social correspondence.

Raygor, A., and Raygor, R. *Effective Reading: Improving Reading Rates and Comprehension*. New York, NY: McGraw-Hill, 1984.

This book presents relevant reading skills in a smooth, logical fashion so that students have ample time to absorb the new skills. It includes skimming, scanning, and rate flexibility techniques that help users significantly improve their reading speed and comprehension.

Smith, Leila R. *English for Careers: Business, Professional & Technical (3rd ed.)*. New York, NY: John Wiley & Sons, 1985.

Topics discussed in this book include: objectives; basic sentence construction; common parts of speech, vocabulary, and spelling development; a business dictionary; basic punctuation; business letter format; and more essentials for basic business English.

Strunk, William, and White, E.B. *The Elements of Style (3rd. ed.)*. New York, NY: MacMillan, 1979.

This classic handbook on grammar and style is highly recommended as a useful working tool. Strunk and White emphasize conciseness and clarity. They select the most common trouble areas or words in communication and explain correct usage.

Visual Education Corporation. *Spelling Made Easy*. New York, NY: McGraw-Hill, 1983.

This text-workbook offers practical instruction for learning to spell those words most commonly used in business correspondence.

Weiss, A. *Write What You Mean: A Handbook of Business Communication*. New York, NY: AMACOM, 1981.

According to the author, the medium is not the message, despite some modern theories on communication. Instead, he says, substance and an understandable style are more important; the sending of real messages to real people is what business is all about. This book encourages direct communication.

Suggested Seminars

The seminars listed here were selected for their appeal to a managerial audience and have received good to excellent ratings from managers attending them.

Because of the dynamic nature of the seminar marketplace, some seminars may have been added, upgraded, or replaced, and others may no longer be offered. Additional information about these seminars may be obtained by calling the vendor directly, or through Seminar Clearinghouse International, a subscriber organization located in St. Paul, Minnesota. Call 612/293-1004 for information.

AMERICAN MANAGEMENT ASSOCIATIONS, P.O. Box 319, Saranac Lake, NY 12983, 518/891-0065.

How To Sharpen Your Business Writing Skills. A practice-based course for all supervisors, managers, and professionals whose responsibilities involve written communications. Program content includes: how to write in a conversational manner, ways to grab the reader's attention, how to organize your writing, choosing the most effective formats for reports and proposals, and how to write persuasive memos.

Length: 4 days
Cost: $795
Locations: Anaheim, CA; San Diego, CA; San Francisco, CA; Washington, DC; Atlanta, GA; Chicago, IL; Boston, MA; New York, NY.

COMMUNISPOND, INC., 485 Lexington Avenue, New York, NY 10017, 212/687-8040.

Speaking on Paper. With individual attention from an instructor, participants will write a benchmark document that will be personally critiqued; learn how to choose your message; visualize your recipient and decide what you expect to happen as a result of your document; learn guidelines on sentence length, colloquial expressions, personal words; acquire skills in using professional jargon; practice editing; and write a final document to be reviewed against your benchmark.

Length: 1 day
Cost: $450
Locations: Newport Beach, CA; San Francisco, CA; Chicago, IL; Boston, MA; New York, NY; Dallas, TX.

INFORMATION MAPPING INC., 275 Wyman Street, Waltham, MA 02154, 617/890-7003.

Effective Reports, Proposals and Memos. In this two-day course, key concepts of the information mapping method are outlined. Applying the research-based principles, a proven approach to organizing the information, refining your analysis and content, and applying the method back on the job are a few of the major topics discussed.
Length: 2 days
Cost: $665
Locations: San Francisco, CA; Washington, DC; Atlanta, GA; Chicago, IL; Boston, MA; New York, NY.

ROBERT S. BURGER & ASSOCIATES, Glen Mills, PA 19342, 215/399-1130.

Effective Writing. This program examines how to avoid superfluous, ill-chosen, or misplaced words and focuses on writing clearly, concisely, and effectively.
Length: 2 days
Cost: $350
Locations: Washington, DC; Atlanta, GA; Chicago, IL; Boston, MA; New York, NY; Columbus, OH; Philadelphia, PA; Dallas, TX.

UNIVERSITY OF MICHIGAN, School of Business Adminstration; Executive Education Center, Ann Arbor, MI 48109, 313/763-1000.

Executive Communication: Improving Speaking and Writing Skills. This five-day program enables participants to analyze and improve their styles of written and oral presentation. It includes analyzing your audience; organizing your material; structuring the communication; written communication issues; oral communications issues; and managing the communications of your subordinates.
Length: 5 days
Cost: $2850 (includes accommodations, meals, materials)
Location: Ann Arbor, MI.

WRITING EXCHANGE, 578 Dell Place, Stanhope, NJ 07874, 201/347-6703.

Write Start. This program includes such topics as: attitudes about writing; contrasts between academic writing and business writing; the number one cause of confusion in writing; clarity and conciseness; organization; effective ghostwriting; sentence variety; formats; managing the writing process; style and tone; and report writing.

Length: 1 day
Cost: $265
Locations: Los Angeles, CA; Greenwich, CT; Atlanta, GA; Chicago, IL; Charlotte, NC; Princeton, NJ; Whippany, NJ; New York, NY; Philadelphia, PA.

FACTOR 5

Personal Adaptability

"Thriving" or "surviving"—which of these words describes your existence as a manager?

If you classify yourself as a survivor, you are probably experiencing problems with balance—balance between your personal and work-related activities and between the needs of the organization, others, and yourself.

On the other hand, the person who thrives in a managerial position has established balance in these areas. This person knows that, to effectively deal with the concerns of the organization and the people in it, one must also ensure that one's own needs receive attention.

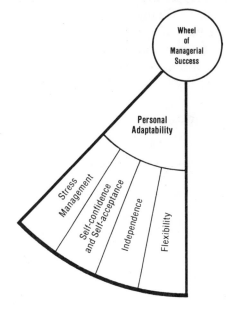

This section contains activities to help you develop this balance in the areas of positive and negative stress, self-confidence and self-acceptance, dependence and independence, and flexibility and adaptability.

Part I: Coping With Stress

Part II: Increasing Self-confidence and Self-acceptance

Part III: Balancing Independence and Dependence

Part IV: Increasing Flexibilty and Adaptability

Tips

- Establish and deepen nonwork friendships. "Let your hair down," be yourself, and talk about sensitive areas without feeling afraid.

- Read Albert Ellis' books and analyze which "Irrational Sentences" you may be telling yourself.

- Do life planning with your mate to develop and maintain common goals.

- Decontaminate your leisure time. Set aside time to have fun and don't let work or thoughts about it intrude.

- Broaden your family activities.

- Expand your recreational activities.

- Take the Dale Carnegie course.

- Be more expressive of your pent-up anger and frustration.

- Look for ways to relax and escape daily tensions.

- Set aside time for vigorous physical exercise and then do it.

- Set aside time for attending to the spiritual side of your life and then do it.

- To control your quick temper, learn to take 10 **slow, deep** breaths through your nose before responding.

- Getting organized and managing your time better may help reduce stress significantly.

- Pay attention to your diet. Learn more about nutrition and drugs, such as caffeine, which impact your stress level or sleep patterns.

- Make sure you don't "catastrophize" events at work. Problems are typical in organizations, but they are not necessarily catastrophic.

- Examine your values and what makes life worth living. Make sure your goals and life habits fit with your deepest values.

- Watch for habits of negative or self-defeating inner conversations or self-talks. Work at replacing them with more positive inner dialogues.

- If you are overcommitted and expect to be great at everything, focus your energy on fewer areas and allow yourself to be average in unimportant matters.

- Seek feedback from your supervisor, trusted peers, and spouse about instances when you may be overly down, negative, or lacking in self-confidence.

- Expect things to turn out well.

- Accept and acknowledge your accomplishments as worthwhile.

- Learn more about your functional area.

- Learn to look at negative feedback and criticism as potentially useful information which you need to understand fully—and unemotionally—before reacting.

- Consciously work at being involved in enough other areas of life to make it likely that you will feel competent even though one area is going wrong.

- Seek additional responsibilities from your supervisor which, when you have successfully achieved them, will increase your self-confidence.

- Try to be less concerned about what others think of you.

- Adopt a more positive approach to your problems instead of being so critical and negative.

- Look for and use the positive side of politics in your organization. Learn to use, and not resist, influence.

- Be more willing to take personal criticism without showing resentment or anger.

- Be more accepting of the constraints imposed upon people in a corporate setting.

- Recognize the potentially self-defeating aspects of your impatience.

- Have your supervisor thrust you into ambiguous situations and coach you on how to cope with them.

- If you are feeling frustrated, analyze whether it is a problem of means or goals. If your goals are OK, but someone else is blocking your methods, try to go along with his or her means as long as your goals still can be achieved.

- Analyze whether your goals are too high. If so, be realistic and adjust them downward without becoming negative and pessimistic in the process.

- Use the serenity prayer daily, "God grant me the serenity to accept what I cannot change . . . ."

Part I: Coping With Stress

Reducing Stress Through Adequate Preparation

You probably know in advance when a situation is likely to be stressful for you. The following procedure will help you increase your confidence and reduce the stress you experience in certain situations. The accompanying chart will help you structure your analysis.

1. Identify situations that cause stress. Then, on the chart that follows, list all of the circumstances and responsibilities that make you feel particularly tense and pressured in a given situation. Assume, for example, that the situation is a group meeting. Circumstances that often cause stress in meetings include:
   - The need to speak in front of a group
   - The presence of high-level managers
   - Lack of knowledge on the meeting topic(s)
   - Interpersonal conflict between you and another group member
2. Take steps to prepare yourself for and cope with stressful circumstances. For example, if interpersonal conflict between you and another group member causes you to feel stressed in a group situation, consider getting together with that person before the meeting to iron out your differences in private.
3. Prepare for the worst. List the worst thing that could happen in each situation and identify ways in which you could handle that outcome.

Situation	Stressful Circumstances	Methods of Coping	Worst Outcome/ Solution

Reducing Your Emotional Involvement in Stressful Situations

If you are very intense in your approach to your work, you may tend to become too emotionally involved in stressful situations. The following suggestions will help you remove yourself emotionally from work-related problems so you can view them objectively and reduce your stress level.

1. First learn to recognize your symptoms of excessive emotional involvement. Because it's difficult to be objective about one's own behavior, you may need help with this step. Ask a colleague to observe your behavior the next time you're involved in a stressful situation and to watch for signs of stress, such as clenched fists, irritability, and so forth. Afterward, ask your colleague to describe your behavior. As you listen to the description, take note of the behaviors that indicate increasing emotional involvement. Try to remember how you were feeling at the time you exhibited these behaviors.

2. The next time you're involved in a similar situation, try to monitor your behavior. In situations involving only one or two people, be flexible in scheduling your time to help alleviate stress. At the first sign that you are becoming too emotionally involved, pull back and set the problem aside for a time. When you feel ready to view the problem objectively, return to it.

   If you are in a situation where you can't set the problem aside, such as in a group meeting, monitor your behavior as if you were an objective third party while you work on the problem. When you see yourself becoming too involved, talk yourself into calming down and becoming objective. For example, if you find yourself getting angry, you might say to yourself, "I'm getting angry about this. I shouldn't take it personally; I should step back a little and calm down."

Reducing Stress by Using Physical Coping Strategies

You probably are already aware of some of the ways in which your physical state affects your ability to cope with stress. For example, most people realize that stress is more difficult to cope with when they are overly tired. Following are additional areas in which your physical state affects your ability to cope with daily crises and demands.

- **General physical fitness.** When your body is not in good shape, it's less efficient in using available energy. Consider starting a three-phase exercise plan that includes body flexibility, muscle strength, and cardiopulmonary endurance. In addition to conditioning your body so that you're better able to cope with stress, physical exercise also helps discharge built-up stress energy that accumulates over time.
- **Use of drugs.** The following three types of drugs can reduce your ability to cope effectively with stress.

- Stimulants. The most common stimulant is caffeine, which is found in coffee, nonherbal teas, chocolate, soft drinks, and many over-the-counter medications. Stimulants provide temporary energy that allows you to push beyond your normal level of endurance for short periods of time. Over the long term, however, these drugs take their toll on your overall fitness level, and, in turn, on your ability to cope effectively with stress.

Consider slowly reducing the amount of caffeine you ingest each day until you reach a point where you no longer rely on it to get you going or keep you going.
- Alcohol. Alcohol is a poison that your body must work extra hard to metabolize. Alcohol abuse also can have interpersonal and personal ramifications that create stress. If you are in the habit of consuming more than one beer, four ounces of wine, or one-and-a-half ounces of hard liquor a day, it's possible that your alcohol use is interfering with your ability to deal with stress. You

may want to consider cutting down on your ingestion of alcohol.

- Nicotine. Nicotine is a stimulant that reduces the body's ability to deal with pressure and stress. If you are smoking a large number of cigarettes each day, it's possible that your nicotine use is interfering with your ability to cope with stress. Consider gradually reducing the number of cigarettes you smoke each day.

Using Support Groups to Cope With Stress

When you're under pressure, other people can help alleviate your stress in two ways.

- Talking to others about problems can provide an outlet for stress energy. In addition, the people you talk to can help generate solutions to the problems.
- If your pressure is a result of an overloaded work schedule, other people can help you get the tasks done.

Thus, it's important to have a strong support network to turn to for both personal and work-related problems. The following procedure and accompanying chart (on the next page) will help you evaluate and build your support network.

1. Evaluate your support network for both your work and personal lives. Using the chart, list the people on whom you can rely in each of the situations listed on the chart.
2. Once you have listed the people in your support network, determine whether your network is adequate. Do you have people who can help you in each area?
3. For areas in which you require a stronger network, generate a plan for building your network. Ask trusted friends and coworkers where they've found support and help. In addition, try to think of other ways in which you can build your network.

For example, to build a stronger network for support with work-related problems, think of people in your organization or other organizations who hold positions similar to yours. Professional organizations and meetings can be excellent means for meeting these people. To build a stronger network for support with personal problems, consider friends of friends, your church, community organizations, health clubs, etc.

Keep in mind that building long-lasting support relationships takes time and requires a lot of give and take.

WORK LIFE	People Who Can Provide Support	PERSONAL LIFE	People Who Can Provide Support
Information/ training		Relaxation and enjoyment	
Relief from overload Advice		Advice Relief from household tasks	
Discussion of issues/values/ problems		Companionship	
Other		Romance Discussion of problems/ sharing of confidences	
		Other	

Relaxing Through Regulated Breathing Patterns

By slowing your breathing cycle, you lower your oxygen intake, which, in turn, slows the function of your body in general and leads to relaxation.

The breathing cycle of a normal adult ranges from 18 to 20 respirations per minute. It's possible to lower this rate to 10 to 14 breaths per minute. To do so, follow these steps.

1. Begin by paying attention to the breath leaving and entering your nostrils. Awareness of this pattern can help you lower your breathing cycle and make it more smooth.

2. Next, pay attention to your nostrils during your breathing cycle (when inhaling and exhaling). Count each breath as it leaves your nostrils. Count to 10 and then begin again very slowly, trying to breathe a little slower. As you do so, consciously begin to breathe gently and smoothly.

Whenever you are stressed, use this exercise to relax.

Relaxing Through Mental Imagery

Mental imagery is very powerful. You can make yourself upset by imagining all of the possible negative aspects of a decision or event. But you can also relax by using positive images. To relax through mental imagery, follow this procedure.

1. Find a comfortable place to sit or lie down. Then close your eyes and take four slow, deep breaths through your nose. Think of the place in which you relax as your personal sanctuary.

2. In your mind, construct a scene that is very pleasant and relaxing for you. This may be a scene from your past or an image you construct just for this exercise. It is preferable that your chosen image not involve activity on the part of yourself or others. For example, you might picture yourself fishing on a beautiful, calm lake or sitting in a comfortable chair in front of a warm fire on a cold winter day.

The secret to using imagery is to develop as vivid a scenario as possible. Use all of your senses to imagine how it would feel to be in that situation— what it would look like, the sounds you would hear, and the diverse aromas in the air.

Set aside five minutes a couple of times a day to take one of these "mental vacations."

Coping With Stress by Managing Your Time

If you are experiencing stress because you can't accomplish everything you need to accomplish or because you sometimes neglect high-priority items, effective time management can help reduce your stress level. To begin a time-management program, follow these guidelines.

1. Use a "time finder" to keep track of how you spend your time over the next week. A time finder is simply a grid with spaces for notating how you spend your time each hour of the day for seven days.

2. When the week is over, analyze the ways in which you spent your time. List the amount of time you spent on each of the following categories:
   - Sleep
   - Work
   - Meal preparation
   - Eating and clean up
   - Transportation
   - Meetings (outside work)
   - Exercise

- Chores
- Relaxation and leisure
- Visiting with friends
- Any other areas (name them)

After you identify the time spent on each area, list these areas in the order of their importance to you. If your time distribution is inconsistent with your rank ordering of importance, it may be contributing to negative stress.

Also, if you spend little or no time on leisure activities, you're not allowing yourself opportunities to "charge your batteries" and recover from the demands placed on you.

3. Read through the "Personal Organization and Time Management" section of this Handbook and select the suggestions most applicable to your situation.

Dealing With Stress That Results from Interpersonal Conflict

Conflict is unavoidable in a dynamic organization. For those who are unable to deal with it constructively, it can create an emotional strain and cause stress. To deal with conflict on the job, follow these suggestions.

1. Analyze the way in which you currently deal with conflict. Over the next month, keep track of situations that involve interpersonal conflict or tension. Note your reactions to these situations. Did you back down? Were you drawn into any win-lose confrontations?

Also keep track of the outcome of each situation. Were you satisfied with the result of the conflict and/or your behavior?

The chart on the next page will help you monitor these situations.

2. Once you recognize sources of conflict and your current way of coping with them, apply the following guidelines each time you become involved in conflict.
  - Reduce antagonism by accepting that others' opinions are just as important to them as yours are to you. Accept the fact that some people will never be completely persuaded to accept your point of view and be willing to compromise.
  - Present your opinions forcefully but tactfully. Try to make a habit of integrating them with the opinions of others rather than being forced to do so.

Conflict Situation	Reactions	Outcome

- Investigate the other conflict management techniques presented in the **Conflict Management and Negotiating** section of this Handbook.
- Evaluate the outcomes of conflict situations to determine if your new methods of handling conflict are reducing the amount of stress you feel.
- Continue to improve your conflict management skills until you are comfortable with your performance in stress situations.

Part II: Increasing Self-confidence and Self-acceptance

Identifying Reasons for Lack of Self-confidence

To build a development plan to increase self-confidence, you must first determine why you lack confidence. The following guidelines can help you do this.

1. Over the next two weeks, pay attention to all situations in which you feel a lack of confidence. Write down what you are thinking to yourself at such times. Be certain to include any negative names, adjectives, or characteristics you apply to yourself. Following are examples of the types of statements that indicate lack of self-confidence:
   - "I just can't handle this kind of situation."
   - "I'm in way over my head; I don't have enough background in this area."

- "I can never make them understand."
- "I'm just not smart enough."

If you have difficulty identifying the types of thoughts that indicate low self-confidence, read the book **How to Make Yourself Miserable** by Greenberg and Jacobs.

2. Next, analyze the thoughts you've recorded. Look for patterns that indicate particular areas of concern, including thoughts that:
   - Suggest that you believe you must be perfect
   - Are self-putdowns or negative self-talk
   - Indicate that you expect impossible things of yourself, such as perfection
   - Refer to your lack of skills or abilities
3. For those thoughts that indicate a lack of confidence due to lack of skills, prepare a plan for increasing your skills. Be sure your plan includes a resolution to think positive thoughts about your increasing skills.

For areas in which you have unrealistic thoughts or put yourself down, use rational, positive statements, such as:
   - "Nobody's perfect, and I shouldn't expect to be either."
   - "I'm not a terrible person just because I made a mistake."
   - "Just because one person didn't like my idea doesn't mean it's a bad idea."

Gradually, as you increase your skills and think positive thoughts about yourself, you will find your self-confidence increasing.

Dealing Constructively With Your Own Failures and Mistakes

Have you made any mistakes in your job over the past three months? If you have, good. That means you are probably stretching yourself to grow. The question is not whether you make mistakes, because good managers always do, but what you learn from those mistakes.

One of the biggest problems managers face as they move up the management ladder is an aversion to taking risks. If success is rewarded and failure is punished, managers might take fewer risks to reduce the possibility of failure. Unfortunately, that approach is counterproductive to creativity and achievement.

When you attempt something and fail, ask yourself, "What have I learned?" rather than kicking yourself or blaming someone else. Discovering the value of your mistakes will make you a better, smarter manager. If you approach it constructively, you can learn more from one mistake than from 100 successes.

Demonstrating Awareness of Your Own Strengths and Weaknesses

Awareness of your strengths and limitations as a manager is a key to your development and your career. It's always more pleasant to look at strengths than at weaknesses, but knowledge of both is essential to success. Objective feedback from others is a necessary part of building this awareness. The following process can help you gather that feedback.

1. Determine what others see as your strengths and limitations. You can use past performance appraisals, discussions with your manager, a trusted peer and subordinates, and tools like the PDI Management Skills Profile to gather this information.

2. When you have compiled as much information as you can, meet with key individuals (your boss, a trusted peer, or subordinates) to share your understanding of the feedback and gather additional insights. Be as open as you can to both negative and positive comments; both are of equal value to your success.

3. Analyze the information you have received and, with your manager, select one or two areas on which to focus for development.

4. Build a development plan for the areas you have selected. The plan should include:
   - Small, measurable steps toward the overall objectives
   - Specific dates for the completion of the steps
   - Room to alter or refocus the plan if necessary

Continue to seek regular feedback from others as you work on developing your skills.

Focusing on Strengths

A lack of self-confidence can have negative effects on your career. It can keep you from aggressively seeking out new responsibilities and leadership opportunities. In addition, it's difficult for others to have confidence in you if you lack confidence in yourself. Thus, it's important to curb any tendencies to be negative about yourself. The following ways of focusing on your accomplishments will help you establish this control.

1. Keep a file on your accomplishments and successes—good performance evaluations, letters of commendation, your own descriptions of difficult and challenging situations in which you performed well. When you begin to doubt your competence, read through this file. Refer to your accomplishments at appropriate times when speaking with others about additional opportunities. For example, an interview for a position you're seeking is the perfect time to stress your qualifications in that area.
2. Seek positive feedback from trusted superiors, peers, subordinates, and friends when you feel a need for support.
3. Be careful to balance your failures by giving equal consideration to your successes.
4. Become involved in off-the-job activities that are rewarding and provide recognition. Again, refer to your successes, when appropriate, as you participate in these activities.

Part III: Balancing Independence and Dependence

Evaluating Your Independence/Dependence Balance

A balance between independence and dependence is important to today's large organizations. Independence is necessary in standing up for your point of view, making your contributions heard and felt, and exhibiting a willingness to take risks. Dependence, on the other hand, is required for good teamwork and for reaching mutually agreed-upon and supported goals.

The following suggestions will help you assess your ability to situationally balance independence and dependence.

1. Over the next few weeks, pay particular attention to how you approach working with others. Note the number of times you exhibit the following behaviors.

Independent Behaviors
- Standing up for your ideas and beliefs, without pushing too hard
- Persistence
- Making decisions on your own
- Taking unpopular stands, when necessary

Dependent Behaviors
- Listening to the ideas of others
- Compromising when your position is not accepted
- Staying involved rather than withdrawing or getting defensive when things don't go your way

2. Evaluate the balance between these two types of behaviors. Do you tend to be overly independent or dependent?
3. If you see a trend that points to excessively independent or dependent behaviors, set goals to balance your independence/dependence in given situations. The following section provides additional suggestions for balancing your behaviors.

Increasing Interdependence

It's possible to be competitive to the point where your actions destroy cooperation. In this case, independence should be tempered to achieve the interdependence necessary for constructive teamwork. The following suggestions will help you achieve this goal.

1. Interdependence begins with the belief that dependence on others is not a sign of weakness. If you doubt that cooperating with others can enable you to achieve more than you could alone, you will have difficulty increasing your interdependence.
2. Next, determine the degree to which you are competitive at the expense of cooperation. Analyze your behavior in meetings and try to gauge the impact of your competitive behavior on the outcomes. Watch for the following tendencies.
   - Pushing your own ideas rather than accepting the ideas of others and compromising
   - Withdrawing from the group psychologically or physically if your ideas are not accepted
   - Behaving in a way that creates a win-lose atmosphere
3. If you observe these tendencies in your behavior, try doing the following.
   - Look for others' suggestions or viewpoints that you can support or agree with.
   - Balance offering your own ideas with accepting others' ideas to create a sense of shared commitment to group outcomes.
   - If you find yourself withdrawing, use this as a cue to begin striving for a compromise position.

- Seek consensus from the group after you've given your opinion. Where consensus cannot be reached, strive for compromise.
4. Evaluate the effects of your new behaviors. Notice if others are becoming more supportive and enthusiastic about implementing shared decisions than they were about decisions made as a result of your aggressiveness. You may wish to ask others to help you evaluate the effects of your behavior.

Increasing Independence

If you're reluctant to make decisions on your own, or if you defer too easily to others, increasing your independence will make you a more valuable contributor and probably help you develop a more positive image of yourself.

Following are some common problems involving overdependence and solutions to such problems.

1. **Difficulty in standing up for what you believe.** If you have valuable ideas that are getting pushed aside, consider the following.

   - Be more persistent in presenting your ideas. You may simply need to restate your opinion more often or speak up more frequently in meetings. Set a goal to state your opinion or put forth your position some time during the meeting, despite any initial discomfort.

   - If you tend to defer to people who are louder or more persistent than you are, push yourself beyond your immediate comfort level and practice fighting a little harder for your position. Often, it's not the best idea that is implemented, but rather the idea whose initiator persisted in fighting for its acceptance.

   - If you tend to compromise too quickly, set a goal to hold out a little longer before compromising. Work toward a position that includes enough of your idea to make you satisfied with the final solution.

   - If you find that you back down because you are unsure of your position, make a point to study the agenda of the meeting, think through your opinions and positions, and gather the necessary supporting data. If you are well prepared, you are less likely to back down due to lack of supporting information.

2. **Concern that taking a stand will cause others to dislike you.** In this case, it's important to distinguish between people who are close to you in your personal life and people who are work-related acquaintances. While acceptance, approval, and closeness are important in personal relationships, they aren't always necessary or appropriate in the work setting.

   When dealing with business associates, remind yourself that it's impossible to be liked by everyone in business and that you need not be overly concerned about your business associates' personal feelings for you. Their professional opinions of your competence are more important.

3. **A need to seek approval before implementing decisions.** To advance in a management career, one must take responsibility for his or her decisions and actions. If you constantly seek approval before proceeding, you may be wasting your supervisor's time and giving the impression that you lack confidence in your decisions.

Before seeking approval, ask yourself whether it's really necessary for your superior to review your decision or action. If you determine that your reason for seeking approval is due to a lack of self-confidence in your work, proceed without checking with your superior.

Part IV: Increasing Flexibility and Adaptability

Understanding Your Reactions to Change

When people are uncertain about the effects of change, they tend to resist it. The following steps will help you determine whether your reactions to change influence your actions and aid you in coping with innovation and change in your work environment.

1. Review your career and list the significant changes that have occurred, including changes in the following areas:
   - Employers or managers
   - Locations
   - Positions
   - Job responsibilities

   Recall how you felt during each of these changes. Were you anxious? Angry? Excited? Determine whether your overall reaction was positive or negative and whether past changes influence your reactions to current events. Briefly summarize the causes of discomfort for each of these events.
2. Use your summary statements as a basis for determining how you can become more accepting of change. For example, if you find that you feel uneasy about how a change will affect your position, arrange to become more involved in planning for the change, thereby reducing your uncertainty. If you can turn changes into positive experiences, you will react more favorably to them in the future.

Increasing Flexibility When Interacting With Others

If you are strongly opinionated, you may tend not to listen to what others are saying. Rather than listening to alternate approaches, you may tend to prepare rebuttals to argue your own case. This may cause others to see you as rigid and inflexible. Try these exercises to increase your flexibility.

1. To make certain that you are listening in order to understand what another person is saying (rather than to strengthen your own position), concentrate on paraphrasing or summarizing the speaker's message.

This will help you pay attention to the speaker and let the speaker know that you are tuned in to his or her message.

2. If you have difficulty seeing the value of another person's viewpoint, reverse sides mentally to see if you can come up with ideas that support that person's position. While your goal is not necessarily to accept the opposite view as your final opinion, understanding the positive aspects of another person's thinking may enhance your own idea and make you appear less rigid.

Increasing Adaptability to Alternate Solutions

If your typical response to a problem is to immediately generate a specific solution, you may find it difficult to give adequate consideration to other possibilities. This tendency can decrease the quality of your decisions. To reduce this tendency, follow these guidelines.

- When you approach a problem, remind yourself that there are many possible solutions to any given management problem and that you must be willing to consider the unique facts about the situation before making a final decision.
- Consciously delay making a final decision. Concentrate on gathering more information so you can gain a thorough understanding of several possible solutions and their unique benefits and drawbacks. Once you understand the solutions, weed out those that are least appropriate, using facts to substantiate your decisions.
- Look for opportunities to combine the best features of several solutions to improve the quality of your final decision.

Adapting to Unstructured Situations

The ability to think on your feet is essential in positions of increasing responsibility. If you are ill-at-ease in situations where you do not know exactly what is expected of you or in which there is no clear leader or structure, the following tips will help you learn to cope.

1. Imagine yourself in situations with which you are unfamiliar and in which responsibilities are not clearly established. Consider how you would respond. For example, would you tend to sit back and wait for someone to take the lead, or step forward to help establish a structure? Your goal should be to picture yourself expanding the range of your behavior—to envision actions you can take to provide structure.
2. Rather than avoiding unstructured situations—such as unstructured problem-solving groups or task forces—seek them out as opportunities

for demonstrating your leadership abilities. Ask trusted participants to give you feedback about your performance and suggestions for how you could be more effective.

Increasing Your Mental Flexibility

Mental flexibility is the ability to quickly adjust to new information when solving problems and to consider a broad range of alternatives. It is the opposite of holding on to a solution or procedure because "that's the way it's always been done." People who think inflexibly generally hold to policy, display rigidity in problem solving by discarding alternatives before thinking them through, and believe that each problem has one right answer.

To become more flexible, try following these guidelines.
- Ask trusted coworkers to provide feedback on situations in which you tend to be overly opinionated or rigid in your thinking. Most people have specific "problem areas." Recognizing the fact that you are becoming inflexible is the first step in initiating change.
- Watch for "snap" reactions. Rather than assuming that the first alternative that enters your mind is the best solution, try writing down your first reaction, then considering other options.

Handling Crisis Situations Effectively

How do you react when a work emergency is brought to your attention? In crisis situations, it pays to keep a cool head and evaluate the seriousness of the situation before reacting. If you find that you tend to react too quickly to crises and make decisions without getting all the facts, you may want to try this technique:
1. Make it a rule to discuss the situation with your boss, a peer, or the subordinate affected before making any decisions.
2. Together, gather all the facts and evaluate the seriousness of the situation. Give the situation a crisis rating from 1 (mild, can wait) to 10 (urgent, immediate attention required).
3. Together, brainstorm alternative courses of action. Select the alternative that best addresses the situation.

This technique can help you put the crisis in perspective and decide if you absolutely must drop everything to react to it. The result of your evaluation may be that you have more time to address the situation than you thought, or that what you initially identified as a crisis may be a small problem—or no problem at all.

Increasing Your Intellectual Curiosity

Looking at problems and issues from different perspectives prevents tunnel vision. Increased intellectual curiosity will also help you become more resourceful in solving problems. The following guidelines will help you broaden your perspective.

- To increase your knowledge of the world around you, get in the habit of reading newspapers and periodicals for current events, technical journals for new developments in your field, and other related books.

- Choose an area of your organization about which you know relatively little. Over the next three months, learn about that area and its perspective. Ask one or two people from that organization to tell you about their responsibilities and problems. Also ask them what they read to keep up with developments in their field.

- The next time you have an opportunity to develop a long-range project for your department or to set up a task force, assemble as diverse a group of people as possible.

Recommended Readings

Burns, David. *Feeling Good: The New Mood Therapy.* New York, NY: Morrow, 1980.

In clear, simple language, Burns, an eminent psychologist, outlines a systematic program for controlling thought distortions that lead to pessimism, lethargy, procrastination, low self-esteem, and other "black holes" of depression. Included in the book: understanding your moods, building self-esteem, handling criticism, defeating guilt, overcoming perfectionism, and coping with the stresses and strain of daily living.

Deal, Terrence E., and Kennedy, Allan A. *Corporate Cultures: The Rights and Rituals of Corporate Life.* Reading, MA: Addison-Wesley, 1984.

The authors of this book, with examples from the nation's best known companies, analyze the inner workings of corporate life and find that the company culture and not attention to the more rational aspects of managing make for the most highly successful companies. They offer managers at all levels explicit guidelines for diagnosing the state of one's own corporate culture and influencing how business gets done, both now and in the future.

Ellis, A., and Harper, R. *A New Guide to Rational Living.* New York, NY: Wilshire, 1977.

This is the most comprehensive book on rational psychotherapy for the intelligent lay person. It presents a self-questioning approach to emotional problems that shows how they can be radically changed by modifying the thinking processes that create them. The topics Dr. Ellis discusses, stressing their relevance in business structures, include: enhancing decisiveness, increasing efficient concentration, improving relations with others, achieving self-discipline, creating self-acceptance, overcoming feelings of hostility, conquering depression, and attacking emotional upsets.

Goldberg, P. *Executive Health: How to Recognize Health Danger Signals and Manage Stress Successfully.* New York, NY: McGraw-Hill, 1979.

This comprehensive guide to good health and physical fitness tailored to the modern business executive was named by Library Journal as one of the ten best business books of 1978. Written in plain language, it provides a basic explanation of the ailments to which business people are most vulnerable, especially problems associated with a high-stress lifestyle.

Greenberg, Dan, and Jacobs, M. *How to Make Yourself Miserable.*
New York, NY: Random House, 1976.

This tongue-in-cheek book tells you how to punish yourself even more
effectively than you already may be doing.

Greenberg, Herbert M. *Coping with Job Stress.* Englewood Cliffs, NJ:
Prentice-Hall, 1980.

This book explains how to deal with such pressures as impossible deadlines,
an excessive workload, bosses, changes in your work environment, and
tension with coworkers. It describes techniques for preventing stress and
tension, and gives instructions on when and how to use them.

Jaffe, D.T., and Scott, C.D. *From Burnout to Balance: A Workbook for Personal
Self-Renewal.* New York, NY: McGraw-Hill, 1985.

This book provides the techniques that prevent or overcome burnout and
suggests those measures easiest to incorporate into life situations. Each
chapter presents a problem area, followed by a self-assessment
questionnaire, and instruction in the self-management skills that can
preserve one's health and ensure a creative and productive existence.

James, Muriel, and Jongeward, D. *Born to Win: Transactional Analysis with
Gestalt Experiments.* New York, NY: NAL Penguin, 1978.

This book is concerned primarily with transactional analysis theory and its
application to the average person's daily life. It is designed to help readers
increase their awareness of the power they have to direct their own lives, to
make decisions, and to understand that they were "born to win."

Kaufman, Gershen, and Raphael, Lev. *The Dynamics of Power: Building a
Competent Self.* Cambridge, MA: Schenkman Publishing Co., 1983.

The author contends that people are never taught how to value themselves,
feel competent, and control their lives. In this book, he offers a framework
for building self-worth and for developing a sense of power in life.

Layden, Milton. *Escaping the Hostility Trap.* Englewood Cliffs, NJ:
Prentice-Hall, 1979.

This book provides simple techniques designed to help the reader
understand and free him/herself from repressed anger and
resentment—emotions known to cause migraine headaches, ulcers, high
blood pressure, and heart disease, and lead to depression, accidents, and
absenteeism at work. Chapter 5 deals specifically with overcoming
depression on the job.

Maultsby, Maxie C. *Help Yourself to Happiness*. New York, NY: Institute for Applied Rational Psychotherapy, 1975.

This work attempts to enable you to pursue happiness and self-mastery at your own pace. It is clear, readable, and includes case histories and many helpful, creative self-analysis techniques.

McKay, Matthew; David, Martha; and Fanning, Patrick. *Thoughts and Feelings: The Art of Cognitive Stress Intervention*. Richmond, CA: New Harbinger Publications, 1981.

This workbook offers simple, concise, step-by-step directions for mastery of techniques such as: systematic desensitization, problem-solving, stress inoculation, values clarification, covert assertion, combating distorted thinking, and visualization. It helps the reader see how thoughts and feelings create his/her stress syndrome and how to determine the techniques which will be most beneficial in dealing with those thoughts and feelings.

Niehouse, Oliver L. "Measuring Your Burnout Potential." *Supervisory Management,* July 1984, pp. 27-33.

The self-administered test included in this article asks the individual twenty questions designed to measure the likelihood of "burning out" in one's job or profession. If the reader's score suggests a high potential for burnout, the author has provided a list of seven simply applied tips for prevention. Additionally, he suggests that to remain capable of making valuable contributions at one's place of employment, one should undertake this self-examination periodically.

Pelletier, K.R. *Mind As Healer, Mind As Slayer*. New York, NY: Dell, 1977.

This book outlines positive steps that people can take to prevent sickness and create a more satisfying life. Included are some guidelines for the evaluation of one's own stress levels, profiles of various disease-prone personalities, and a practical section on the prevention of stress-related diseases through such techniques as meditation and biofeedback.

Peters, Tom. *Thriving on Chaos: A Handbook for a Management Revolution*. New York, NY: Alfred A. Knopf, 1987.

Peters maintains that organizations merely aspiring to be excellent will prove disastrous; the only winning companies will be constantly adapting ones. Developing such flexibility will require a revolution in both management theory and day-to-day management practice. *Thriving on Chaos* is the essential guide to this revolution. Forty-five prescriptions specify what managers at every level must do if the organizations are to survive and flourish in today's and tomorrow's environment.

Quick, J.C., and Quick, J. *Organizational Stress and Preventive Management.* New York, N.Y.: McGraw-Hill, 1984.

Emphasizing diagnosis and preventive management and methods, this new book provides a straightforward, comprehensive approach to organizational, medical, and psychological viewpoints.

Suggested Seminars

The seminars listed here were selected for their appeal to a managerial audience and have received good to excellent ratings from managers attending them.

Because of the dynamic nature of the seminar marketplace, some seminars may have been added, upgraded, or replaced, and others may no longer be offered. Additional information about these seminars may be obtained by calling the vendor directly, or through Seminar Clearinghouse International, a subscriber organization located in St. Paul, Minnesota. Call 612/293-1004 for information.

LEARNING INTERNATIONAL, 200 First Stamford Place, P.O. Box 10211, Stamford, CT 06904, 203/965-8400.

Interpersonal Managing Skills. The new Interpersonal Managing Skills system prepares professionals for the demands of today's changing organizations. Participants learn techniques for encouraging subordinates and peers to contribute the best work they have to offer, giving constructive criticism, crediting good performance, clarifying and confirming understanding, acknowledging the value of other people's contributions, and managing differences.
Length: 3 days
Cost: Call vendor
Locations: Marina Del Rey, CA; San Francisco, CA; Atlanta, GA; Chicago, IL; Schaumburg, IL; Boston, MA; Bloomington, MN; New York, NY; Pittsburgh, PA; Dallas, TX; Houston, TX; Bellevue, WA. The above seminar is offered in other U.S. cities. For additional locations, contact the vendor.

NTL INSTITUTE, P.O. Box 9155, Rosslyn Station, Arlington, VA 22209, 703/527-1500.

Centering for Personal and Professional Development. This program covers finding one's physical and mental point of equilibrium, greater clarity about the self, and finding one's own "unique center."
Length: 12 days
Cost: $995
Location: Bethel, ME.

Developing the Organizational and Personal Self. This program is based on the premise that success is based on self-awareness. Given that, topics included in this workshop are: boundaries; reintegration; acceptance of

ourselves; removing self-diminishing myths and behaviors; improving interactions with others; and speaking more clearly, directly, and candidly.
Length: 8 days
Cost: $765
Location: Bethel, ME.

Holding On and Letting Go. Participants in this program: explore in depth your personal identity, gain awareness of your own emotions, and clarify issues you may confront when working with groups.
Length: 7 days
Cost: $1095
Location: Bethel, ME.

Successful Transitions in Life and Work. This program enables participants to learn how to understand stress and transition, establish your own strategies for coping with transitional stress, identify transitional stress in others, and discover ways to enter new situations.
Length: 6 days
Cost: $765
Location: Bethel, ME.

WEIR ASSOCIATES INC., 621 Woodbridge Street, San Luis Obispo, CA 93401, 805/544-1754.
Weirlabs For Personal Growth. Weirlabs are designed for adults, couples and teams, managers, workers, and professionals to use the methods of laboratory education to discover and teach the principles and practices of personal growth. These seminars are educational experiences and should not be considered a substitute for psychotherapy or for relief of severe emotional distress.
Length: 1 week
Cost: $850
Locations: St. Helena, CA; Poconos, PA.

Personal Adaptability

Notes:

Notes:

FACTOR **6**

Personal Motivation

Over the past several months, Ellen has become more and more aware of her dissatisfaction with her job. She has difficulty getting going in the morning, and by the end of a typical day, she has a nagging headache. Ellen realizes that her greatest problem with her job is that the tasks that were once challenging are now routine and mundane. She is just plain bored!

Ellen also realizes that her sinking level of motivation has begun to adversely affect her staff. Her subordinates, who once viewed her as a model of the level of drive and enthusiasm expected in the organization, are confused by her lack of motivation.

What Ellen finds most discouraging, however, is the fact that her boss has not mentioned any opportunities for promotion or change for a long time.

At some point in their careers, most managers find themselves in Ellen's position. They've been in the same job for too long and need a change. Unfortunately, too many of these managers expect the organization to solve their problems; they wait for someone to offer a promotion or to suggest a new, more interesting position. And chances are that most of them wait a long time!

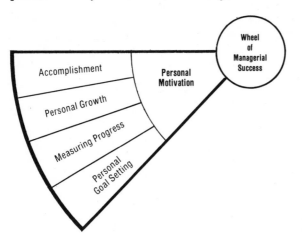

345

Personal Motivation

In the area of personal motivation, no one knows your needs and interests better than you do. And no one can decide how and when you should make changes to meet these needs. Thus, this section offers development activities that will help you take charge of your own motivation program.

- Setting Personal Standards (p. 350)
- Making Your Job More Interesting (p. 351)
- Displaying a High Energy Level (p. 352)
- Persisting at a Task Despite Unexpected Difficulties (p. 352)
- Willingly Working Long Hours When Required (p. 353)
- Seeking Increased Responsibility on the Job (p. 353)
- Preparing a Plan for Personal Growth (p. 354)
- Identifying Management Role Models to Serve as Sources of Personal Motivation (p. 355)
- Clarifying Personal Goals by Identifying Opportunities Within Your Organization's Management Network (p. 356)
- Measuring Progress by Establishing Short-term Goals (p. 357)
- Measuring Progress by Establishing Long-term Goals (p. 358)

Tips

- Look for ways to make a unique contribution to your organization. Take calculated risks to demonstrate that contribution.

- Refrain from saying "It can't be done" and focus on how you "can make it happen."

- Avoid negative "self-talk."

- Reinforce yourself with gifts (new suit, new car, etc.) for achieving goals.

- Discuss satisfactions to be expected from your career with company associates and your spouse.

- Discuss your personal values and goals with your boss, friends, or spouse.

- Introspect about your personal goals.

- Consider the importance to your happiness of doing the kinds of things you ultimately expect to be doing.

- Take an annual audit of where you are by asking yourself: "How am I doing," "Where am I going?," and "Is this the way I want to be?"

- Think through your values to determine how committed you are to them and whether you are willing to change them in order to promote your career.

- Show initiative by suggesting new ways to make or save money for your organization.

- Ask yourself what you need to do to feel excited about going to work.

- Have your job enlarged and enriched to make it more challenging.

- Determine whether to 1) specialize more intensively in your own functional area, 2) go into broader areas of professional management, or 3) find another functional area in which to go.

- For work to become a more central feature in your life, seek and generate additional challenges and let people know that you want additional responsibilities and personal growth.

- Become more energetic on your job and more committed to it by gaining experiences in various management areas through job rotation or management development seminars.

- In order to develop your work motivation, examine the outcomes you want from a job.

- Get involved in activities that make you feel excited and alive, both at work and in your personal life.

- Attend the Leadership Development Program offered by Personnel Decisions, Inc., in Minneapolis, MN.

- Work an extra hour or half hour per day—enough to make a difference.

- Be willing to sacrifice in the short-term for long-term gains in the welfare of your organization.

- Buy a set of motivational tapes and listen to them when commuting to and from the office.

- Undertake a daily exercise program to increase your energy level and endurance.

- Talk to people in higher management levels about their roles and what it takes to be successful.

- Recognize that informal time after hours is often the best time to build networks of support and achieve understanding. Plan to use that time well.

- Talk with someone in your manpower planning group about your goals within the corporation and try to map out a career plan.

- Discuss with company officials what career paths might lead to your long-range career objectives.

- With your boss, define your personal objectives and seek ways to integrate them with organizational goals.

- Try to discover how well your personal goals can be satisfied by job opportunities in your own company by questioning high level executives.

- Routinely set goals that are challenging but achievable for yourself in each area of your life.

- Make some form of public commitment to your goals so others will encourage you to reach them.

- Use mental imagery to visualize attainment of your goals.

- Spend 10 minutes every day visualizing yourself attaining your goals and already having arrived.

- When you set goals, make sure they are for accomplishments **you** really want and not what others want or what you think you **should** want.

- Keep your goals in front of you at all times in some way, such as on the mirror, in your desk drawer, etc.

- Read *If You Don't Know Where You Are Going, You Will Probably End Up Someplace Else* by David Campbell.

- Review your goals with significant others in your life to test them for reality.

- Decide on a clear-cut, long-range goal for yourself and then establish what you will need to do and what attitudes you will need to have in order to achieve it.

- Become more energetic on, and committed to, your job by engaging in a series of goal-setting interviews with your supervisor.

- Set high but realistic goals for yourself and be more of a risk taker.

Setting Personal Standards

Although recognition, increased status, and other rewards are important, your satisfaction with your performance is the ultimate reward. These guidelines will help you develop standards for your performance.

1. Perform a job analysis of your work and set your own objectives using the following procedure.
    - Write down your five most important job duties or responsibilities—those that make the difference between success and mediocrity on your job.
    - For each duty, identify the factors that lead to success. What types of knowledge, skills, abilities, or other characteristics are important for achievement in this area?
    - Describe the characteristics of superior performance in each area.
    - Describe the characteristics of inferior performance in each of the five areas.
    - Using these extremes, set personal standards for yourself in each area. Try to make the standards challenging yet attainable.

The following chart will help you structure your analysis.

Most Important Job Duties	Success Factors	Superior Performance	Inferior Performance	Personal Standards

2. On a regular basis—such as weekly or monthly, depending on the nature of the standards—monitor your performance based on your personal standards. Compare your actual performance to your standards.

3. When you accomplish a goal or meet a standard, take time to congratulate and reward yourself, and enjoy the feelings of personal accomplishment that accompany these achievements.

4. After six months, compare your assessment of your work with the feedback and recognition you receive from others to determine if your self-assessment is accurate.

Although praise and support from others is important, your personal assessment of your achievements should become increasingly important as a source of reward. It can help you emphasize task accomplishment and continual improvement in your work instead of focusing too heavily on status and recognition.

Making Your Job More Interesting

If you've held a job so long that many of your assignments have become routine, you may have difficulty developing and maintaining enthusiasm for your work. There are several methods you can try for revitalizing your job and regaining your enthusiasm.

1. Make a list of your job duties. Then identify the tasks that have become so routine they no longer interest you. To regain your enthusiasm for these tasks:
   - Ask yourself whether you are performing them with maximum efficiency. Is your method the best possible method for performing each task? Try to generate several ideas for improving the accomplishment of each task, such as eliminating a step or adding a step that will improve the end product.
   - Consider whether the tasks should be delegated. Routine tasks usually provide excellent opportunities for preparing a subordinate for advancement. What seems routine to you may be challenging for a subordinate.

2. Prepare a job description for an improved version of your job. Include any current tasks that you find stimulating and list additional, related tasks that you would like to be given the opportunity to perform. In addition, think of duties that would prepare you for advancement.

When you have finished your description of your ideal job, set it aside for a day or two. Then review it to determine if the modifications you would like to make are realistic. Eliminate unrealistic changes from your description.

As a final step, show your description to your superior and negotiate any major changes. Then implement the changes gradually.

3. Change your schedule so that you alternate between high-interest and low-interest tasks. This will allow you to avoid large blocks of time spent on unpleasant duties.

Evaluate the changes you made based on these three suggestions after a month or two. Determine whether they are helping you change your overall attitude toward your job and resulting in improved job performance.

Displaying a High Energy Level

If you find it difficult to maintain a high energy level on the job, you may want to assess your fitness level, giving consideration to:

- *Nutrition.* Examine your eating habits. If you typically rush out of the house in the morning without breakfast and take lunch on the run, you may not be getting the balanced diet you need to sustain energy on the job.
- *Exercise.* Regular physical exercise, whether it be a brisk evening walk or an intense nightly workout, can go a long way toward making you feel energetic and alert all day.
- *Sleep.* While the amount of sleep needed varies with each individual, you may need more, or less, than you're getting right now. Examine your sleeping pattern and decide the right amount for you.
- *Work Schedule.* It is typical for most managers to work 50 to 60 hours per week. If you find you are working more than that on a regular basis, you may want to examine how effectively you are managing your time on the job.
- *Stretch Breaks.* Long periods of intense work effort can create lethargy and drowsiness. Break up these sessions with short "stretch breaks." Take a short walk outside or do some simple calisthenics to relieve tension and relax stiff muscles.

Persisting at a Task Despite Unexpected Difficulties

Despite evidence to the contrary, persistence does **not** mean banging one's head on an obstacle until one or the other gives way. When you find that your progress toward your objectives is impeded, try asking yourself these questions:

- How does this obstacle affect the key results I am trying to obtain?
- Are there other, more vital things I should be doing rather than attacking this obstacle?

- Might this obstacle go away by itself if I leave it for a while?
- If I cannot avoid dealing with the obstacle, is the head-on approach best, or should I look for less direct solutions?
- If I can't solve this problem myself, whom can I get to help me look at it objectively and brainstorm possible solutions?

If you determine that reaching other goals is more important than overcoming the present difficulty, put it aside for the time being and attend to more important issues. Sometimes a little "incubating time" will help you discover an obvious solution at a later date. And, if the obstacle must be overcome immediately, seek help as soon as you run into a dead end in your own thinking.

Willingly Working Long Hours When Required

There will undoubtedly be times when you will be required to make an extended effort to complete a project or get caught up on your routine responsibilities. When such a situation arises, it is important to take a constructive approach to completing the work at hand. The following techniques can help:

- Determine the larger goal and take the initiative to break it into smaller, yet challenging steps. Set up a personal rewards system and reward yourself when you reach each smaller goal.
- Look for the long-term payoff that working extended hours will bring. Showing that you are willing to "go the extra mile" will reflect positively on your performance appraisal and will let others know that you are willing to do what is necessary to get the job done. As a consequence, you will likely find yourself involved in many interesting and challenging projects.

Seeking Increased Responsibility on the Job

Taking the initiative to assume broader responsibilities demonstrates your commitment to the organization and increases the variety and challenge of your job. The following process can get you started:

1. Identify projects or assignments which are of interest to you, but for which you are not currently responsible.
2. Be realistic about what you can handle. Consider your strengths and weaknesses, and set your goals accordingly. Don't try to take on too much at one time.
3. Talk with your boss about your desire to broaden the range of your responsibilities. Indicate your interests, and discuss with him or her possible action steps.

Preparing a Plan for Personal Growth

By identifying areas in which you would like to see personal growth on the job and preparing a plan for achieving this growth, you can channel your achievement motivation toward the objectives that will bring the greatest reward. Following is a process for preparing your plan.

1. Identify areas for improvement by:
   - Making a complete list of the skills required for your job. For each skill, identify your personal strengths and weaknesses by checking the appropriate column on the chart that follows. A developmental feedback instrument such as the Management Skills Profile (MSP) offered through Personnel Decisions, Inc., may be helpful. It provides specific feedback on your management skills from the perspectives of your boss, subordinates, and/or peers. Then identify one or two target areas in which improvement is needed. By improving your skills in these areas, you will become a better performer in your immediate position. For more information, write to Personnel Decisions, Inc., 2000 Plaza VII Tower, 45 South Seventh Street, Minneapolis, MN 55402, (612) 339-0927.

- Identifying additional skills that, although not required, would be assets to your performance either in terms of your personal motivation or in preparing you for future positions. Be sure to identify a range of skills, including technical, analytical, communications, and interpersonal skills. Again, identify one or two target areas for improvement, using your long-range career goals as the basis for your selection. Improvements in these areas will help you prepare for future positions.

The following chart can help you structure your analysis.

Required Skills	Strengths	Weaknesses	Development Ideas
Additional Skills			

2. Prepare a plan for developing the identified skills. Sources of development ideas for your plan include this Handbook (check the section titles to see if they match your desired skills), your superior or persons in positions to which you aspire, and references that are available through your organization's personnel department.

Identifying Management Role Models to Serve as Sources of Personal Motivation

Association with a variety of managers and executives will allow you to observe a number of different approaches to management. This exposure can help you in the following ways.

1. Observing approaches and talking to managers about how they do their jobs can help you identify and implement behaviors that contribute to successful leadership.

2. Asking managers about significant events in their careers can give you a better view of the experiences and challenges you are likely to face as you assume greater management responsibility in your company.

3. Discussing with managers their views on the events of their careers enables you to understand the motivations behind their advancement and, perhaps, to clarify your perspective on your own goals and aspirations.

You can gain exposure to these managers by:
- Joining a local business club or association
- Registering with the local chapter of the Society for the Advancement of Management (SAM)
- Becoming active in a community-based project in which you know other managers are involved
- Studying the organization chart for your company and watching for opportunities to observe and talk with other managers on the chart (for example, task forces, company-sponsored events, and speeches given by these managers)

Clarifying Personal Goals by Identifying Opportunities Within Your Organization's Management Network

Persons new to an organization or to the management function may be unaware of the career opportunities available to them. Investigating the levels and functions of various management positions within your organization will help you identify the direction in which you wish to channel your career energies. This is particularly true if you are part of a large organization. To gain an understanding of the available opportunities, follow these guidelines.

1. Obtain an organization chart for your company and for your organization within the company. You will use this chart to identify positions and individuals you wish to investigate. (If no formal organization chart exists, you may have to construct one as you go through this process.)

2. Ask your superior to help you identify positions (and the persons in them) that would be particularly interesting in terms of their relationship to your career goals.

3. To gain exposure to these positions:
   - Schedule interviews with several of these individuals (after obtaining your superior's approval). Prepare for each interview by compiling a list of questions whose answers will help you determine your career goals and construct your development plan. Examples of such questions include, "What are the most important skills required for a position such as yours?" and, "What is the best way to obtain these skills?"
   - Talk with your peers about their interests and experiences in various management areas to learn more about the rewards and problems of their jobs.
   - Arrange to visit other departments within the company to learn the specific functions of each. Try to contact at least one department each month, and continue until you feel that you have a perspective on the way in which each department contributes to the functioning of the company as a whole.
4. After learning about the various positions available, identify those that may fit into your long-range career plan. Recognize that positions may change as the goals of the company change, and be prepared to be flexible in identifying the steps in your career path.

Measuring Progress by Establishing Short-term Goals

In both their personal and professional lives, people are motivated by their progress toward their goals. By establishing short-term goals, you will be better able to gauge your progress, thereby attaining an increased sense of achievement.

To set short-term goals and monitor progress, follow these guidelines.
1. At the beginning of each day or week, prepare a list of the things you wish to accomplish and the dates by which you wish to accomplish them. Use the list as the basis for your daily activities.
2. Compare your actual accomplishments with your scheduled accomplishments. Determine whether you are satisfied with your achievements during your established time period.
3. If you determine that you would like to accomplish more during a given period of time, gradually increase the demands you make of yourself by adding activities to your list. Establish a pace that will enable you to attain your goals, and set interim dates for individual activities so that all activities have been completed by the end of your chosen time period.

Continue to work toward your goals until you find yourself accomplishing an average of 90 percent of your established goals.

4. If you have difficulty achieving your goals, consider your use of time management techniques. If you feel that you could use your time more effectively, consult the **Personal Organization and Time Management** section of this Handbook for suggestions on creating a development plan in this area.

5. Periodically evaluate your progress to determine whether your achievement level is satisfying your need to realize your progress toward your goals.

Measuring Progress by Establishing Long-term Goals

Whereas short-term goals provide the motivation for your daily activities, a strong long-term goal orientation is important for an individual's growth within an organization. It is a key to achievement motivation—the will to strive for advancement and improvement.

These guidelines can help you establish long-term goals.

1. Identify several goals you want to attain over the next three to five years. These goals can be for either yourself or your department and should be realistic yet challenging enough to encourage you and others in your department to "stretch" to achieve them.

   If you are unaccustomed to setting long-term goals, ask your superior for assistance in identifying appropriate goals. Your superior, however, should not set your goals for you. You will be more highly motivated if you set these goals yourself.

2. Prepare strategic plans for attaining each goal. Outline the steps required to attain it, and set a schedule for achieving the steps.

   To ensure your commitment to your goals, ask your superior or others to help you ensure that you achieve them. For example, you might set a deadline for a development activity, inform others of your deadline, and ask them to inquire about your progress as the deadline approaches.

3. Monitor your progress toward your goals, making adjustments as necessary.

4. As you make progress toward your goals, take time to congratulate yourself on your achievements and to appreciate the sense of accomplishment that comes with continued progress.

Recommended Readings

Rosen, Betty. *How to Set and Achieve Goals: The Key to Successful Management.* Englewood Cliffs, NJ: Prentice-Hall, 1982.

This book offers step-by-step, practical tools for helping managers determine what they want to accomplish, figuring out the best way to do it, and then doing it within a stated period of time. It explains how to define functions and responsibilities, identify payoff areas, select priority objectives, write concrete goal statements, prepare workable action plans, and establish a review system.

Souerwine, Andrew H. *Career Strategies: Planning for Personal Achievement.* New York, NY: AMACOM, 1980.

The author describes how to develop a practical career strategy for personal fulfillment, then outlines a step-by-step plan for putting this strategy into action. He shows how workers can—and why they must—enlist the help of their bosses and companies in achieving personal satisfaction on the job rather than just sitting back and waiting for things to happen.

Stuart-Kotze, Robin, and Roskin, Rick. *Success Guide to Managerial Achievement.* Reston, VA: Reston Publishing Co., 1983.

This book presents a tightly integrated system for increasing achievement by focusing on motivation, leadership, communication, and decision making. It will help you discover your own strengths and weaknesses and teach you what to do, and when and how to do it, to become an effective manager.

Suggested Seminars

The seminars listed here were selected for their appeal to a managerial audience and have received good to excellent ratings from managers attending them.

Because of the dynamic nature of the seminar marketplace, some seminars may have been added, upgraded, or replaced, and others may no longer be offered. Additional information about these seminars may be obtained by calling the vendor directly, or through Seminar Clearinghouse International, a subscriber organization located in St. Paul, Minnesota. Call 612/293-1004 for information.

BLESSING WHITE, 900 State Road, Princeton, NJ 08540, 312/642-5565.
   Managing Personal Growth. This two-day program helps participants examine the specific requirements of their jobs; clearly identify personal goals, satisfiers, values, limitations, talents, and development needs; create personal development plans comprising of action steps to increase satisfaction and improve performance in the current job; and actively seek the support and feedback of their immediate supervisors when they return to the job as a means of making the most necessary performance improvements.
   Length: 2 days
   Cost: $2000
   Locations: San Francisco, CA; New York, NY.

CARLSON COMPANIES, 12755 State Highway 55, Plymouth, MN 55441, 612/557-2232.
   Adventures in Attitudes. Through the group-dynamic process, this program explores ten major areas: communication skills; self-understanding; self-confidence; understanding others; making your personality pleasing; getting through to people; awareness of how you appear to others; secrets of motivation; the role of the ego; and time management.
   Length: 1 week
   Cost: $850
   Locations: Denver, CO; Minneapolis, MN; San Francisco, CA. For additional locations, contact vendor.

DALE CARNEGIE & ASSOCIATES, INC., 1475 Franklin Avenue, Garden City, NY 11530, 516/248-5100.
   The Dale Carnegie Course. The 14 sessions of this course cover a variety of subjects designed to maximize the innate abilities of any individual.

The skills covered in a given session are put into practice and reemphasized in succeeding sessions. The topics include expressing ideas easily and naturally, thinking straight, stimulating action without arousing resistance, and earning enthusiastic cooperation.
Length: 2 days
Cost: $325
Location: For location information, contact vendor.

PERSONNEL DECISIONS, INC., 2000 Plaza VII Tower, 45 South Seventh Street, Minneapolis, MN 55402, 612/339-0927; 800/633-4410, ext. 875 (outside Minn.).
The Emerging Manager: Skills & Strategies For Sucess. The Emerging Manager is a week-long (40-hour) program presenting a full range of management and leadership skills for first level managers at an early stage in their careers. Participants not only gain knowledge but also build skills and self-awareness in the following areas: interpersonal skills, adaptability skills, cognitive (thinking) skills, communication skills, personal motivation skills, administrative skills, and leadership skills.
Length: 5 days
Cost: $1750
Location: Minneapolis, MN.

UNITED LEARNING INSTITUTE, 7121 27th Street West, Tacoma, WA 98466, 206/565-3131.
Increasing Human Effectiveness. This four-day program, taught in a relaxed lecture/discussion format, provides participants with the tools that will enable them to tap the vast wellspring of potential that exists within them.
Length: 4 days
Cost: $595
Location: Tacoma, WA.

UNIVERSITY OF MINNESOTA. 423 Management & Economics Building, 271 19th Avenue South, Minneapolis, MN 55455, 800/328-5727 (outside Minn.), 800/742-5685 (in Minn.), 612/624-5525.
Career Development Systems. Program objectives include learning about changing work life values and work life cycles, individual differences and vocational patterns, how to better develop individual career plans, the 'state of the art' in organizational orientation, and training and career development programs.
Length: 2 days
Cost: $325
Location: Minneapolis, MN.

UNIVERSITY OF WISCONSIN. Business Outreach, Schneider 113A, Eau Claire, WI 54701, 715/836-5637.

Executive Self-development: Cultivating Emotional Toughness. This program helps participants discover more about themselves. It focuses on coping with pressures, frustrations, tensions inherent in executive positions, flexibility, and becoming non-defensive, personally secure, and self-confident.
Length: 4 days
Cost: $595
Location: Cable, WI.

UNIVERSITY OF WISCONSIN, The Wisconsin Center, 702 Langdon Street, Madison, WI 53706, 800/362-3020 (in Wisc.), 800/262-6243.

Personal Growth and Self-development for Managers and Supervisors. A three-day program focusing on understanding one's personal growth and development, eliminating self-defeating behaviors, increasing self-management, obtaining high-level wellness, developing self-esteem—assessment and fine tuning, and getting (it) (you) (myself) (us) together.
Length: 3 days
Cost: $545
Location: Madison, WI.

FACTOR 7

Occupational/Technical Knowledge

"Knowledge is power"

In the past, it was possible for workers to train for specific jobs and to hold those jobs for the rest of their working lives. Now, however, the world's information base doubles every three years. As a result, it is not uncommon for people to hold numerous different positions during their professional careers as more old jobs become obsolete and new ones take their place.

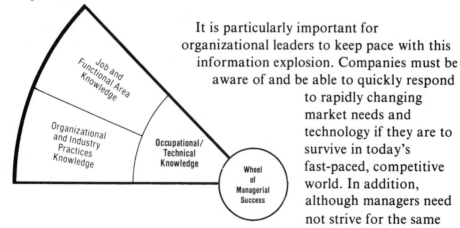

It is particularly important for organizational leaders to keep pace with this information explosion. Companies must be aware of and be able to quickly respond to rapidly changing market needs and technology if they are to survive in today's fast-paced, competitive world. In addition, although managers need not strive for the same high level of technical competence as that of their subordinates, they must have sufficient knowledge to make sound hiring decisions and to address training and development needs.

This section explains how increasing your knowledge of organizational and industrial practices and trends can help you improve your professional competence as well as your promotional opportunities.

Occupational/Technical Knowledge

Tips

- Read the latest books in your field.

- Develop one or more specialty areas where you will be considered the expert in your organization.

- Have lunch with a colleague to discuss innovations in your mutual areas of interest.

- Lay out a career plan specifying the moves that will help assure acquisition of the functional, occupational, or technical knowledge needed to achieve your goals.

- Work for someone who is particularly competent in a field you want to learn.

- Seek a job rotation to a lateral position in your function in another department.

- Ask your supervisors, both immediate and higher, to identify the most important job assignments you need to maximize your knowledge.

- Try to write down the ten emerging technological advances most likely to impact your field.

- Hire people with superior technical knowledge who will challenge you.

- Ask your subordinates to list your three strongest and three weakest technical areas.

- Identify a mentor outside of your chain of command who will serve as a career counselor for you.

- Discuss with people in other functional areas their job responsibilities and satisfactions and consider a functional change for yourself.

- Seek opportunities to interact with people in different managerial functions.

- Try to get task force and project assignments in functional areas other than your own.

- Volunteer to take on a technically challenging project.

- Seek a job rotation to a lateral position in another function.

- Be willing to take a pay cut to acquire broader knowledge and lay the base for future rapid pay growth.

- Read the primary journals in your profession and industry.

- Join the primary professional associations of your industry and professional area.

- Meet people in your industry upon whom you can call for advice.

- Write a journal article in your field.

- Get involved in the program committee of your professional association.

- Network with people you can meet with occasionally to discuss professional matters.

- Speak to a professional group in your field.

Knowing and Understanding the Requirements of Your Job

To perform at your full potential, you need to understand fully the requirements of your position. This can be accomplished by using the following procedure for writing specific objectives for your position. At minimum, this should be done on an annual basis.

1. Begin by reading through previous job descriptions or objectives for your position to get a feel for the required responsibilities and goals and how these have changed over the years.
2. Describe the current mission or purpose of your role in the organization.
   - Why does your position exist?
   - What would be the effect if it didn't exist?
   - How do you see your position's role or mission changing over the next year?
3. Detail the three to seven key result areas in which effective performance is critical for the achievement of your organizational mission. Focus on the critical few areas rather than the trivial many.
4. Identify indicators for measuring performance in each key result area. For example, in sales it might be revenues; in customer service it might be average time in responding to customer complaints; in word processing it could be turnaround time or number of error free pages produced per day.
5. Set specific objectives for each indicator. For example:
   "Respond to 95% of customer complaints within 24 hours and 100% within 48 hours, effective 1/1/19XX."
6. Define what level of performance each objective represents. For example, is the objective (such as in step 4 above) meeting job requirements or exceeding them? If you determine that the objective is at the "meets requirements" level, how would it have to be changed to exceed requirements?
7. Meet with your boss to get his or her input. Get your boss's assurance that your objectives cover the key areas of your job and get his or her agreement on the level of performance your objectives represent.
8. Share your objectives with your subordinates and others in the organization with whom you work closely.
9. Periodically review your performance against your objectives and update your objectives when neccessary.

Relying Effectively on Your Own Expertise

If you are uncomfortable relying on your expertise at times, the result may be that you turn to others for help in areas where they expect you to be knowledgeable. This situation may indicate that you need to further develop your skills in some areas. The following guidelines can help you determine where you may lack the skills you need to perform more independently.

1. Keep a log for one month of the problems related to expertise that you encounter on the job.
2. After one month, study the log, paying attention to:
   - The types of problems you have most frequently
   - Whom you go to most often for help or advice
3. Determine what knowledge or skills this person possesses that you may be lacking.
4. Prepare a development plan to address these weaker areas, particularly those that cause you to seek help most frequently.

The Management Skills Profile (MSP) is a professionally designed instrument which provides feedback to assist in identifying areas of strength and development needs. The Successful Manager's Handbook is designed to accompany the MSP and contains an index referencing special development suggestions for each item contained in the MSP (p. 445). For more information, write to Personnel Decisions, Inc., 2000 Plaza VII Tower, 45 South Seventh Street, Minneapolis, MN 55402.

Developing and Using Your Expertise to Resolve Technical Problems and Questions

One indication of your technical expertise is the extent to which others come to you with questions or ask for your help in resolving technical problems. These techniques can help you increase your expertise and help ensure that coworkers benefit from your knowledge.

- Over the next two weeks, keep track of the number of times people come to you with questions about projects which they are working on.

  After two weeks, if this number seems low, go out and talk to others in your area about their current projects. Show a genuine interest in their work and, if appropriate, mention projects of a similar nature on which you are working or have completed.
- Offer to serve as a sounding board to others if they run into technical difficulties and ask them to do the same for you.
- When people do come to you with questions, be supportive and work with them to solve the problem rather than solving the problem for them. It is important that they leave your office not feeling foolish or incompetent because they were unable to resolve the problem independently.

- To chart your long-term progress, periodically monitor the number of times people come to you with technical questions.

Increasing Knowledge About Specific Job Areas

Many positions, especially those held early in one's career, require knowledge in specific technical areas. Some areas of technical knowledge relate to an individual's specific function in the organization. For example, a compensation manager would have specialized technical knowledge about the task of managing compensation in an organization. Positions such as this require employees to handle specific functions in the organization, and the skills needed for doing so must be developed as fully as possible.

Other positions require knowledge about specific products or specialized techniques. For example, a person who supervises programmer analysts should keep informed on state-of-the-art developments in both systems technology and specific applications.

Although the type of required technical knowledge varies from one position to the next, some sources of information can provide general knowledge. The following suggestions apply to a cross section of positions.

1. Read manuals, books, articles, research publications, and specialized technical literature that contain information about areas related to your job.
2. Take courses offered by your organization, local universities or community colleges, adult education programs, or other institutions.
3. Seek opportunities to observe, work with, and get feedback from individuals (your supervisor, a colleague, or someone from another part of the company) who are highly skilled in your specific job area.
4. Request assignments and tasks that will broaden or increase your technical knowledge. Depending on your job and the knowledge you want to acquire, these assignments may involve more difficult tasks, a greater variety of tasks, new categories of tasks, or areas of greater specialization. Whenever possible, arrange to receive coaching and/or feedback on your performance of these assignments.
5. Solicit feedback on your performance—either your overall performance or your way of handling specific activities or situations. You may want to ask for a more formal appraisal (by your supervisor) or several informal ones (by colleagues or subordinates).

Increasing Knowledge About Functional Areas

Many positions are part of a broad functional area. A personnel department, for example, usually has specialized positions in areas such as compensation, training and development, recruitment and employment, and employee counseling. Many employees advance in their careers as they move from specialized positions to jobs within broader functional areas.

The following guidelines for developing professionally within a functional area are similar to those for increasing one's technical knowledge; they simply take a broader view. Instead of focusing on his or her specific position, the person concentrates on the functional area. Again, the development possibilities depend on the functional area and organization in question.

1. Observe the actions and practices of those in positions similar or related to yours within your functional area. You may want to ask them if you can try working with them on tasks, interview them formally or informally to learn their secrets for success, or associate with them more often to develop a relationship.

2. Make opportunities to talk with individuals, both inside and outside your organization, who have expertise in particular areas. Look upon committees, task forces, and department meetings as chances to enhance your understanding of your functional area and to communicate with other specialized groups or individuals within it.

3. Obtain and read reports and documents that describe procedures, practices, and other information related to your functional area.
4. Attend courses and seminars that could give you a broader perspective of how your position fits into the functional area.
5. Join professional organizations related to your functional area. For example, a compensation manager might want to get involved in a professional organization that encompasses areas of personnel other than compensation.

Increasing Understanding of Organizational Practices

In many cases, employees' promotional opportunities and success are based, at least in part, on their awareness of how other parts of the organization function. This awareness is not always easily developed, however. As companies become larger and more geographically fragmented, opportunities for employees to learn about other parts of their organization decrease. Time constraints, distance, and limited interface with potentially helpful individuals can prohibit this learning process.

Many employees rely on publications or other such organized forums for information about other parts of their companies. Some seek the data on their own. The following guidelines present a framework for increasing your knowledge about your company's organizational practices.

1. Read books, articles, and marketing literature that describe your company. Books have been written about the founders of many large organizations. Product literature, articles in business journals, and your company's annual report can also increase your understanding.
2. Learn about the history of your company by reading or talking with others. Find out how it was founded, what changes in organizational structure have been made, how products and services have evolved, and who the leaders have been at various points in time. Try to determine the effect of the company's history on its current structure, products, philosophy, and management style.
3. Study all available documents that describe strategic plans for the company (or specific divisions or departments). Organizational goals and philosophy statements are also good sources of information.
4. Read job descriptions for your position and others in your work area. If they are available, also read job descriptions for the heads of your division, your functional area, and related functional areas.
5. Compile a list of things you'd like to find out about the company that could help you perform more effectively. Seek out individuals or documents that can provide the information you want.

6. Meet with individuals who are at your level in the organization but who work in different functional areas. Talk informally about what they do and how their functional areas operate.
7. Broaden your contacts and associations within the company. Informal clubs, recreational outlets, and individuals you've met on work assignments and task forces can help you form these contacts.

Increasing Understanding of Industry Conditions, Developments, and Trends

Based on the products and/or services it offers, your organization can be described as fitting into one or more industry categories. Such classification may be based on the nature of the products/services or on the market for those products and services. Typically, one's understanding of how his or her organization fits into a category increases as that person moves up in the organization.

Information on a particular industry is made available by industry members who have worked cooperatively to develop it and to ensure its availability. Restrictions on the availability of industry-related data are due to competition and confidentiality.

The following guidelines are provided to help you develop your knowledge and understanding of your industry's standard practices.

1. Get involved in one or more industry associations. This involvement can consist of reading association journals, attending meetings and seminars, and getting involved in committees and legislative bodies.
2. Join groups that get together on a formal or an informal basis to exchange information. For example, the personnel directors of several farm cooperatives meet both formally and informally to exchange ideas and develop a working relationship. These types of affiliations can be based on any number of common bonds—type of business, organization size, manufacturing processes, market, and so on. Some groups form because of geographical proximity. Others form because their members want to associate with people who are in similar businesses but who serve a totally different market area. This practice promotes the exchange of ideas without the threat of competition.
3. Look for books, publications, and research information on practices in specific industry categories or on industry categories related to your own. Associations, governmental sources, universities, cooperative programs, and libraries are sources of these documents.

Keeping Up-to-date on Technical Developments Related to Your Work

Keeping up-to-date with the technical advancements related to your work is important for continued growth and development for both yourself and your organization. Following are some suggestions on resources to consult and activities to pursue to help you do this:

- Join professional organizations in your community.
- Subscribe to trade journals and professional publications.
- Attend conferences on your professional specialty. Consult professional or organizational newsletters for dates of these conferences.
- Offer to present a paper at a conference on a project you've completed.
- Become a program chairperson for your professional organization's conventions or conferences.
- Build an informal network of peers in similar organizations through which you exchange ideas and discuss issues relevant to technical advancements in your field.

Recommended Readings

Because of the highly specialized nature of the information specific to the multitudinal occupational and technical areas, a comprehensive list of available books and articles would be beyond the scope of this book. For detailed information about your area of expertise, contact your local library, professional/trade association, or university.

Suggested Seminars

The seminars listed here were selected for their appeal to a managerial audience and have received good to excellent ratings from managers attending them.

Because of the dynamic nature of the seminar marketplace, some seminars may have been added, upgraded, or replaced, and others may no longer be offered. Additional information about these seminars may be obtained by calling the vendor directly, or through Seminar Clearinghouse International, a subscriber organization located in St. Paul, Minnesota. Call 612/293-1004 for information.

AMERICAN COMPENSATION ASSOCIATION, 6619 North Scottsdale Road, Scottsdale, AZ 85223, 602/951-9191.

Total Compensation: A Basic Overview. This workshop provides an overview for human resource generalists. Topics include: complying with governmental regulations; job analysis and job evaluation; methods of pay; costing of compensation; benefits; and performance appraisal.
Length: 3 days
Cost: $490
Locations: Oakland, CA; Chicago, IL; Boston, MA; New York, NY.

AMERICAN INSTITUTE OF CHEMICAL ENGINEERS, United Engineering Center, 345 East 47th Street, New York, NY 10017, 212/750-7526.

Marketing for Engineers and Scientists. The topics covered in this two-day program include: organizing for marketing; product life cycles; product planning and development; deleting unsuitable products; bringing R&D results to the marketplace; pricing policies and strategies; market research; the marketing plan; and the marketing and product audit.
Length: 2 days
Cost: $495
Locations: Denver, CO; Washington, DC; New Orleans, LA.

AMERICAN MANAGEMENT ASSOCIATIONS, P.O. Box 319, Saranac Lake, NY 12983, 518/891-0065.

Fundamentals of Marketing—Modern Concepts and Practices. A five-day program including such key topics as: an introduction to marketing and marketing management; marketing environment and the marketing mix; marketing research and the marketing plan; demand analysis and market segmentation; formulating product and pricing strategies; selling and sales management; and marketing communications and advertising.

Length: 5 days
Cost: $895
Location: San Francisco, CA; Washington, DC; Orlando, FL; Atlanta, GA; Chicago, IL; Boston, MA; Cambridge, MA; New York, NY; Philadelphia, PA.

COUNCIL ON EDUCATION IN MANAGEMENT, 321 Lennon Lane, Walnut Creek, CA 94598, 415/934-8333.

Basic Personnel Law for Employers and Managers. Key topics of this program include: regulations employers must follow; posting and record retention requirements; dealing with anti-discrimination laws—lawful hiring practices; overtime regulations—exempt/non-exempt rules; special concerns with pregnancy, age, and handicap; sexual harassment; AIDS and drugs; defamation risks; designing and enforcing company standards; discipline, discharge, and the law; wrongful discharges and company personnel practices; employee privacy protection; and employee handbooks.
Length: 2 days
Cost: $395
Locations: Scottsdale, AZ; Costa Mesa, CA; Los Angeles, CA; San Diego, CA; San Francisco, CA; San Jose, CA; Chicago, IL; Boston, MA; Teaneck, NJ; Cincinnati, OH; Houston, TX; Seattle, WA. For additional locations, contact the vendor.

Personnel Law Update 1988. This program provides an understanding of topics such as: wrongful discharge update; handling your discharged employee's case: a plaintiff attorney's perspective; examination of a personnel director on trial; administering your employee benefit programs with reduced legal risk; employee recordkeeping; what employers should know about libel, slander, and emotional distress in employment; your employee handbook from a legal perspective; preventing abuse of your company's workers' compensation insurance; recent developments in EEO, including age, pregnancy, and handicap; legal aspects of workforce reduction in the eighties; and AIDS discrimination.
Length: 2 days
Cost: $495
Locations: Phoenix, AZ; Scottsdale, AZ; Anaheim, CA; San Francisco, CA; San Jose, CA; Atlanta, GA; Minneapolis, MN; Kansas City, MO; St. Louis, MO; Cincinnati, OH; Pittsburgh, PA; Houston, TX. For additional locations, contact the vendor.

NEW YORK UNIVERSITY, 310 Madison Avenue, Room 1412, New York, NY 10017, 212/682-1435.

Human Resource Management: Legal Issues. A two-day program covering content such as: preventing employee-related liabilities; handling worker drug/alcohol abuse; employee health and saftey considerations; understanding employer-employee laws and regulations; and trends and directions in human resources law.
Length: 2 days
Cost: $750
Locations: Washington, DC; New York, NY.

PERSONNEL DECISIONS, INC., 2000 Plaza VII Tower, 45 South Seventh Street, Minneapolis, MN 55402, 612/339-0927; 800-633-4410, ext. 875 (outside Minn.).

Internal Consulting Workshop. This intensive three-day learning experience is designed to help human resource professionals become more effective internal consultants. Focus is on three themes: knowing and using yourself effectively as a consultant; managing the consulting process; helping individuals and organizations deal with change.
Length: 3 days
Cost: $895
Location: Minneapolis, MN.

Developing Managers: How To Make It Happen. This program enables the internal consultant to diagnose a manager's strengths and development needs, lay out an action plan to address those needs, consult individually with managers, and lead a Development Planning Workshop for managers. As a participant, the manager receives feedback on how others perceive his/her skills using a powerful survey feedback instrument, the Management Skills Profile (MSP). The MSP provides comprehensive feedback from the workplace and guides each manager in designing a specific action plan. Workshop teaches human resource managers and licensees of the MSP how to use the MSP in their organizations.
Length: 2 days
Cost: $750
Location: Minneapolis, MN.

TECHNOLOGY TRANSFER INSTITUTE, 741 Tenth Street, Santa Monica, CA 90402, 213/394-8305.

James Martin Seminar. This seminar is designed for participants who want to learn how dramatically new technologies will affect corporations. It discusses such issues as fourth generation languages; techniques for

maximizing DP productivity; high bandwidth networks; information engineering; the integration of AI into MIS; and the end-user revolution.
Length: 5 days
Cost: $1695
Locations: Los Angeles, CA; San Francisco, CA; Washington, DC; Atlanta, GA; Chicago, IL; Boston, MA.

UNIVERSITY OF MICHIGAN, School of Business Administration, Executive Education Center, Ann Arbor, MI 48109, 313/763-1000.

Marketing for the Non-marketing Manager. The key topics in this three-day workshop include orientation to marketing, the marketing environment, product and promotion management, pricing and distribution management, and marketing planning strategy.
Length: 3 days
Cost: $1560
Location: Ann Arbor, MI.

UNIVERSITY OF MINNESOTA, 423 Management & Economics Building, 271 19th Avenue South, Minneapolis, MN 55455, 612/624-5525: Ext. 97, 800/328-5727 (in Minn.), 800/742-5685 (outside Minn.).

Introduction to the Personnel Function. Program topics in this workshop address issues of job analysis and job descriptions, staff function, compensation and benefits, performance management, legal issues affecting the employment process, and skills required for effective personnel management.
Length: 3 days
Cost: $425
Location: Minneapolis, MN.

FACTOR **8**

Cognitive Skills

Reports, budgets, speeches, publications, computer data bases, media presentations—these are just a few of the numerous information sources available to today's managers. The way in which managers approach and use these sources makes the difference between keeping up with and keeping on top of the management job.

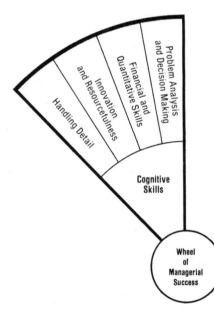

Successful managers must be able to gather and process large amounts of information. They must efficiently sift through masses of detail to obtain the facts required for sound decisions. In addition, in this era of rapid change, managers must be creative and resourceful to keep ahead of the competition. And, to make the most of limited resources, they must be able to effectively balance creativity and resourcefulness—to decide whether to start from scratch or to build upon what already exists.

This section presents development activities in the following four cognitive skills areas.

Problem Analysis and Decision Making: effectively and efficiently identifying problems and recognizing the symptoms, causes and potential solutions.

Financial and Quantitative Skills: drawing accurate conclusions from financial and numerical data in order to apply these conclusions to management problems

Innovation and Resourcefulness: developing original approaches and encouraging the creativity of others

Handling Detail: processing and generating information without overlooking important items or bogging down in technicalities

Problem Analysis and Decision Making

Following are a few of the numerous problems confronting managers on a typical day:

- "I don't have enough information to make a decision."
- "If we buy the machine now, we can really increase our productivity on this project, but what if we don't get enough future business to make the payments? It's a risky move."
- "We spend so much time solving the small daily problems that we never seem to get around to solving our serious problems."

Analyzing problems and deciding on the best solutions to those problems is a process involving several steps. Over the years, Personnel Decisions, Inc. has developed a model to describe this process. This dimension presents a collection of the development suggestions clients have found most useful for each step for the model.

Tips

- Identify the most important decision you have to make this quarter. Be sure you've started gathering the input to make it.

- Write out the steps and information required for a future major decision. Get the input of others early.

- Search for improved ways to collect and analyze data for your decisions.

- Allow yourself plenty of time to work on the big problems and work on them in several sittings.

- Be prepared to write down your thoughts which occur while sleeping, taking a shower, running, etc.

- Determine whether immediate action is required before making an overly hasty decision.

- Gather as much information as possible before making decisions.

- Talk to colleagues about their approaches to a difficult decision. See what you can learn from their approaches.

- Review the Kepner-Tregoe process of decision-making (forcefield analysis) and use it in defining problems.

- In order to learn to search for more alternative solutions to a problem, write a summary of the problem and then list all the solutions you can think of **before** evaluating them.

- Ask for input from those closest to the problem.

- Write out the alternative solutions to a problem. There usually are more than you first imagine.

- Try reformulating or restating the problem in different words or from different perspectives to uncover new alternatives.

- Keep a systematic record of problems as they arise in your job, and then analyze it to develop other approaches to the solutions.

- Generate more alternatives and weigh their consequences before making decisions.

- Learn to be open to the possibility of changing your decisions when new information comes in. Seek feedback from your supervisor about some of your decisions that might have been changed after being informed of new developments.

- If you shoot from the hip, ask yourself what else you should know before going with your first reaction.

- Study Vroom and Yetton's decision-making model and try to apply it in situations involving subordinates.

- Discuss your planning and decision-making skills with your superior and seek feedback about the quality of your decisions.

- In order to become less impulsive in your decisions, seek feedback from your boss regarding what may have been inappropriate snap decisions that you have made.

- Ask yourself, "What is the worst thing that could happen if I made the decision without more information?"

- If you are slow to make decisions, make a preliminary decision before you feel you have all the data. Compare it to your final decision after all the data are in.

- Identify two kinds of decisions required of you which you make least effectively and identify ways to improve your approach.

- Identify routine decisions which can be made easily or automatically by yourself or others.

- Go to your boss with your analysis and a recommended solution rather than with the problem.

- Use your best time of the day for your biggest decisions and problem solving.

- If you are slow at making decisions, push yourself by deciding quickly in low risk decision areas.

- Be willing to accept the risk in decisions where you cannot possibly improve your information and analysis.

Step 1. Identifying the Information Needed to Solve a Problem

The first step in solving a problem involves: 1) identifying the information required to formulate a solution and 2) determining how that information can best be obtained. To accomplish this step:

1. Make a list of what you need to know to solve the problem effectively. For example, you may require a better description of the problem from people affected by it, data that shows how other organizations have handled similar problems, historical information about your organization to determine whether the problem has occurred in the past, or input from experts inside or outside your organization.

2. Consider how each type of information can best be obtained. The possibilities include:
    *   Interviews
    *   Discussions
    *   Questionnaires
    *   Reference materials
    *   Observation

Once you have completed this procedure, you can begin to gather the necessary information.

Step 2: Gathering the Required Information

Using Written References to Obtain Information

Written references of which you are not currently aware may be available for solving the problem you're facing. The following procedure can help you identify and become familiar with such information sources.

1. List several general problem areas in which you could benefit from additional information. Examples of these include statistical quality control and time management.

2. List any references of which you are already aware.

3. Ask colleagues and/or superiors to list any references they feel would be valuable. Also ask them to identify the portions of these references likely to be most helpful.

4. Locate and become familiar with the references suggested by others. You may wish to create a schedule for doing so, such as one reference per week, to help you stay on track with your reading. As you review

each reference, determine which parts could be valuable to you in problem solving. On your list of resources, you may wish to summarize the ways in which each resource is helpful. If the resources are your own, highlight useful sections in some way so that you can locate them easily when you need them.

Using Active Questioning and Listening to Gain Information

When interviewing others to gain information on problem solving, you can use two techniques to increase your efficiency and effectiveness. These techniques are called active questioning and active listening.

- Active questioning involves asking open-end questions that require more than one- or two-word responses. Examples of active questions include those that begin with such phrases as "What do you think..." or "Tell me about...." Avoid questions that encourage passive responses—questions that begin with the words "did" or "is" and that can be answered with a simple "yes" or "no." In addition to limiting the amount of information you gain, a string of closed-end questions usually results in an interview that seems more like an interrogation and tends to alienate the listener.

- Active listening involves listening closely to responses and determining how well you have listened by rephrasing the person's comments and then asking the person whether you have understood correctly. You may also wish to take notes and, to summarize the interview, quickly review them with the interviewee to determine if they are correct.

Keep an open mind when listening. Take care not to judge the speaker's suggestions or to convey, verbally or nonverbally, that you disapprove of the information you are receiving. If you do not remain open to the information you are soliciting, your speaker will sense that his or her input is not really appreciated and will stop trying to communicate with you.

Analyzing and Improving Your Interviewing Techniques

Interviewing to gain information is a technique you probably use more often than you realize. Each time you ask someone a question, you are using interviewing skills. Sometimes the characteristics of the person being interviewed determine the success of your communication. Often, however, the difference between effective and ineffective communication will be determined by your behavior. To determine the effectiveness of your interviewing techniques:

1. Make a special effort, over the next several weeks, to be aware of the situations in which you are interviewing others to gain information.
2. Analyze each interview situation to determine the techniques that:
   a) are especially effective, and b) hinder or block communication.
3. Make an effort to incorporate the effective behaviors and to eliminate the ineffective behaviors whenever you interview.

Establishing a Network to Gain Information

Often, the information you need to solve a problem may be as near as the colleague next door. Your peers can be valuable sources of information. The following suggestions will help you tap the knowledge of those around you.

- Make an effort, over the next several months, to identify people outside your organization who hold positions similar to yours. Choose one or two people with whom you share common job concerns and problems. For example, the manager of an applications programming department decided to serve on an interdivisional task force as a means of getting to know other managers. She discovered that one manager of a systems programming department had established an excellent system for managing complex, lengthy programming projects and that she could apply much of this system to large projects within her own department.

- Encourage informal communications between you and other professionals to build a network of people you can consult when you need information about how others have handled problems similar to yours. For example, you might suggest taking coffee breaks or having lunch together once a week.

Step 3: Determining the Cause of the Problem

Discovering Sources of Problems: Preventive Problem Solving

Do you ever have days when it seems that you are constantly "fighting fires" rather than doing meaningful work? Although some problems are unavoidable, preventive measures can be taken to forestall many of them. If you find yourself in a constant state of crisis management, you may wish to complete the following exercise in preventive problem solving.

1. Over the next few weeks, keep a list of the unforeseen problem situations that require your attention. Although it may seem inconvenient at the time, the most important time to compile such a list is when you're inundated by a large number of unanticipated crises.
2. For each problem on the list, ask yourself:
   - What was the cause of this problem?
   - Could this problem have been prevented?
   - If so, what action could have prevented the problem?
   - Who should have taken preventive action? Me? My subordinates? My superior?
   - What could be done to prevent the recurrence of this problem?
3. After you have analyzed the problem, determine whether their causes can be grouped into general categories, such as inadequate oral communications, failure to delegate, or lack of employee development. Use the PDI Wheel to identify possible categories.
4. For skill areas in which either you or your subordinates require development, prepare and implement development plans.
5. After several months, repeat this process to determine if the number of unforeseen problems has decreased.

Increasing Efficiency in Problem Diagnosis

The ability to discover the source of a problem quickly is helpful when you must solve problems under pressure. Following are two ways to increase your efficiency in diagnosing problems.

The first way is to cut down on the time wasted pursuing unlikely alternatives. Follow these steps when diagnosing problems over the next few weeks until you are satisfied with your ability to quickly eliminate "dead-end" alternatives.

1. For each problem, generate a list of all possible causes in order of probability.
2. For each cause, determine what must be done to verify it.
3. Rate the effort required for verification investigation on a scale from 1 to 5, with "1" representing the least effort.
4. Balance the probability of the cause with the amount of verification investigation required. Based on this analysis, determine the order in which you will investigate the causes and identify any alternatives that should be dropped altogether.
5. Review your analysis with a colleague who is familiar with the situation and ask for reactions. Adjust your investigation plan, if necessary.
6. Conduct your investigation. Record the number of potential causes to be investigated before locating the problem source. Over time, the number of causes investigated should decrease as you develop your ability to quickly determine the most likely causes.

The chart on the following page will help you structure your analysis.

Reducing Time Spent Collecting Unnecessary Data

A second way to increase speed in diagnosing problems is to reduce the time spent collecting unnecessary data—data that you don't really need but that you collect to "make sure."

The next time you reach a tentative solution when solving a problem, answer these questions:
- What additional information could be collected?
- What information is absolutely necessary?
- What information should make you feel better but probably would not cause you to change your decision?

After answering these questions, stop yourself from gathering information you've identified as unnecessary.

Potential Cause	Investigation	Effort Required	Order of Investigation
		1 2 3 4 5	
		1 2 3 4 5	
		1 2 3 4 5	
		1 2 3 4 5	
		1 2 3 4 5	

Step 4: Analyzing Alternate Solutions and Making a Decision

Curbing Impulsiveness

If you often make decisions and later wish you'd waited until you had more information or more time to think, you're making decisions impulsively. Knowing the reasons for your haste can help you refrain from impulsiveness. Does one of the following apply to your situation?

- Do you feel pressured into making decisions that you are not ready to make? If so, learn to "buy time" in decision-making situations. When possible, tell the person(s) applying the pressure that you need more time and name a date by which you will announce your decision.

- Do you make decisions emotionally, for instance, when you're upset or angry? If so, try waiting a few hours, if possible, so you can judge whether the decision is really the best or simply the one that seemed right at the time.
- Do you often sense that you are "leaping to a solution" because you have a desire for action? If so, create a decision-making plan that will result in action. Write down who will be involved in the decision-making process, the types of information you will need, the criteria you will use to judge solutions, and a time frame for action.

Suspending Judgment and Considering More Alternatives

Follow these steps each time you encounter a major problem until you have made a habit of considering more alternatives. The chart on the next page will help you structure your analysis.

1. State the problem at the top of the chart.
2. Along the left side, record, in order of priority, the criteria to be considered when making a decision. Examples include:
   - Public relations
   - Schedule
   - Profitability
   - Superior's acceptance
   - Available technology
3. Write down several possible alternatives across the top of the chart.
4. Determine the degree to which each solution meets the criteria you have listed. Write the pros and cons of each on your chart. Choose the solution that most completely satisfies the most important criteria.

Being More Decisive

Indecision is often confused with flexibility. But flexibility is a willingness to entertain alternatives in the decision-making process, whereas indecision is the tendency to either leave the decision making to someone else or be tentative.

If you tend to divert decision-making responsibility to others, try the following actions.

1. Make a list of the major areas in which you have decision-making responsibility. Examples of such areas include capital expenditures, staffing, delegating, and policy making.

Criteria	Solution: _____ _____	Solution: _____ _____	Solution: _____ _____

PROBLEM: _____

2. Identify the areas in which you tend to divert responsibility by determining which of the following decision-making processes you usually use in each area.
   - Make decisions on your own
   - Formulate alternatives, select what seems to be the best alternative, then ask for the opinions of others
   - Formulate alternatives but have problems determining which is best
   - Ask for others' opinions immediately

   For example, you may feel comfortable making decisions on capital expenditures and often make decisions in this area on your own. You may feel less comfortable making policy decisions and may tend to ask for others' opinions immediately.

   If you often use the third or fourth approach for a particular area, you may have a tendency toward indecisiveness in that area.

3. If you have difficulty determining which of several alternatives is best, don't use that as a cue for going to others for a decision. Instead, force yourself to choose one of the alternatives and develop a rationale for why that alternative is best. Only then should you seek input. Tell the other person(s) what your alternatives and recommendations are, then ask for opinions.

4. If you turn to others immediately, before you've even formulated any alternatives, ask yourself why. Do you need more information? If so, make that clear to others when you approach them. Gather the facts, then formulate alternatives on your own.

If you turn to others out of habit or because you are uncomfortable making decisions alone, force yourself to formulate alternatives and make a recommendation on your own before seeking the help of others. This should help you break the habit and gain confidence in making decisions, especially if others agree with your recommendations.

5. Many people have a tendency to push their decision-making responsibilities upward. If you notice that you have a problem in this area, get in the habit of presenting recommendations rather than problems to your superior.

If you tend to make tentative decisions, consider these suggestions.
- Watch how you present your ideas, both orally and in writing. Look for tentative phrases that lessen your impact, such as "sort of," "kind of," "I guess," and "I'm not really sure, but...." Once you have identified such phrases in your presentations, make a conscious effort to eliminate them.
- Setting deadlines may help you to be more decisive. For major decisions, make a commitment to arrive at a decision by a certain date. For minor decisions, try to make your judgments within a few minutes.
- Once you've made a decision, stand by it. Avoid reopening the decision-making process unless new information strongly indicates the need for reconsideration.

Overcoming Procrastination

The opposite of impulsive decision making is procrastination. Most people do not procrastinate every time they make a decision; rather, they tend to delay decisions under certain circumstances. It is important that these people learn to identify these circumstances and determine how to handle them in the future. The following suggestions should help.

1. For most people, procrastination stems from some problem they have in completing a task. Each time you find yourself delaying a decision, ask yourself the reason for the delay. Some of the more common reasons include:

cBUSH

- Lack of information
- Unclear course of action, especially in subjective matters
- Lack of time for thought
- Fear of negative consequences, such as anger on the part of those affected or having the decision prove unsuccessful

2. Once you have determined why you procrastinate, begin a focused attack; plan a way to substitute decisive behavior for the delaying tactics you wish to eliminate. Following are some possible alternatives.

   - For situations in which you lack information, use the information-gathering suggestions in this Handbook to acquire more data. Construct a plan for how you will gather the information, and implement your plan immediately.
   - When a course of action is unclear, choose what appears to be the best plan and implement it on a temporary basis. A trial run of a plan may turn up unanticipated drawbacks and benefits of the plan. Even if the plan doesn't work, the trial run may produce

alternatives that have more credibility than any that could be generated without the benefit of this experimentation.

- If you lack sufficient time for focused, concentrated thought, block out time on your schedule for decision making when you are confronted with a major issue. This will help ensure that you are not so wrapped up in the details of the daily routine that you have no time left to work on top-priority items.

- If you fear negative consequences in making a decision, face your fears. Seek the involvement of those you believe would resist your decision; a participative process is usually better in this kind of situation. If you are worried that your plan will fail and that your career may suffer as a consequence, inform your superior of the risks involved and ask for approval to proceed.

In almost all situations, it is helpful to designate a time frame for decision making. You might want to create a flow chart of the decision-making process, with deadlines for each part of it. You also might want to request the assistance of someone who can help ensure that you meet your deadlines.

Considering the Consequences of Decision Alternatives

Frequently, the reason solutions don't work is that they affect certain people so negatively that these people set out to either change the solution decision or circumvent it. This is especially true when the people affected by the decision have not been involved in the decision-making process. To avoid this problem, get in the habit of performing the following analysis before making a decision.

- For each alternative you are considering, ask yourself how the decision will be accepted by each of the following:
  - Your employees
  - Your superior
  - Other departments
  - Informal leaders in the organization

Write down the pros and cons for each alternative according to who will support or resist the alternative and why. A chart similar to the one shown here can help you structure your analysis.

Persons Affected	Alternative Pros Cons	Alternative Pros Cons	Alternative Pros Cons
Your employees			
Your superior			
Other departments			
Informal leaders			

- Considering the consequences of decision alternatives does not mean that the most popular decision is the one that you should choose. Rather, the information you gather should be used to construct your implementation plan and to "sell" your decision and plan. Those who are most resistant will require the most attention in the implementation phase.
- When making decisions in controversial areas, it is extremely important to involve those who will be affected by the decisions as early as possible in the problem-solving process.

Increasing Your Willingness to Take Calculated Risks

Every decision involves an element of risk. Sometimes, however, sound decisions or decision alternatives are avoided or discarded because they appear too risky or because the decision maker feels uncomfortable with unproven alternatives.

Calculated risk taking implies that a decision is made with a thorough understanding of the potential risk and benefits involved. The ability to recognize and take calculated risks is a skill for managerial advancement.

Following are some of the problems commonly experienced in the area of risk taking and suggestions for overcoming each type of problem.

- **A need to gather too much data.** Fact finding is a necessary step in the decision-making process. It can, however, be carried to the point where valuable time is wasted. If you find that you tend to gather too much information in an attempt to make sure that your decisions are well formulated, try making a decision at an earlier stage in the process. Before all data has been collected, force yourself to make a decision and write it down. Then analyze the additional data and make a final decision. Compare your final decision to your preliminary one to determine whether the additional information was needed. If you consistently find that the additional data was not needed, you should begin to feel confident making decisions based on less information.

- **Lack of knowledge of the true risk level.** At times, you may feel uneasy about the level of risk involved because the pros and cons of the alternatives have not been clearly specified. In such cases, write down each alternative and its associated risks and benefits. Try to choose the one that provides the greatest benefit, even if it involves some risk.

- **Discomfort about the consequences of risk taking.** It's not unusual for people to become so uncomfortable about the possible consequences of a risky decision that their discomfort prevents them from taking risks altogether. If you tend to overemphasize the possible negative results of a decision, try the following.

  - Ask yourself, "What is the worst thing that could happen as a result of this decision?" Then ask yourself how much of an impact that "worst thing" would have on you personally or on the organization. These questions will help you put risks in perspective.
  - If you find yourself concentrating on the negative aspects of an alternative and deemphasizing its benefits, try substituting positive statements or thoughts for negative statements. This process will help you determine whether the negatives are really as strong as you thought or whether you have gotten yourself into a "rut" in which the drawbacks of alternatives receive too much emphasis.
  - Develop a strategy for reducing risks. Some risks can be reduced by good planning.

- **Discomfort due to unknown risk factors.** In some cases, you may have a vague feeling that a solution carries with it some unknown risks. Rather than allowing these feelings to keep you from trying the solution, analyze your implementation process. Determine points where the process could be halted—the "go/no-go" decision points.

Inform others of these points so they will not be surprised if you decide to discontinue the process at some point. Then, if the risk becomes too great, stop the process at one of these points.

- **Discomfort in selected areas.** If you analyze the various areas in which you must make decisions—hiring, capital expenditures, work flow, organizational structure, and advertising expenditures, to name a few—you will probably find that you are very comfortable with certain kinds of risks and less comfortable with others.

When dealing with areas of discomfort, turn to others in your organization who seem particularly skilled in making decisions that involve these kinds of risks. Talk with these individuals about how they take risk factors into account in their decisions, and study the way they make their decisions. Then apply what you have learned from these people to your own decision-making process.

Getting Others Involved in Your Decision Making

When a decision is not of a crisis nature and does not require confidentiality, it is wise to use a participative decision-making process, especially if the decision will affect a large number of people. The increased time spent on making the decision will be regained during the implementation process. When people have been involved in making a decision, they are more likely to help carry it out.

The following process will help you get others involved in your decision making.

1. When you first learn that a decision must be made, quickly determine whether the decision should be solely your own or made collectively. To help you decide, put yourself in the place of those who will be affected by the decision. Would you want to have a say in this situation if you were they?

2. If you determine that the decision should be made collectively, solicit the ideas of others. There are many ways to collect these ideas: you can call a meeting, send a memo requesting written feedback, or interview the individuals involved, to name only a few. In problem-solving situations, meetings are often the best; a group's solution to a problem is generally superior to the solution proposed by any one person. At this meeting, you can play the role recorder and group facilitator, with the others acting as idea generators.

3. Inform your subordinates of the criteria you use to determine whether a decision must be solely yours or whether it should involve others.

Choosing Solutions that Work

Frequently, a solution that looks good on paper or sounds feasible at first does not work when implemented. Following are ways of testing the practicality of decisions to increase their probability of success in the work setting.

- After making a decision, get in the habit of asking yourself whether that decision is workable. Be sure to consider the specifics of your situation; the fact that a solution was effective in another environment or situation does not mean it will be effective in the situation at hand. When asking this question, try to put yourself in the shoes of those who will be affected by the solution. Attempt to assess the impact of the decision and whether others are likely to accept it. In completing this analysis, remember to consider individuals in other units who may be affected by changes you initiate. These people can be as instrumental in determining the success of your plan as those within your own group.
- Ask people who are likely to be affected by your decisions for their opinions on the practicality of those decisions.
- Ensure that a good solution does not fail because of a poor implementation plan. A complete plan includes the correct sequence of steps and persons responsible for ensuring the success of each step. While preparing your plan, arrange to spend time with all groups or departments that will be affected by the changes you are implementing. If you understand the problem from their perspectives, you increase the likelihood that your plan will be accepted and supported.

Despite the most careful analysis and planning, there will be times when a seemingly sound solution proves unworkable. Be aware of this fact and don't let such cases deter your future efforts to choose and implement the best solutions.

Step 5: Reconsidering Decisions on the Basis of New Information

You've probably encountered situations in which a policy or procedure has outlived its usefulness. Such situations can produce frustration and inefficiency if the person who originally implemented the decision cannot be convinced that it's time to change.

Thus, it's important to remain open to the possibility that a decision should be reconsidered. The following suggestions should help you remain flexible.

- Encourage others to contribute new information and to challenge decisions they feel have become outdated.
- Listen to the new information and gather new data about decisions or solutions you have implemented. Based on this information, decide whether to reopen the decision-making process.
- When a decision must be reconsidered, remind yourself that even the best decisions, solutions, procedures, and policies require reworking as the organization and its people change. The fact that a change must be made does not indicate that the decision was wrong in the first place; rather, it indicates that it has outlived its usefulness.

Step 6: Preparing for Typical Problem Situations

- It's Saturday. The company's computer system has crashed, and you must get it up and running by Monday.
- A customer complains about a new sales representative, saying that the new rep doesn't understand his needs the way the last rep did.
- An employee has been missing work consistently on Mondays and Fridays.

Many problems can be anticipated and prevented. Others, however, such as those listed above, cannot be prevented but must be solved as they arise.

The following exercise will give you practice in solving problems that are likely to occur in your particular work setting.

1. Talk to your supervisor or an experienced colleague to determine problems that can be expected to arise in your unit. Ask this person to limit the information he or she gives you to a description of each problem. It will be up to you to diagnose the cause and prepare solutions.
2. For each problem, list several possible causes. Then describe how you would investigate the problem to recommend a solution for each possible cause and determine the true cause.
3. Review your analyses with the person who described the problems to determine if they are complete and appropriate.
4. Keep your notes for use when the problems actually arise.

Recommended Readings

Ackoff, Russell L. *The Art of Problem Solving—Accompanied by Ackoff's Fables.* New York, NY: John Wiley & Sons, 1978.

This book synthesizes Ackoff's years of experience in creatively recasting constraints unnecessarily imposed by the problem solver through inadequate or unfounded conceptual sets. The "applications" section provides lengthy case examples for the techniques and approaches described in the first section. Managers who are looking for a readable discussion of creativity and problem solving, replete with interesting examples, should find this book appropriate.

Adair, J. *Training for Decisions.* New York, NY: Gower Press, 1978.

This is a successful and lively guide to improving decision making, problem solving, and creative thinking. It presents general principles followed by case studies to which the principles can be applied. Different training approaches are then described and reviewed, and the book concludes with details of several experimental training sessions.

Albert, Kenneth J. *How to Solve Business Problems: The Consultant's Approach to Business Problem Solving.* New York, NY: McGraw-Hill, 1983.

The problem-solving techniques used successfully by professional management consultants are detailed in this guide for managers and small business owners. The basics of problem analysis are presented, along with specific approaches for nine common problem areas, guidelines for establishing problem-solving systems, and tips on when and how to seek outside help.

Heyel, C., ed. *The VNR Concise Guide to Management Decision Making.* New York, NY: Van Nostrand Reinhold, 1980.

Designed for executives who wish to expand their knowledge beyond their specialty, this book covers many areas involved in management decision making. Each chapter deals with a specific function of management decision making and is written by an expert in that function.

Huber, George P. *Managerial Decision Making.* Glenview, IL: Scott, Foresman and Company, 1980.

This book is about making good decisions. The author takes a three-way approach, providing: 1) an overview of decision making, 2) methods of improving the decisions of individual managers, and 3) an examination of difficulties in evaluating data correctly. He also explores related areas, such as the use of committees, study teams, and other groups that help in the decision-making process.

Kaufman, Roger. *Identifying and Solving Problems (a Systems Approach) (3rd ed.).* San Diego, CA: University Associates, Inc., 1982.

This book offers a unique, illustrated approach to solving problems. The author describes how to use the technique of systems analysis to maximize the effectiveness of the decision-making process. This work is an easy-to-use tool for analyzing and closing the gaps between current and desired goals.

Keegan, Warren J. *Making Judgments, Choices, and Decisions In Business: Effective Management Through Self-Knowledge.* New York, NY: John Wiley & Sons, 1984.

The author contends that one's approach to problem-solving and decision-making is, more than anything else, a function of your management style. The book enables the reader to better understand his/her management style and develop others, rather than consistently relying on one. The reader is encouraged to draw on all aspects of his/her personality, rather than just one or two, in reacting to the unpredictable and making decisions that reflect the specific nature of each problem as it arises.

Suggested Seminars

The seminars listed here were selected for their appeal to a managerial audience and have received good to excellent ratings from managers attending them.

Because of the dynamic nature of the seminar marketplace, some seminars may have been added, upgraded, or replaced, and others may no longer be offered. Additional information about these seminars may be obtained by calling the vendor directly or through Seminar Clearinghouse International, a subscriber organization located in St. Paul, Minnesota. Call 612/293-1004 for information.

CENTER FOR CREATIVE LEADERSHIP, 5000 Laurinda Drive, P.O. Box P-1, Greensboro, NC 27402, 919/288-7210.

Targeted Innovation. This six-day workshop presents the tools of the trade for creative problem solving and focuses on the applied side of the creative process.
Length: 6 days
Cost: $1800
Locations: San Diego, CA; Greensboro, NC.

CREATIVE EDUCATION FOUNDATION, 437 Franklin Street, Buffalo, NY 14202, 716/884-2774.

Creative Problem Solving Institute (CPSI). This institute is designed for those who feel that they have little or no previous experience in the study of creative problem solving. Three major tracks are available: business/industry; creative learning; and heterogeneous—for those seeking an expanding experience involving a variety of resources within the group.
Length: 5 days
Cost: Call vendor
Locations: San Diego, CA; Orlando, FL; Buffalo, NY.

EXECUTIVE DEVELOPMENT INCORPORATED, 7200 France Avenue South, Suite 238, Minneapolis, MN 55435, 612/835-1183.

Decision Focus. A two-day program covering key topics such as situation analysis, problem analysis, decision analysis, and problem prevention.
Length: 2 days
Cost: 395
Location: St. Paul, MN.

KEPNER TREGOE, Research Road, P.O. Box 704, Princeton, NJ 08542, 800/223-0482, 609/921-2806, 800/268-6685 (in Canada).

Problem Solving and Decision Making. A dynamic, intensive learning experience that focuses on results on the job, the key topics of this workshop include making decisions, solving problems, planning projects, and managing complex issues.

Length: 3 days

Cost: $795

Locations: Anchorage, AL; Anaheim, CA; San Francisco, CA; Washington, DC; Chicago, IL; Boston, MA; Baltimore, MD; St. Louis, MO; Princeton, NJ; Buffalo, NY; New York, NY; Seattle, WA. For additional locations, contact the vendor.

LEARNING INTERNATIONAL, 200 First Stamford Place, P.O. Box 10211, Stamford, CT 06904, 203/965-8400.

Problem Analysis and Decision Making. A two-day program enabling participants to size up the situation, be involved in problem analysis, information evaluation, decision making, and stimulating creativity.

Length: 2 days

Cost: Call vendor

Locations: Marina Del Rey, CA; San Francisco, CA; Stamford, CT; Atlanta, GA; Chicago, IL; Schaumburg, IL; Dallas, TX; Houston, TX; Bellevue, WA.

UNIVERSITY OF CHICAGO, Office of Continuing Education, 5835 S. Kimbark Avenue, Chicago, IL 60637, 312/962-1724.

Executive Decision Making. Key topics included in this three-day workshop are: introducing the key issues, the framing of decisions, information gathering and synthesis, coming to conclusions—deciding, taking action; implementation and feedback; and emerging decision technologies.

Length: 3 days

Cost: $795

Location: Chicago, IL.

WEINBERG AND WEINBERG, Rural Route Two, Lincoln, NE 68520, 402/781-2542.

Problem Solving Leadership Workshop. This program focuses on the process aspects of problem solving leadership. The purpose is not merely to convey thoughts, but to change behavior.

Length: 6 days

Cost: $725

Locations: Jacksonville, FL; Lincoln, NE; Portland, OR.

WORCESTER POLYTECHNIC INSTITUTE, Office of Continuing Education, Higgins House, Worcester, MA 01609, 617/793-5517.

Creative Problem Solving and Decision Making. This workshop presents the tools for creative problem solving and focuses on becoming aware that a situation is developing, defining the problem, problem/decision analysis, and implementing the solution.

Length: 2 days
Cost: $695
Locations: Marlboro, MA; Natick, MA; Worcester, MA.

Financial and Quantitative Skills

Many sections of this Handbook focus on the people-related aspects of management. But the management function is, in part, a "numbers game," too. This section presents guidelines for learning more about your organization's finances.

- Increasing Your Familiarity With the Financial Aspects of Your Organization (p. 411)
- Using Microcomputers and Software Programs for Financial Analysis (p. 412)
- Analyzing Financial Information Quickly (p. 413)
- Using Statistical and Quantitative Information (p. 413)
- Improving Your Math Skills (p. 414)
- Incorporating Financial and Quantitative Data Into Your Decision Making (p. 415)
- Improving Financial Data Submitted by Subordinates (p. 416)
- Becoming More Comfortable Using Financial Information (p. 416)

Tips

- Arrange a monthly meeting with a controller or financial accounting person in your organization to discuss information you most need to understand how to do your job better.

- Plan to talk with all department heads in the finance/accounts functions about their departments' duties and how they fit into the overall picture of the company.

- Always carry a small hand-held calculator with you.

- To understand budget items, go to the department, plant, etc., and "walk the floor" so you know the origins of each line item.

- Take charge of handling the financial responsibilities for your church or community organization.

- Ask an accounting friend to explain the annual report of your own and one other organization.

- Develop and maintain a detailed household budget.

- Subscribe to and read **Money** magazine.

- Develop a "spread sheet" for your department by using a personal computer and one of the appropriate software packages currently available.

- Take a course in algebra at a local college.

- Help your kids with their math homework.

- Take a computer-assisted course in basic math skills.

- Take a course at a local college to address math anxiety.

- Ask for special assignments or additional duties that will require more financial/quantitative knowledge.

FINANCIAL AND
QUANTITATIVE SKILLS

- Read one of the many books available on "finance for nonfinancial managers."

- Avoid getting bogged down in the data by determining only the two or three major implications from the data.

- Read your company's annual report and try to forecast the impact of the balance sheet on your department.

- Compensate for your weakness by delegating financial work to someone with strong skills in this area.

- Learn to compute ratios such as ROI, ROA, etc., on a calculator by using data available to you in your job.

- Assemble a mock portfolio of stocks based on financial reports and track their progress weekly.

Increasing Your Familiarity With the Financial Aspects of Your Organization

Every organization must have sound financial control in order to survive. Your development in the area of finance can help you prepare for advancement and do your part to maintain your organization's financial system. Following are suggestions for increasing your familiarity with the financial aspects of your organization.

- **Learn to read and analyze annual reports.** With the help of reference materials or a knowledgeable colleague, learn to read and analyze annual reports. Then obtain copies of your organization's reports for the last several years. Study them and look for trends. Predict the impact of your department's tasks, decisions, and outcomes on the balance sheet. Then discuss your perceptions with someone in the organization who is knowledgeable in financial report analysis.

- **Become involved in the budgeting process.** If you don't currently participate in your organization's budgeting process, ask your superior if it would be possible for you to become involved. As you begin the budgeting cycle, ask for your superior's perspective on the budgeting and forecasting process and how your department's budget fits in with that of the total organization.

- **Learn your organization's system of financial reporting.** Obtain coaching from someone who understands your organization's system of financial reports. Your superior or someone from the accounting organization would be a likely choice. Ask your coach to explain:
  - The purpose of each report in the system
  - Who is responsible for the completion of each report
  - Which reports are incorporated into other reports (for example, a departmental financial statement may be combined with other departmental statements in the preparation of a divisional statement)
  - How often each report is updated
  - The process by which each report is updated

- **Obtain other perspectives on financial reporting.** Explore the possibility of talking with people from outside your unit to obtain their perspectives on the financial report system. Ask these people to explain their jobs, their views of your department, how your department fits in with the rest of the organization, and which financial skills would be most important to you as you assume advanced responsibilities.

- **Develop your analytical skills.** People who are uncomfortable with numbers tend to skip over them when reading reports. If you are one of these people, force yourself to pay attention to numbers, and ask yourself whether the numerical data supports the conclusions of the reports. In addition, develop an analytical attitude toward all conclusions reached on the basis of numerical data. Look for inaccurate data and data that has been excluded. In doing so, you will begin to notice situations for which the conclusions are not adequately supported by data.

Using Microcomputers and Software Programs for Financial Analysis

With the cost of microcomputer hardware and software programs rapidly decreasing, more and more managers are using these tools in financial analysis. Following are suggestions to help you gain familiarity with microcomputers and spread-sheet programs.

- Visit a computer store to learn about microcomputers and financial software programs. Most stores offer informational literature on the machines and programs they carry. Often, salespeople will give demonstrations of the capabilities of the machines and programs. Some stores even offer seminars at little or no cost.
- Obtain coaching from a person experienced in using microcomputers for financial analysis. More and more people are using microcomputers. You'll be surprised at the number of people who will be glad to share their knowledge with you once you have expressed an interest.
- Create your own programs. If, through your study of microcomputers and software, you find that these tools could help you perform your job, learn to use the programs. The reports you can easily create using spread-sheet programs include:
    - Cash flow
    - Sales forecasts
    - Budget forecasts
    - Break-even analysis

Data-base programs can be used to create any type of report that requires the listing and sorting of data. For example, a data-base program can: tell you how many purchase orders have been written to a given company and the total amount of these orders, list outstanding invoices and their amounts, and list inventory items that have fallen below the reorder point.

Other types of programs are also available, including general ledger programs and financial programs geared to specific businesses.

Analyzing Financial Information Quickly

Unfortunately, financial reports and budget information are usually structured to meet the needs of a wide variety of people within the organization. As a result, they often contain far more information than any one person in the organization requires.

A second common problem with financial information, especially when it is computer-generated, involves the readability of the data. Computer program designers are often more concerned with the "number crunching" aspects of the program than with the readability of the reports it produces.

In an ideal world, you could attack these problems at their roots by asking for reports tailored to meet your needs and by suggesting computer program modifications to make the reports easier to read. These solutions, however, often involve considerable time and expense for the organization as a whole.

You can, however, use the following process to help analyze financial information more quickly.

1. Identify the departmental or organizational reports you have difficulty using efficiently. If you work with numerous reports, select a subset of reports that have one or more of the following characteristics:
   - Most important to your job
   - Used most frequently
   - Most difficult to analyze
2. Ask your manager or a peer in finance or accounting to go over the reports with you, focusing on the items of importance for you and your department.
3. Compare the key items on each report across earlier issues of the same report. Correlate the differences among the items to what has been happening in your department or business.
4. Create a "crib sheet" for each report. This "crib sheet" should contain definitions of key items and a step-by-step procedure for analyzing the report.

Using Statistical and Quantitative Information

Managers are often barraged by periodic computer reports and summaries, some of which contain valuable information for the operation of the department and some of which do not. To determine the difference, you need to understand clearly the information contained in these reports. Follow these guidelines each time a computer report appears in your in-basket.

1. Take the report back to the department from which it came and have someone thoroughly explain the report to you.
2. Make notations and take notes on any information contained in the report relevant to projects in your department. The report may contain helpful feedback for monitoring the achievement of your departmental or organizational goals.
3. File the report and your notes on it for quick reference should you need it at a later date.

Improving Your Math Skills

Many people avoid financial analysis because of the low level of their math skills. Some have become "rusty" at math because of the years that have lapsed since they learned the concepts. Some took too few classes in

school. Others have decided that they don't have the ability to learn math skills (these people are said to have "math blocks" or "math anxiety"). If your math skills are deficient, for whatever reason, improving them will help you become more comfortable with financial data. The following suggestions will help you develop your skills.

- **Overcoming math anxiety.** Although specialized mathematical analysis requires a specialized math aptitude, anyone who is capable of learning to read and write is also capable of learning mathematics up through higher-level algebra—an adequate level for most managerial positions. Yet if you have math anxiety, you may believe that this is not true. Fortunately, because so many people have the same problem, many training programs have been designed that can help you overcome your anxiety. Survey the course and seminar catalogs of your local university and community colleges. Look for a program geared toward people with math anxiety or one that diagnoses skill levels so that you can be placed in the appropriate class.

- **Brushing up or learning new skills.** If you need a math review or want to learn new math skills, survey the catalogs of your local university and community colleges for courses that meet your needs. Many managers take such courses as business math, managerial accounting, advanced math, and statistical analysis. You might wish to buy one of the numerous programmed learning texts on the subject of your choice. If you choose this option, be sure to set a deadline for finishing each section of the book to help prevent procrastination in finishing the program.

Incorporating Financial and Quantitative Data Into Your Decision Making

Financial and/or quantitative data is required to support many business decisions. The following suggestions will help you develop the ability to identify and prepare such data.

- Make a list of the major types of decisions in which you are involved during the year. For each decision area, note the kind of financial or quantitative data you need to make your decisions or support your conclusions. For example, the total number of work hours projected for the year is a number often used to justify the hiring of additional staff. Savings in labor dollars and projected work hours per machine can be used to justify the purchase of equipment. Based on your analysis of the type of information required, create a plan to collect the information.

- Review your reports and recommendations with your superior to determine whether they can be improved with quantitative data.
- With the help of your superior, identify a project in your organization that requires a close working relationship with financial or accounting managers.

Improving Financial Data Submitted by Subordinates

In many cases, subordinates submit financial reports or forecasts to their managers, who, in turn, use them in preparing reports that they submit to their superiors. In such instances, the subordinates' reports may lack data, include inaccurate data, or contain unrealistic forecasts. Or, in the case of expense tracking, perhaps costs in some expense categories exceed budgeted figures. To improve the accuracy of your reports, and to develop the report-writing abilities of your subordinates, try the following activities.

- Instead of asking your subordinates to submit their reports directly to you, hold a review meeting at the time of submittal. Ask subordinates to make transparencies of their reports and to present them to the staff as a group. Ask group members to comment on any favorable data or problem areas they observe.
- In the area of expense control, focus on one major area each reporting period. Meet with your subordinates as a group to discuss ways in which expense control can be improved.
- Ask subordinates to assist you in compiling your reports to help them understand the ultimate purpose of the reports. Rotate this assignment among qualified subordinates each preparation period so that, eventually, your entire staff will be qualified to prepare the data.

Becoming More Comfortable Using Financial Information

People who are uncomfortable with numbers tend to skip over them in reports. Follow these guidelines until you become more comfortable with financial data.

1. Force yourself to go through the numbers and ask yourself whether the data supports the conclusion. Develop an attitude of being more critical of the conclusions someone reaches based on numerical or financial data. You will probably begin to notice areas of data that have been excluded and areas in which conclusions are advanced that do not fit the data.
2. Approach your superior and ask for involvement in the budgeting process if you do not already have it. It would be helpful for you to

understand the budgeting and forecasting process from his or her perspective. Your goal, too, is to understand how your area's budgeting and forecasting fit in with that for the total organization.

Recommended Readings

Clark, John J., and Clark, Margaret T. *A Statistics Primer for Managers.* New York, NY: The Free Press, 1983.

The authors explain how to choose data to support or challenge business decisions, avoid costly unused computer capacity, and understand the shortcuts and limitations of the computer. Using clear language, they explain basic statistical concepts such as probability, sampling, time-series analysis, correlations, and index numbers.

Detterman, D.K., and Sternberg, R.J., eds. *How and How Much Can Intelligence Be Increased.* Norwood, NJ: Ablex, 1982.

This book presents a reasonably comprehensive survey to current work on efforts to modify intelligence. Even if there is no precise answer to how and how much intelligence can be increased, the work presented here demonstrates a number of ways the question can be asked with hope of an eventual answer.

Targett, David. *Coping with Numbers: A Management Guide.* New York, NY: Basil Blackwell, 1983.

The author has written a book with non-mathematical managers in mind. It demonstrates what is practical and useful for managers, giving them guidelines in day to day tasks of number handling. There are techniques for manipulating numbers and converting them into information, as well as the concepts and practical aspects of more complex areas, so that the manager can at the very least participate sensibly in discussions with the experts.

Tobias, Sheila. *Overcoming Math Anxiety.* Boston, MA: Houghton Mifflin, 1980.

Written to those who have avoided math and don't feel comfortable with numbers and measurements, this book covers gender differences and math, the "non-mathematical mind," word problem solving, basic statistics, an introduction to calculus, and techniques and suggestions for beefing up your mathematical background. The author has put together a very clear and readable presentation.

Walgenbach, Paul H.; Dittrich, Norman E.; and Hanson, Ernest I. *Financial Accounting: An Introduction (4th ed.).* New York, NY: Harcourt, Brace, and Jovanovich, 1985.

This book presents a complete and balanced treatment of the concepts, procedures, and uses of financial accounting. Among the topics discussed are double-entry accounting systems, the accounting cycle, mass processing of transactions, cash controls, trade accounts and notes, inventories, assets, liabilities and investments, capital stock, and corporate dividends.

Cognitive Skills

Notes:

Suggested Seminars

The seminars listed here were selected for their appeal to a managerial audience and have received good to excellent ratings from managers attending them.

Because of the dynamic nature of the seminar marketplace, some seminars may have been added, upgraded, or replaced, and others may no longer be offered. Additional information about these seminars may be obtained by calling the vendor directly or through Seminar Clearinghouse International, a subscriber organization located in St. Paul, Minnesota. Call 612/293-1004 for information.

AMERICAN MANAGEMENT ASSOCIATIONS, P.O. Box 319, Saranac Lake, NY 12983, 518/891-0065.

Fundamentals of Finance and Accounting for Non-financial Executives. This course is recommended for individuals who want to learn the fundamentals of finance and accounting. It covers a crash course in accounting language, setting up financial statements and reports, interpreting your company's financial signals, annual reports, financing business—way of obtaining funds, profit planning and budgeting, and return-on-investment.

Length: 3 days
Cost: $795
Locations: San Diego, CA; San Francisco, CA; Ft. Lauderdale, FL; St. Petersburg, FL; Tampa, FL; Boston, MA; Chapel Hill, NC; Raleigh, NC; Morristown, NJ; Parsippany, NJ; White Plains, NY; Columbus, OH. For additional locations, contact the vendor.

COLUMBIA UNIVERSITY, Graduate School of Business, 807 Uris Hall, New York, NY 10027, 212/280-3395.

Accounting and Financial Management for the Non-financial Executive. This program provides an overview of the financial tools and techniques needed in an increasingly complex business environment. Particular emphasis is placed on understanding financial performance measures and the role the measures play in the planning and control of business operations.

Length: 6 days
Cost: $2850
Location: Harriman, NY.

MICHIGAN STATE UNIVERSITY, 7 Olds Hall, East Lansing, MI 48824, 800/428-4284 (in Mich.), 517/353-4284.

Reading and Analyzing Financial Statements. This course shows you how to read and analyze balance sheets, income statements, and cash flow analyses. Get the financial background you need to demystify financial statements. Use time-tested financial tools for making better, more informed decisions. This program is designed for corporate executives, general management, small businessmen, bank loan officers, individuals responsible for credit analysis, managers, and those who are seeking a good working knowledge of financial statement analysis.
Length: 1 day
Cost: $295
Locations: East Lansing, MI; Troy, MI.

PENNSYLVANIA STATE UNIVERSITY, College of Business Administration, University Park, PA 16802, 814/865-3435.

Financial Concepts for General Management. Two-week program offering the following topics: financial strategies and corporate strategies; corporate financial objectives; managerial accounting; capital structure and the cost of capital; capital budgeting; working capital management and banking relationships; evaluation of capital markets; mergers and acquisitions; lease financing; and international business.
Length: 2 weeks
Cost: $4200
Location: University Park, PA.

UNIVERSITY OF PENNSYLVANIA, Office of Executive Education, Vance Hall, Philadelphia, PA 19104, 215/898-1776.

Finance and Accounting for the Nonfinancial Manager. The seminar emphasizes comprehensive coverage of the most salient features of financial accounting and financial statements. It stresses the interpretation, analysis and application of accounting data toward informed decision making. Through the use of lectures and case studies, the seminar develops systematically the language and important concepts of accounting in order to facilitate the clear understanding of financial statements.
Length: 5 days
Cost: $2750 (includes accommodations, meals)
Location: Philadelphia, PA.

UNIVERSITY OF VIRGINIA, The Colgate Darden Graduate Business School Sponsors, P.O. Box 6550, Charlottesville, VA 22906, 804/924-3000.

Financial Management for Nonfinancial Managers. This seminar is designed to provide, at a basic level, sufficient familiarity with financial information to enable the nonfinancial manager to interpret and comfortably utilize financial data in daily decisions. The program aims at the uses of the information rather than its preparation.
Length: 5 days
Cost: $2500
Location: Charlottesville, VA.

UNIVERSITY OF WISCONSIN, Management Institute, 432 North Lake Street, Madison, WI 53791, 608/262-8890, 800/362-3010 (in Wisc.), 800/262-6243 (outside Wisc.).

Finance and Accounting for the Nonfinancial Executive. This three-day workshop is designed to enable participants to develop an understanding of the terminology, concepts, and practices of finance and accounting. The key topics include: an introduction to financial statement concepts; working capital management; fixed assets and depreciation; income taxes and profit; financial analysis; evaluating capital expenditure proposals; and using management accounting for decision making.
Length: 3 days
Cost: $645
Location: Madison, WI.

UNIVERSITY OF WISCONSIN, Management Institute, 423 North Lake Street, Madison, WI 53706, 608/262-8891, 800/362-3020 (outside Wisc.), 800/262-6243 (in Wisc.).

Finance & Accounting for the Non-financial Executive. Topics included in this three-day seminar are planning and budgeting for results, interpreting financial statements, evaluating expenses, managing working capital and cash flow, improving asset use, and lease-versus-purchase. To benefit most from this program, you need a limited background in financial basics.
Length: 3 days
Cost: $695
Location: Madison, WI.

STANFORD ALUMNI ASSOCIATION, Bowman Alumni House, Stanford, CA 94305, 415/497-2027, 415/497-2021.

Financial Seminar for Non-financial Managers. Three-day course designed to provide a working knowledge of the complexities of financial

management in both for profit and nonprofit organizations. The curriculum covers reading a financial report, the use of ratios in financial analysis, interrelationships of key financial variables, forecasting financial requirements, and financial leverage.
Length: 3 days
Cost: Call vendor
Location: Stanford, CA.

VANDERBILT UNIVERSITY, Owen Graduate School of Management, Office of Executive Education, Nashville, TN 37203, 615/322-2513.
What Executives Should Know About Finance & Accounting. Among the topics discussed in this five-day program are communicating with financial personnel, designing effective profit planning and control systems, selecting financial measures for usefulness in monitoring crucial variables for effective organizational control, negotiating loan provisions with banks, and dealing effectively with other funding institutions.
Length: 5 days
Cost: $1450
Location: Nashville, TN.

Notes:

Innovation and Resourcefulness

Progress and growth are impossible if you always do things the way you have always done things.

—Author unknown

In the workplace as in other facets of life, innovation often occurs when people develop new ways of looking at old ways of doing things. By studying existing practices and procedures, you can determine which of their elements would best be combined with your own ideas for developing programs suited to your work group's unique needs.

This section is divided into two parts.

Part I: Personal Development contains guidelines for:
- Capitalizing on Experiences (p. 425)
- Making Use of Existing Information (p. 425)
- Thinking Positively When Faced With Obstacles (p. 425)
- Overcoming Mental Blocks (p. 426)
- Creating New Approaches to Your Work (p. 426)
- Increasing Your Mental Flexibility (p. 427)
- Increasing Your Intellectual Curiosity (p. 427)

Part II: Encouraging Innovation in Others presents suggestions for:
- Brainstorming (p. 428)
- Encouraging Innovations in Your Department (p. 429)

Tips

- Once you have identified the problem, ask yourself, "What would my critics say the problem is?"

- Once you've made a risky decision, pour lots of energy into it to make it work and modify it as needed.

- Suspend your critical judgment, that part of you that says "it won't work." Generate far-out and crazy ideas; be silly to loosen up your blocked thinking.

- Talk about the situation with someone from a different discipline, order, or perspective.

- Talk to others in the organization to see how they have addressed similar situations or problems.

- Develop more originality in your decision making by being less cautious and conservative and by taking more risks.

- Generate as many options in the problem-solving process as you can for both the problem-cause phase and the generation-of-alternatives phase.

- If you run out of ideas try reconceptualizing the problem, redefining it, turning it 90 degrees, and looking at it from a different perspective.

- Fantasize a "different universe" with a different set of natural laws. What possibilities exist for solving this problem?

- Avoid stereotyping people and ideas. Think of their unique qualities and try to use them productively.

- Figure out a way to make it happen!

- Don't be satisfied with your first idea. Push yourself to generate other ideas before committing.

- Practice coming up with what may at first seem like "dumb" and way-out ideas to get your creative juices flowing and reduce your self-criticisms.

- Allow yourself quiet time to generate as many ideas as possible in 15 minutes.

- When considering alternatives, ask yourself and others "Why not?" instead of "Why?"

- Avoid premature censoring of ideas, and don't be concerned about whether or not ideas are flowing in a logical sequence.

- Refrain from imposing a prematurely structured solution on a problem without first considering alternative solutions.

- Use group idea generation techniques only as brainstorming and nominal group techniques.

Part I: Personal Development

Capitalizing on Experiences

Day-to-day experiences can be used to promote resourcefulness. The suggestions that follow will help you make the most of these experiences.

- Approach new situations and people with the attitude of, "What can I learn?"
- After a meeting or discussion, take a few minutes to think about what you have learned and how it relates to your job.
- Keep a file entitled "New Ideas." Each time you hear or see something related to your job, write it down and file it.

Making Use of Existing Information

Innovation does not require doing, making, or thinking something that has not existed before. For example, if you are charged with creating a training program, don't "reinvent the wheel," or create a program similar to those already in existence. This is a waste of time, and you are likely to miss some key factors. But if you learn as much as you can about how others have done the task, you may be able to use their ideas, along with your own, to design a unique but solid program that suits the needs of your organization.

To put this concept into practice, follow these guidelines.

1. Choose one area related to your job in which you think innovation could be beneficial.
2. Go to the library or any resource center and read relevant books and articles. Jot down ideas others have had related to the area in question and any new ideas you develop from reading the ideas of others.
3. Talk to people who are knowledgeable in your chosen area and capitalize on their ideas.

Thinking Positively When Faced With Obstacles

When you feel that a task is impossible or that an obstacle cannot be overcome, stop yourself from thinking these negative thoughts, which actually "close down" your mental processes and prevent you from being resourceful.

When negative thoughts occur, think of the most resourceful person you know and imagine how that person would resolve the problem. Say to yourself, "I know there is a solution to this." If necessary, take a break from the problem and return to it later in the day or week.

Overcoming Mental Blocks

When every alternative for a problem seems inadequate, you can overcome your feeling of being "stuck" by using the following techniques.

- The most important step is to acknowledge that you are stuck; once you realize that your problem-solving processes are blocked, there are a number of techniques you can use to get past the block.
- Think positively. Instead of telling yourself that the task is impossible, tell yourself that you have reached a momentary impasse and that a solution does exist and will eventually come to you.
- Take a break if you can. While you are working on something else, your mind will work on the problem on a subconscious level. When you return to the problem, you will probably approach it from a different perspective.
- Don't hesitate to let others know that you are stuck or to ask them for help. When a new perspective on the problem is required, others may be able to help you develop this perspective. Consider seeking out people with perspectives or backgrounds different from your own. Briefly outline the characteristics of the problem without offering your solutions. Then ask these people for their suggestions.

Creating New Approaches to Your Work

From time to time, you should critically analyze your routines to eliminate or modify inefficient procedures. The following process will help you structure your analysis.

1. Select a procedure that you find outdated, overly time-consuming, or difficult.
2. Evaluate the procedure from a general perspective by asking:
   - What is the purpose of this procedure?
   - In which areas is it failing to meet its objectives?
3. Generate as many alternate procedures as you can that would meet the same objective. Concentrate on innovation rather than on limiting implementation factors.
4. Evaluate the procedure in detail, criticizing each step. Ask yourself:
   - Is this step necessary?
   - What is the purpose of this step?
   - Could this step be eliminated or combined with another step to save time?

5. Generate alternatives to each step in the procedure, again concentrating on quantity rather quality or sheer practicality.
6. Review your potential alternatives, both at the general and detailed levels. Try combining them in different ways to arrive at a new approach. It may be possible to combine the best elements of several alternatives to obtain one superior solution.

Increasing Your Mental Flexibility

Mental flexibility is the ability to adjust to new information when solving problems and to consider a broad range of alternatives. It is the opposite of holding on to a solution or procedure because "that's the way it's always been done." People who think inflexibly generally hold to policy, display rigidity in problem solving by discarding alternatives before thinking them through, and believe that each problem has one right answer.

To become more flexible, try following these guidelines.
- Ask trusted coworkers to provide feedback on situations in which you tend to be overly opinionated or rigid in your thinking. Most people have specific "problem areas." Recognizing the fact that you are becoming inflexible is the first step in initiating change.
- Watch for "snap" reactions. Rather than assuming that the first alternative that enters your mind is the best solution, try writing down your first reaction, then considering other options.

The list of references at the end of this section includes several publications that can help you combat inflexibility.

Increasing Your Intellectual Curiosity

Looking at problems and issues from different perspectives prevents tunnel vision. Increased intellectual curiosity will also help you become more resourceful in solving problems. The following guidelines will help you broaden your perspective.
- To increase your knowledge of the world around you, get in the habit of reading newspapers and periodicals for current events, technical journals for new developments in your field, and other related books.
- Choose an area of your organization about which you know relatively little. Over the next three months, learn about that area and its perspective. Ask one or two people from that organization to tell you about their responsibilities and problems. Also ask them what they read to keep up with developments in their field.

- The next time you have an opportunity to develop a long-range project for your department or to set up a task force, assemble as diverse a group of people as possible.

Part II: Encouraging Innovation in Others

Brainstorming

When a number of people gather to solve a problem, one idea can help generate others. This is especially true in an environment that encourages idea generation. To encourage the sharing of ideas in your organization, try following these guidelines.

1. Organize an informal brainstorming session to discuss new approaches to persistent departmental problems or innovative applications of existing products and/or services. The purpose of the session should be

to generate as many novel ideas as possible (for example, 50 ideas within a 30-minute session). Limit the number of participants to seven to nine to ensure the active participation of all members.

2. To create the proper environment, announce these ground rules at the beginning of the session.
    - The emphasis is on quantity rather than quality. Avoid blocking creative thinking with unnecessary concentration on detail. For the moment, implementation constraints should be ignored.
    - No criticism of ideas allowed. All ideas will be evaluated at a later time.
    - Feel free to add to ideas or to combine ideas.

3. Present a clear definition of the problem, remind participants of the ground rules, and then let loose. As chairperson, you are responsible for:
    - Stopping criticism and preventing judgments
    - Trying to get everyone to participate
    - Ensuring that all ideas are recorded

4. At the end of the meeting, review the ideas. You can perform this review yourself, get other group members involved, or send the ideas to a preselected committee for evaluation. Your mission at this point is to identify the ideas that could actually be implemented. The results of the evaluation, in terms of the number of implementable ideas, should be reported to the brainstorming group. The specific ideas chosen or rejected should not be part of this report.

When the group is comfortable with this process, you may wish to consider inviting individuals from different levels in your department/division to participate. A brainstorming session can serve as a communications bridge, helping people to work together as a team.

Encouraging Innovation in Your Department

Most people are reluctant to voice new ideas if they fear they will look foolish. To encourage innovation, you must create a climate in which individuals feel free to present their ideas without fear of criticism. To foster this type of climate over the next month, implement two or three techniques for generating new ideas in group discussion. Examples of these techniques follow.

- Set aside time at your regular staff meeting to discuss new, innovative ideas. Stress the fact that ideas need not be fully considered.

- Promote a climate in which people initially encourage rather than criticize new ideas by asking people to first discuss what they like rather than what they dislike about an idea.
- On an experimental basis, initiate two or three sessions dedicated to brainstorming. These need not be formal sessions; if a problem arises during a staff meeting, suggest that the group brainstorm to generate as many solutions as possible. (See the preceding subsection.)

As people's fear of criticism is reduced, you will see your department's climate change and hear people voice more new ideas.

Recommended Readings

Ackoff, Russell L. *The Art of Problem Solving—Accompanied by Ackoff's Fables.* New York, NY: John Wiley & Sons, 1978.

This book synthesizes Ackoff's years of experience in creatively recasting constraints unnecessarily imposed by the problem solver. Part 1 of the book presents the basic framework. Part 2, Applications, provides case examples of the techniques and approaches described in the first section. This book is appropriate for managers who are looking for a readable discussion of creativity and problem solving.

Buzan, Tony. *Use Both Sides of Your Brain.* New York, NY: E.P. Dutton, Inc., 1983.

The author discusses how the mind works and how to use it to the best advantage. He offers practical tips on how to read faster and more efficiently, to study more effectively, to solve problems more readily, and to increase the power of your memory.

Kanter, Rosabeth Moss. *The Change Masters: Innovation for Productivity in the American Corporation.* New York, NY: Simon and Schuster, 1983.

The Change Masters vividly demonstrates that when environments and structures are hospitable to innovation, people's natural inventiveness and power skills can make almost anything happen. Dr. Kanter's book is an indispensable guide for individuals who seek to realize their entrepreneurial potential, for corporate leaders who want to see their companies grow, and for all those concerned with the economic future of the nation. Included are some searches for innovation by companies such as Hewlett-Packard, General Electric, Polaroid, General Motors, Wang Laboratories, and Honeywell.

LeBoeuf, M. *Imagineering: How to Profit From Your Own Creative Powers.* New York, NY: McGraw-Hill, 1980.

The author attempts to show how personal creativity and idea-generating can be increased, learned, and systematically practiced. The book explains ways to create an inner and outer environment most conducive to creativity and provides a full range of tested techniques for generating ideas which insure judgment-free spontaneity, evaluating ideas objectively, and putting these ideas into action.

Notes:

Suggested Seminars

The seminars listed here were selected for their appeal to a managerial audience and have received good to excellent ratings from managers attending them.

Because of the dynamic nature of the seminar marketplace, some seminars may have been added, upgraded, or replaced, and others may no longer be offered. Additional information about these seminars may be obtained by calling the vendor directly, or through Seminar Clearinghouse International, a subscriber organization located in St. Paul, Minnesota. Call 612/293-1004 for information.

BATTELLE, 4000 Northeast 41st Street, P.O. Box C-5395, Seattle, WA 98105, 206/527-0542 (in Wash.), 800/426-6762 (outside Wash.).

Creative Thinking Strategies for Scientists, Engineers and Project Managers. This program focuses on inventive thinking, styles of thinking, creative climate strategies, and strategy contrasts and mode interaction.

Length: 2 days

Cost: $675

Location: Palo Alto, CA; Washington, DC; Chicago, IL; Cincinnati, OH; Seattle, WA.

CENTER FOR CREATIVE LEADERSHIP, 5000 Laurinda Drive, P.O. Box P-1, Greensboro, NC 27402, 919/288-7210: ext. 351.

From Idea to Market Entry: Managing the People Process. This program focuses on creative problem-solving technology in applied managerial settings. Topics include: techniques that will tap the knowledge and creativity of your group; communicating goals and empowering individuals with responsiblity for achieving them; how to structure your department's environment to stimulate your people's creativity; important considerations in developing new product ideas; an overview of the total process of bringing a product to the marketplace; how to adapt your decision-making style to specific situations to ensure quality, acceptance, and timeliness; and better integration of the "links" in the innovation process through planning and decision making.

Length: 5 days

Cost: $2100

Location: Greensboro, NC.

Implementing Innovation. Three to five participants attend from each organization: research and development, marketing, and manufacturing.

Their goal will be to learn specific structures for coordinating their organizational functions.
Length: 4 days
Cost: $1700
Location: Greensboro, NC.

International Creativity Symposium. This program, originally Creative Week, explores the integration of imagination and practical experience. It challenges participants and presenters to expand their thinking about innovation in the workplace.
Length: 4 days
Cost: $1000
Locations: San Diego, CA; Greensboro, NC.

NTL INSTITUTE, P.O. Box 9155, Rosslyn Station, Arlington, VA 22209, 703/527-1500.

Implementing Innovative Ideas. Participants in this four-day program will gain an understanding of the innovation process and develop analytical and behavioral skills for communicating with and influencing stakeholders.
Length: 4 days
Cost: $665
Location: Bethel, ME.

STANFORD ALUMNI ASSOCIATION, Bowman Alumni House, Stanford, CA 94305, 415/723-2027.

Stanford Program on Managing Innovation. This three-day program focuses on innovation and developing an enterpreneurial attitude within your company; reviewing with the innovators themselves the practices of companies that have survived and flourished in spite of increasing competition; and learning how to fuse the functional units involved in the development of new products and services.
Length: 3 days
Cost: $1750
Location: Stanford, CA.

UNIVERSITY OF WISCONSIN, Department of Engineering, 432 Lake Street, Madison, WI 53706, 800/362-6020 (in Wisc.), 800/262-6243 (outside Wisc.).

Creative Action in Engineering and Science. Three-day program offered in Madison, Wisconsin. Course focuses on process, content, and practice.
Length: 3 days
Cost: $800
Location: Madison, WI.

Notes:

Handling Detail

Our life is frittered away by detail. Simplify, simplify.
　　　　　　　　　　　　　　　—Henry David Thoreau

Thoreau would probably be unimpressed by the amount of documentation generated in today's world of business. Paperwork is nonetheless a staple of everyday office life, and a certain amount of detail is needed in communicating the events of the day to supervisors, subordinates, and others who need information.

The key to complete, succinct communication is deciding what needs to be said and what doesn't. The same general rule concerning detail applies in decision making and problem solving: Which details need to be considered and which don't? Project planning and information tracking (trends, production levels, deadlines, and so on) also require attention to detail.

This section suggests ways for:
- Introducing Less Detail in Reports and Presentations (p. 437)
- Avoiding Excessive Detail in Decision Making (p. 438)
- Providing Complete, Accurate Information (p. 438)
- Considering Important Details When Solving Problems (p. 439)
- Attending to Detail When Processing Paperwork (p. 439)
- Attending to Detail in Project Plans (p. 439)
- Keeping Track of Details (p. 440)

Tips

- Have subordinates provide you with lists of the pros and cons of each issue to identify critical areas needing more analytical attention.

- If you lack substantive detail, support your ideas or opinions with at least two or more facts.

- When solving problems, making decisions, planning, or organizing, consciously and deliberately determine what details are necessary to 1) make a critical decision, 2) check the validity of projected results, and 3) make the plan complete. Then, list examples of facts that might be needed to answer these questions.

- Acquire the habit of double-checking important decisions and actions to see if you have neglected salient details.

- Ask for feedback from your manager about what types of details you tend to overlook.

- Work with your secretary to establish procedures for documenting important details.

- Develop a checklist of details that need to be handled when making certain decisions.

- Have your supervisor monitor your performance carefully and call your attention to details that may have slipped by you.

- Keep a flow chart of your daily activities and a checklist of the details involved.

- Underline key points in memos and write notes to yourself in the margins.

- When writing or talking, provide information on a "need to know" basis.

- Force yourself to move from details to the "big picture" periodically to gain a broader perspective.

- Observe others who go into too much detail in speaking, writing, or decision-making and avoid similar patterns for yourself.

- Identify problems resulting from lack of attention to detail and establish procedures to insure that they don't recur.

- To avoid getting bogged down in details, ask yourself how various items relate to your overall objectives.

- Practice presenting your idea in a succinct form to friends and coworkers and see if they still get your main point.

- Insist that subordinates provide you with a one-page summary of all documents they write.

Introducing Less Detail in Reports and Presentations

Unnecessary detail wastes your time and the time of those to whom you are presenting your ideas. In addition, the impact of your message can be lost if the reader or listener must sift through unimportant data in order to determine the key points. To reduce extraneous detail, follow these guidelines.

- Before reviewing masses of information to prepare a report or presentation, list the items you really need to cull from these materials. Then skim the materials, giving your primary attention to important items and little or no attention to others.
- To develop more succinct writing, go over your memos and see if you can cover the same content in half the words.
- Learn more about your method of handling detail. Ask trusted colleagues to give you feedback on your concern with detail and to suggest any ways in which you might improve your use of detail.

- When preparing a report or presentation, discuss your task with your superior. Ask which details can be bypassed and which are critical. When the report is finished, ask your superior to review it to determine if the appropriate amount of detail has been included.
- Delegate detailed work to subordinates whenever appropriate.

Avoiding Excessive Detail in Decision Making

Considering too many details can prevent you from making timely decisions. To determine the level of detail required, try making your decisions in two phases.

- First, limit yourself to 15 minutes for gathering data and making a preliminary decision. Record your decision.
- Next, spend as much time as you would under normal circumstances gathering additional information and reaching a final decision. Compare your final decision to the preliminary one to determine if the extra time spent was worthwhile.

Continue to make decisions in this way for several months. Keep track of the results each time you apply the process. At the end of this time period, evaluate your results to determine whether you should reduce the amount of detail you collect before making a decision.

Providing Complete, Accurate Information

The following three guidelines will help you provide and elicit complete, accurate information.

- To ensure that information you supply to others is complete, take notes during the request for information. Review the notes with the person making the request to ensure that you understand what is required. Then, before you provide the information, compare it to your notes to ensure that you have satisfied all requirements.
- To ensure that you receive complete information, give a written list of requirements to the person supplying the information. Keep a copy of the list for yourself. Then, when the information is presented to you, compare it to your list.
- To ensure that information you supply is accurate, compare the information you have copied to the original source and restate information supplied verbally to the person providing the information.

Considering Important Details When Solving Problems

To ensure that you consider all important details before making a decision, follow these guidelines.

1. Make a list of all details required for the decision.
2. Conscientiously search through information sources until you have located each required item.
3. Acquire the habit of checking each decision to determine if the necessary details have been considered at the time the decision is made.

Attending to Detail When Processing Paperwork

Recognizing and attending to important details is necessary in order to be an effective administrator. Over the next several months, each time you process documents:

1. Glance through each piece of paperwork quickly to get an initial understanding of its contents and impact.
2. Place the documents in order of priority.
3. Read the documents carefully, highlighting underlined key points which are important for you to be aware of, or which will influence future actions.
4. In the margin indicate references to other documents which contain information relevant to this particular piece of paperwork.
5. Before taking action on the document, refer back to the underscored points and any noted references in additional documents to ensure your action is based on a complete understanding of all factors.
6. File the document where it will be easily accessible.

Attending to Detail in Project Plans

The most successful plans are complete plans. When preparing a plan, use the following list of plan components to determine if you have included all necessary details. In addition, review this list with your superior to determine additional requirements.

Plan Components
- A complete listing or description of each task to be accomplished
- Staffing requirements (the number of people, the types and levels of expertise required, how and where these people will be obtained, which tasks each person will be expected to accomplish)
- Information resource requirements for each staff member
- Equipment requirements for each staff member

- Schedule requirements (date by which each task must be completed)
- Supplies requirements
- Anticipated problems and possible solutions
- Budget constraints

Keeping Track of Details

Almost all managers and professional-level employees must keep track of some amount of detailed information. Trends, production levels, significant dates, goals, and efficiency data are examples of the types of detail most often tracked.

The following chart can be used to identify information to be tracked and the method of tracking it. To use this chart:
1. Set aside time for a planning session to determine information tracking requirements.
2. Determine the information the organization needs to function effectively.
3. Determine the best sources of that information.
4. Determine the frequency with which the data should be collected.
5. Determine the method to be used for recording the information.
6. Identify the person responsible for collecting the information.
7. Determine the method by which the information will be retained. Filing systems, binders, and notebooks are examples of methods by which data can be retained. If your information retention needs are great, consider an automated system, such as a computer data-base application.

Information Required	Sources	Frequency of Collection	Method of Recording	Person Responsible	Method of Retention

Recommended Reading

Buzan, Tony. *Use Both Sides of Your Brain.* New York, NY: E.P. Dutton, Inc., 1983.

Chapter 4 of this book offers suggestions on how to wade through information and retain the important details. Techniques of creating and recalling key words and concepts in order to improve efficiency and memory are discussed.

Suggested Seminars

The seminars listed here were selected for their appeal to a managerial audience and have received good to excellent ratings from managers attending them.

Because of the dynamic nature of the seminar marketplace, some seminars may have been added, upgraded, or replaced, and others may no longer be offered. Additional information about these seminars may be obtained by calling the vendor directly, or through Seminar Clearinghouse International, a subscriber organization located in St. Paul, Minnesota. Call 612/293-1004 for information.

AMERICAN MANAGEMENT ASSOCIATIONS, P.O. Box 319, Saranac Lake, NY, 12983, 518/891-0065.

Time Management. Two-day practical course designed to help participants at all levels make the best possible use of time. Program topics include: taking charge of your time clock; Pareto's principle; priority systems; real vs. stated objectives; managing vs. doing; clarifying objectives; tracking time use patterns; matching activities to objectives; wiping out timewasters; and turning your team on to time management.
Length: 2 days
Cost: $795
Locations: Irvine, CA; San Francisco, CA; Washington, DC; Atlanta, GA; Chicago, IL; New York, NY.

CENTER FOR CREATIVE LEADERSHIP, 5000 Laurinda Drive, P.O. Box P-1, Greensboro, NC 27402, 919/288-7210.

Targeted Innovation. This six-day workshop presents the tools of the trade for creative problem solving and focuses on the applied side of the creative process.
Length: 6 days
Cost: $1800
Locations: San Diego, CA; Greensboro, NC.

CONTROL DATA CORPORATION, 1450 Energy Park Drive, St. Paul, MN 55108, 800/638-6590, 612/642-3300.

Critical Thinking Skills for the Technical Professional. This program is designed to build skills in the areas of situation analysis, potential opportunity analysis, and creative process.

Length: 3 days
Cost: $995
Locations: San Diego, CA; San Francisco, CA; Denver, CO; Washington, DC; Chicago, IL; Minneapolis, MN; New York, NY; Dallas, TX.

FRED PRYOR SEMINARS, 2000 Johnson Drive, P.O. Box 2951, Shawnee Mission, KS 66201, 800/255-6139.

How To Get Things Done. Participants attending this program learn how to waste less time, as well as gain tips for digging out from under, how to produce more—better, faster & easier, delegating, and how to make the most of your work style.
Length: 1 day
Cost: $98
Locations: Hartford, CT; Arlington Heights, IL; Chicago, IL; Boston, MA; Framingham, MA; Detroit, MI; Grand Rapids, MI; Kalamazoo, MI; Morristown, NJ; Hempstead, NY; White Plains, NY; Allentown, PA. For additional locations, contact the vendor.

WILLIAM ONCKEN CORPORATION, 8344 East R. L. Thornton Freeway, Suite 408, Dallas, TX 75228, 214/328-1867 (in Dallas), 612/473-2404 (in Minneapolis).

Managing Management Time. Also known as "Get Them Monkeys Off Your Back," this program goes beyond the "daily diary" approach—it examines the causes and effects of time management problems and deals with the realities of getting performance through other people.
Length: 2 days
Cost: $450
Locations: Washington, DC; Chicago, IL; New Orleans, LA; Minneapolis, MN; Dallas, TX; Houston, TX; Seattle, WA.

INDEX OF MANAGEMENT SKILLS PROFILE (MSP) SUGGESTIONS

The following index will direct you to the Successful Manager's Handbook for suggestions, seminars, and readings related to each MSP item. The MSP item is shown in bold type, followed by Handbook suggestions (sometimes more than one relates to an MSP item) and the Handbook page on which each appears.

FACTOR 1. Administrative Skills

PLANNING

Successful Manager's Handbook

FACTOR 2. Leadership Skills

LEADERSHIP STYLE AND INFLUENCE

FACTOR 3. Interpersonal Skills

HUMAN RELATIONS SKILLS

FACTOR 4. Communication Skills

INFORMING

LISTENING

WRITTEN COMMUNICATIONS

FACTOR 5. Personal Adaptability

FACTOR 8. Cognitive Skills

PROBLEM ANALYSIS AND DECISION MAKING

PERSONNEL DECISIONS, INC.
Building Successful Organizations

2000 PLAZA VII TOWER • 45 SOUTH SEVENTH STREET • MINNEAPOLIS, MN 55402-1608 • 612/339-0927

YES, I would like to know more about what PDI can do for my organization.

☐ Please place me on the mailing list for your newsletter: PDI Perspectives.

My business phone number is _____

Name _____

Title _____

Organization _____

Address _____

_____

_____

(Please print or affix your business card)

I'm especially interested in:

ASSESSMENT SERVICES
☐ Individual Assessment
☐ Assessment Centers
☐ Reliability/Security Screening
☐ Selection Systems & Methods

MANAGEMENT DEVELOPMENT SERVICES AND PRODUCTS
☐ Management Skill-building Workshops
☐ Management Development Center
☐ Executive Development Center
☐ Leadership Development Program
☐ Individual Coaching for Effectiveness
☐ Management Skills Profile (MSP)
☐ Successful Manager's Handbook
☐ Executive Success Profile (ESP)
☐ Individual Development Profile

ORGANIZATIONAL EFFECTIVENESS SERVICES
☐ Organizational Effectiveness Audit (OEA)
☐ Customized Attitude Surveys
☐ Looking Glass, Inc.
☐ Organizational Restructuring/Change Management
☐ Team Development
☐ Human Resource Systems

CAREER TRANSITION
☐ Career Counseling
☐ Outplacement
☐ Dual Career Program

PERSONNEL DECISIONS, INC.
Building Successful Organizations

2000 PLAZA VII TOWER • 45 SOUTH SEVENTH STREET • MINNEAPOLIS, MN 55402-1608 • 612/339-0927

HBK4

YES, I would like to know more about what PDI can do for my organization.

☐ Please place me on the mailing list for your newsletter: PDI Perspectives.

My business phone number is _____

Name _____

Title _____

Organization _____

Address _____

_____

_____

(Please print or affix your business card)

I'm especially interested in:

ASSESSMENT SERVICES
☐ Individual Assessment
☐ Assessment Centers
☐ Reliability/Security Screening
☐ Selection Systems & Methods

MANAGEMENT DEVELOPMENT SERVICES AND PRODUCTS
☐ Management Skill-building Workshops
☐ Management Development Center
☐ Executive Development Center
☐ Leadership Development Program
☐ Individual Coaching for Effectiveness
☐ Management Skills Profile (MSP)
☐ Successful Manager's Handbook
☐ Executive Success Profile (ESP)
☐ Individual Development Profile

ORGANIZATIONAL EFFECTIVENESS SERVICES
☐ Organizational Effectiveness Audit (OEA)
☐ Customized Attitude Surveys
☐ Looking Glass, Inc.
☐ Organizational Restructuring/Change Management
☐ Team Development
☐ Human Resource Systems

CAREER TRANSITION
☐ Career Counseling
☐ Outplacement
☐ Dual Career Program

BUSINESS REPLY MAIL

FIRST CLASS   PERMIT NO. 13372   MINNEAPOLIS, MN

POSTAGE WILL BE PAID BY ADDRESSEE

PERSONNEL DECISIONS, INC.

2000 Plaza VII Tower
45 South Seventh Street
Minneapolis, MN 55402-9891
612/339-0927

NO POSTAGE
NECESSARY
IF MAILED
IN THE
UNITED STATES

BUSINESS REPLY MAIL

FIRST CLASS   PERMIT NO. 13372   MINNEAPOLIS, MN

POSTAGE WILL BE PAID BY ADDRESSEE

PERSONNEL DECISIONS, INC.

2000 Plaza VII Tower
45 South Seventh Street
Minneapolis, MN 55402-9891
612/339-0927